From Gentlemen
to Townsmen

FROM GENTLEMEN TO TOWNSMEN

The Gentry of
Baltimore County,
Maryland
1660-1776

CHARLES G. STEFFEN

THE UNIVERSITY PRESS OF KENTUCKY

Library of Congress Cataloging-in-Publication Data

Steffen, Charles G., 1952–
    From gentlemen to townsmen : the gentry of Baltimore County,
Maryland, 1660–1776 / Charles G. Steffen.
        p.   cm.
    Includes bibliographical references and index.
    ISBN 0–8131–1829–8
    1. Gentry—Maryland—Baltimore County—History.   2. Baltimore
County (Md.)—History.   I. Title.
F187.B2S74   1993
975.2'71—dc20   92–44321

To Allyson and Brendan

Contents

Illustrations, Maps, Figures, Tables

Acknowledgments

My thanks go to many people. The efficient, courteous, and knowledgeable staff of the Maryland State Archives made my visits to Annapolis pleasurable and profitable. I cannot imagine a better place to do historical research. The Committee on Institutional Studies and Research of Murray State University provided invaluable financial support for research and writing. Ken Wolf, Charlotte Beahan, Terry Streiter, Lois Green Carr, Jack Greene, and James Henretta made insightful comments on early versions of several chapters. I owe a special debt of gratitude to Joseph Cartwright, my former chairman and eternal friend, who struggled mightily to create a department in which scholarship was recognized and rewarded. The entire manuscript was read by Gregory Nobles, Richard Beeman, and Allan Kulikoff, whose probing questions opened my eyes to many things I had not seen before.

The dedication is to a pair of countervailing forces. Brendan did everything in the power of a determined three-year-old to prevent his father from finishing this book. Allyson did everything in the power of a devoted teacher, busy mother, and loyal *compañera* to see that it did get finished. Between the two of them, I have had the best of both worlds.

Introduction

During the past twenty years, a growing number of historians has been exploring and mapping the social terrain of the two colonies that encircle the Chesapeake Bay, Virginia and Maryland. It has been a truly collaborative enterprise, with each new insight simultaneously building upon and calling forth another. To name everyone who has helped revolutionize our understanding of the early Chesapeake would produce a long list and a weary reader.[1]

But four contributors deserve to be named, because their sweeping interpretations have established the thematic framework and research agenda for those of us who write narrowly focused monographs about the small places and silent people of the Chesapeake. In numerous essays and his magnum opus, *France and the Chesapeake*, Jacob M. Price has traced the institutional maturation of the transatlantic tobacco economy. No single work has more poignantly captured the tragic interplay of race, class, and slavery in Virginia than Edmund S. Morgan's *American Slavery—American Freedom*. In *The Transformation of Virginia*, Rhys Isaac has offered a profound analysis of the structure and process of cultural hegemony among the tidewater gentry. Finally, the demographic and economic underpinnings of class formation in the Chesapeake have been the subject of Allan Kulikoff's masterful synthesis, *Tobacco and Slaves*.[2]

Each of these historians, in turn, owes a tremendous debt to the formidable standards of methodological sophistication and empirical rigor set by the "Maryland school." With single-minded determination, Lois Green Carr, Lorena S. Walsh, Russell R. Menard, David W. Jordan, and Paul G.E. Clemens have been draining every ounce of possible significance from probate, tax, and court records to reconstruct the economic and social conditions of early Maryland. Their quantitative approach to such questions as price movements, life expectancy, and mobility rates has reached a culmination in *A Place in Time*, Darrett B. Rutman's and Anita H. Rutman's richly researched book on Middlesex County, Virginia.[3]

Yet in spite of this ambitious effort to illuminate every hidden feature and dark corner of Chesapeake life, from the great house and sleeping chambers to the slave quarters and family parlor, one group has not emerged from the shadows. This group, which I have called the "county gentry," is the subject of the present study.

The claim that the gentry has somehow eluded scholarly scrutiny should raise more than a few eyebrows. After all, if one group has been privileged by historians of the colonial South, it is the class of privilege. Many outstanding studies of the gentry spring to mind: Jack P. Greene's meditations on the political culture of the Virginia gentry, Richard R. Beeman's and Albert H. Tillson, Jr.'s examinations of the transplantation of gentry culture to the Virginia backcountry, Aubrey C. Land's exploration of the multifaceted investments that sustained upper-class fortunes, T.H. Breen's decoding of the cultural meanings attached to the gentry's economic behavior, Kenneth A. Lockridge's psychological profile of one of Virginia's foremost gentlemen, David Hackett Fischer's search for the Old World determinants and continuities of gentry life, and Daniel Blake Smith's and Jan Lewis's investigations into the inner dimensions of the gentry family. The list could go on to include older works such as Charles Sydnor's analysis of the paradoxical blend of popular elitism that characterized gentry politics, Louis B. Wright's treatment of the considerable intellectual attainments of the provincial gentry, and Thomas J. Wertenbaker's and Bernard Bailyn's accounts of the consolidation of gentry rule in Restoration Virginia.[4]

How then can it be said, given this richly textured and broadly conceived body of scholarship on upper-class life in the colonial Chesapeake, that historians have not given the gentry its fair due? The answer becomes clear when we look closely at the specific individuals and families whose experiences have formed the basis of the most widely accepted generalizations about the gentry as a whole. One need read only a few pages of the key studies on gentry life to find extended discussions of Thomas Jefferson and George Washington of Virginia, Charles Carroll of Carrollton and Daniel Dulany of Maryland, and such multitentacled clans as the Lees, Carters, Byrds, Burwells, Addisons, Bennetts, and Ludwells. If we look more closely still, we see two men crowding out all the rest: William Byrd of Westover and Landon Carter of Sabine Hall, who left behind a pair of unique diaries on which several generations of historians have lavished textual analysis of Talmudic precision. No two sources have so thoroughly shaped our notions of gentry life.[5]

The Byrds, Carters, Jeffersons, and Washingtons were to their society what the Rockefellers, Carnegies, Morgans, and Vanderbilts were to theirs. No one would attempt to write about the pioneering industrialists of the Gilded Age by looking exclusively at these economic giants. Why? Because they *were* giants. To understand fully the manufacturing community of their day we would need to lower our sights to the small- and medium-sized employers who comprised the numerical bedrock of industrialists and who articulated a collective identity frequently at odds with that of the Rockefellers and Carnegies. Only then could we begin to appreciate the complicated and unpredictable ways in which these two segments of the larger industrial elite interacted to form a whole. Only then could we begin to ask whether they comprised a class in and for itself.

What is true for the industrializing United States is no less true for the preindustrial Chesapeake. Behind the mighty Byrds and Carters stood thousands of gentlemen now sunk in obscurity, who counted themselves lucky if they had a dozen slaves, a thousand acres of land, and a seat on the county court. None of them ever attained the immense work forces, sprawling plantations, and political dynasties of the masters of Westover, Sabine Hall, Monticello, or Mount Vernon. But they called themselves gentlemen, and they were accepted as such by their neighbors. Thus it is necessary to draw a distinction between gentlemen whose interests, attitudes, and aspirations spanned the entire province and gentlemen whose horizons were largely circumscribed by the counties in which they lived. Greene has put the point well in his discussion of the Virginia gentry: "the only common denominator among all of the members of the broad *social category* of gentry was possession of more than ordinary wealth. Within that broad category, however, was a much smaller, cohesive, and self-conscious *social group*, at the core of which were about forty inter-related families that had successfully competed with other immigrants for wealth and power through the middle decades of the seventeenth century and consolidated their position between 1680 and 1730."[6] The fact that in this study I have substituted the terms *county gentry* and *provincial gentry* for Greene's "social category" and "social group" should not obscure our agreement on the fundamental point: the Chesapeake gentry was internally differentiated into a small but solid upper rank and a large but diffuse lower rank.

Baltimore County might seem an odd place for studying the Chesapeake gentry. Established around 1660 and eventually encompassing the northern reaches of the Western Shore, Baltimore remained at the

margins of Chesapeake society throughout the seventeenth century. By
the third quarter of the eighteenth century, as vast economic and political forces began to redefine the regional identity of northern Maryland, Baltimore found itself being pulled into the economic orbit of
the Middle Atlantic colonies. That left a period of two or three generations, from roughly 1700 to 1760, when Baltimore could be said to
belong to the social order of the Greater Tidewater. So if we were
seeking a mature Chesapeake county with the full panoply of tidewater
institutions, Baltimore would be a bad choice.

But Baltimore is a good choice for a study of the county gentry,
precisely because it was not typical of tidewater Virginia or lower
Maryland. Except for one or two cases, Baltimore did not have families of tidewater scale who could hold their own alongside the provincial gentry. Even the top local clans such as the Ridgelys or Halls,
whose economic and political aspirations could not be contained
within the confines of county life, would have been sorry matches for
the likes of a William Byrd or a Landon Carter. My goal has been to
draw attention away from the provincial gentry to the county gentry,
so what better place to start than Baltimore, where gentlemen of lesser
rank did not have to share the stage with the provincial giants?

Thus far we have avoided the most basic question of all: Who were
the gentry? Colonials never gave a clear-cut answer, since one of the
things that transformed a man into a gentleman was that most elusive
of qualities, his character. He had to be cultivated but not stuffy. He
had to be a congenial companion but not a backslapper. He had to have
a deeply ingrained sense of honor but not a half-cocked temper. Being
a gentleman amounted to a kind of delicate balancing act, and the man
who mastered it was instantly recognizable to those around him. But
how do we recognize him two or three hundred years later? We can
thumb through the pages of any colonial record book and find many
people with "Gent." appended to their names, but as disdainful European visitors were quick to point out, parvenues readily assumed
the title without anything to back it up. Historians need something
more tangible, a mark of gentry standing that can be easily identified
and measured.

The one thing a gentleman had to have was wealth or access to it.
Although wealth alone did not elevate a man to gentry status, a gentleman was nothing without it. Fortunately, the information on
wealthholding in the colonial Chesapeake is immense. The Maryland
probate courts kept careful records of inventories of estates, listing every bit of personal property a person owned at his death. The chief

problem in using the inventories is that they do not include land. Attempts to estimate the value of landholdings have had limited success, because we often do not know exactly how many acres a person owned or what improvements had been made to the property. The omission of land from the inventories is a drawback but not a fatal one: in Baltimore, the people who owned the most personal property also owned the most real property.[7]

In this book the gentry is defined as those people who owned the largest personal estates at their deaths (see appendix 1). Identifying them involved the following steps: First, I calculated the estate value for every decedent in Baltimore between 1660 and 1776 whose inventory was recorded in the provincial or county courts. Second, I adjusted the estate value for price inflation with a deflator generously provided by Lois Green Carr and Lorena S. Walsh of the St. Mary's City Commission. Finally, I selected the richest 10 percent of decedents for the period before 1690, and for each succeeding decade until 1776.

The result was that 1,810 Baltimore County inventories for the entire colonial period yielded a total of 181 individuals whom I have labeled *the economic elite*. Drawing the cutoff point at 10 percent is admittedly arbitrary. Although very few historians have been willing to venture an estimate on the number of gentry families in any one place or time, no one has suggested they comprised over 10 percent of the population, much less 10 percent of the probated population. My estimate might well err on the liberal side and include some men who hovered around upper-middling status or who fell outside the privileged circle altogether. But closing the door at 5 percent or 2 percent would have excluded many men who behaved like gentlemen. All in all, 10 percent strikes me as a reasonable figure.[8]

Another group that appears prominently in this study is made up of merchants, whose names I have combed from county land records (see appendix 2). These volumes contain tens of thousands of conveyances, mortgages, leases, assignments, gifts, powers of attorney, and more. They touch virtually every side of commerical enterprise. In Baltimore about one-half of the parties who registered a deed at the county court listed an occupation or an honorific. It is possible that some small-time traders slipped through the records without listing their occupations, and a few important merchants might have escaped undetected during the seventeenth century when transactions were less frequent. Yet the sheer volume of deeds, coupled with the high percentage of people reporting occupations, convinces me that any merchant worthy of the name would appear at some point or another in the land records. An examination of every land deed recorded before 1776 resulted in a total of 201 resident merchants active in the county.

An examination of these 349 Baltimoreans (181 members of the elite plus 168 merchants who did not belong to the elite) enables us to test certain widely held ideas about the Chesapeake gentry, ideas derived largely from the experiences of the great tidewater planters. The standard argument goes like this: By the first decades of the eighteenth century a gentry class had emerged in the Chesapeake characterized by stability, permanence, and continuity. The restoration of order following Bacon's Rebellion in Virginia and the Protestant Association in Maryland cleared the way for a coterie of interrelated families to consolidate its power in each county. Generation after generation, these same families clung to their privileged positions at the top of the wealth and status hierarchies. The pillars of their economic power were labor, land, and credit; the bases of their political power were the court, church, and assembly. In using such terms as *oligarchies, aristocracies,* and *dynasties* to describe the leading families who held sway in colonial Virginia and Maryland, historians have highlighted the closed nature of this class. Whatever we choose to call them, the gentlemen who rose to power in the colonial Chesapeake constituted, according to the prevailing view, one of the most socially cohesive, economically entrenched, and politically conscious ruling classes in all of British North America.

The 349 Baltimoreans examined in the pages that follow do not easily fit this pattern of development. If stability and permanence were hallmarks of the provincial gentry, openness and fluidity characterized the county gentry of Baltimore. In chapter 1 I suggest that at no point during the seventeenth century did anything remotely resembling a gentry class emerge in Baltimore. According to the arguments presented in chapter 2, after 1700 the county gentry was marked by a high degree of openness, in both economic and political terms. The main point of chapter 3 is that openness and instability also defined labor arrangements on gentry plantations, producing a distinctive type of hybrid work force. Chapter 4 focuses on one of the principal factors contributing to the high rates of turnover among the gentry, partible inheritance. Chapter 5 is an examination of Baltimore's large and active merchant community, whose rise to prominence was emblematic of the openness of upper-class life. In chapter 6 I argue that the overall fluidity at the upper reaches of society found institutional expression in an established church that opened its doors to a wide spectrum of the white community. The conclusion reached in chapter 7 is that the dramatic rise of Baltimore Town after 1760, the explosive growth of the merchant community, and the sudden emergence of new revolutionary leadership were logical outcomes of the same process of social formation that produced the open gentry in the first place.

The qualities of openness, fluidity, and impermanence that I have discerned among the county gentry of Baltimore contrast sharply with the stability, continuity, and cohesiveness that so many historians have associated with the leading tidewater families. But my interpretation and theirs are not necessarily incompatible, and for a simple reason—we are dealing with two distinct segments of the gentry. How and under what circumstances these segments interacted to form a self-conscious class—assuming they did—can only be addressed by examining localities that, unlike Baltimore, contained both a county gentry and a provincial gentry. Yet if this study has any broader application to the region of which Baltimore was a part, historians should not be surprised to discover among the life-sized gentlemen who comprised the backbone of the Chesapeake upper class a world far removed from that of William Byrd or Landon Carter.

1

Baltimore County

Baltimore County was a victim of its own geography. During the seventeenth century between 100,000 and 150,000 European immigrants reached Virginia and Maryland in search of rich soil, flat lands, and navigable rivers. They found all these things in the wide Coastal Plain that stretches from the James to the Patuxent River. As one moves north beyond the tidewater heartland, the plain becomes a narrow triangle of land wedged between the Piedmont Plateau and the Chesapeake Bay. At the Patapsco River, which marked the southern boundary of Baltimore throughout the colonial era, the plain virtually disappears. So while Baltimore had abundant natural resources, from rich outcroppings of iron ore to vast stands of virgin timber, it did not have enough of the one thing Englishmen wanted most—fertile, flat, accessible land.[1]

Those who settled in Baltimore endeavored to knit their separate lives into a viable community, but they battled against the sheer rawness of the Chespeake frontier. No Maryland county was as thinly populated as Baltimore. Further, the familiar landmarks of the social landscape already taking shape in the prime tobacco-producing areas—gentlemen, slaves, merchants, court, and church—were barely visible in the straggling settlements between the Patapsco and Susquehanna rivers. Clearly, Baltimore was a backwater. If tidewater Virginia and southern Maryland constituted the demographic and institutional core of early Chesapeake society, Baltimore occupied the underdeveloped periphery. Emblematic of its backwardness was the unlikely assortment of small-time planters and politicians, merchants and ministers, slaveholders and servant holders, who passed for a gentry.

The river was not exactly impressive but it did have one interesting characteristic. At low tide, one could see a ribbon of red clay cliffs running along the river bank. The bright color reminded Capt. John Smith of *bole armeniac,* a medicinal substance popular in his day. The self-promoting Smith never missed a chance to leave his personal

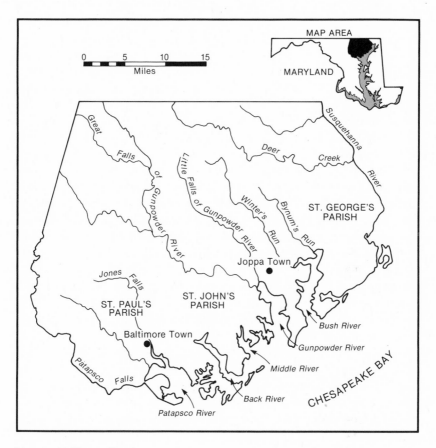

Map 1. Baltimore County

mark on the North American map, so he christened the river the Bolus (see Map 1). What he did not know, or chose to ignore, was that native peoples who hunted in the area already had a name for this body of water. They called it Patapsco.[2]

If not the first Englishman to see the place that would become Baltimore County, Captain Smith was the first one to write about it. The red cliffs came into view about June 14, 1608. A few weeks before, Smith had assembled a small expeditionary force in Jamestown, consisting of one "Doctor of Physicke," six "Gentlemen," and seven "Souldiers." He packed them all into a small "Barge" and set out to explore the Chesapeake Bay. The crew got only as far north as the Bush River before turning back. But a few months later Smith organized a second expedition to complete his exploration of the bay. This time he reached the Susquehanna River.[3]

As his barge bobbed its way along the shoreline between the Patapsco and the Susquehanna, Smith quickly sized up his discovery. He did not especially like what he saw. No great waterways offered easy entrance to the interior. If the Patapsco River itself was a small matter compared to the Potomac, the Back, Middle, Gunpowder, and Bush rivers seemed scarcely worth mentioning. Smith dismissed them as "4 small rivers, 3 of them issuing from diverse bogges." No great Indian nations offered opportunities for trade and conquest. In fact, there were no Indians at all. The powerful Susquehannocks, whose main settlements were located some thirty miles up the river that bears their name, had blocked Algonquian-speaking peoples from settling north of the Patapsco, creating a kind of uninhabited demilitarized zone. Most damning, no great expanse of accessible farm land offered promise for husbandry.

Captain Smith hoped that the account of his exploration, published in 1612, would encourage immigration to the new lands. But anyone reading his description of the future Baltimore would have thought twice before settling there. "[T]he Westerne shore by which we sayled," he wrote, "we found all along well watered, but very mountanous and barren, the vallies very fertill, but extreame thicke of small wood so well as trees, and much frequented with Wolves, Beares, Deere and other wild beasts."[4]

This was not Eden. Looking out from the cramped barge, the estuaries of the Patapsco, Gunpowder, and Bush rivers offered a disquieting vista to a seventeenth-century Englishman. These rivers are situated on the northern rim of the geographical unit we call the Chesapeake. Smith already had some idea that the region encompassed two physiographic zones, the Coastal Plain and the Piedmont Plateau. On the hard-rock plateau, waters from the Appalachians race through relatively shallow, rock-strewn courses. Upon entering the plain with its softer soils, they carve out wide channels navigable by sailing vessels of Smith's day. The plateau and plain meet at the fall line. For land-hungry Englishmen the navigable rivers and arable lands below the fall line were magnificent gifts from their God. But God had been stingy on the northern Western Shore, squeezing the Coastal Plain into a narrow strip only a few miles wide. And it was not the relatively flat land Smith had left behind in Jamestown. The terrain of Baltimore County falls rapidly toward the bay in a series of terraces, the highest reaching some 500 feet near today's Loch Raven, ten miles north of downtown Baltimore. By contrast, the same drop in elevation is spread over a hundred miles on the Potomac River. It is no surprise that when Captain Smith sat down to record his impressions of Baltimore, what he remembered most vividly was "high mountaines."[5]

Englishmen wanted nothing to do with high mountains, so they abandoned Baltimore to the occasional explorer, fur trader, and Susquehannock hunter. In 1628 George Calvert, the first Lord Baltimore, scouted out the Chesapeake with an eye to establishing a colony there, and he might have caught a glimpse of Baltimore. English fur traders did business around the Bush and Susquehanna rivers. None was more determined than William Claiborne of Virginia, Lord Baltimore's inveterate enemy, who sent his employees and servants to the northern Chesapeake in an attempt to yoke the Susquehannocks into a commercial partnership for their mutual benefit. But Englishmen who came to Baltimore in the two decades following Captain Smith's visit did not stay there long.

The formal creation of Maryland brought no immediate improvement to the situation on the northern frontier. In 1634, two years after the Calverts secured their charter, the first permanent settlement was established on a tributary of the Potomac River. Thanks to a better grasp of the challenges at hand and the absence of a significant Indian threat, St. Mary's was spared the worst horrors of Jamestown. Even so, the new colony faced problems that delayed the settlement of the upper Chesapeake. The Roman Catholic Cecilius Calvert, who in 1632 became second Baron of Baltimore, spent many years navigating the storms of the English Civil War and the Interregnum. Fighting for his political life at home and abroad, Lord Baltimore had little time for the deer hunters, fur traders, and occasional adventurers who passed through the northern reaches of his colony.[6]

But events were slowly forcing the upper Chesapeake onto the proprietor's agenda. In 1652 Maryland negotiated a treaty with the Susquehannocks, which permitted white settlement in their traditional hunting grounds above the Patapsco River. Three years later Dutch forces conquered the small Swedish outpost on the Delaware River, an act that drew attention to the northern frontier, now dangerously exposed to a formidable military and commercial threat. In 1660, with the restoration of Charles Stuart to the throne, Cecilius Calvert could finally count on friends at court. As his old enemies scrambled for cover, Lord Baltimore could get back to the business of running his colony. Among the many backlogged problems demanding decisive action was the unregulated northern frontier, and action came sometime in 1659 or 1660 when the assembly passed an act for the establishment of Baltimore County.[7]

The new county was big enough to be a colony. It encompassed all of northern Maryland, although the assembly probably expected additional counties to spin off as population increased. On the Western Shore, Baltimore began at the Patapsco River; on the Eastern Shore, at the Chester River. The northern boundary was staked at the fortieth parallel to embrace the lower Delaware Valley. Over the years this unwieldy jurisdiction was pruned to a more managable size. In 1674 the Eastern Shore territory became Cecil County; the Delaware claim was eventually abandoned in negotiations with Pennsylvania; and in 1773 the area north of the Gunpowder River became Harford County. For practically all of its colonial existence, Baltimore extended thirty-five miles in a straight line from the Patapsco River to the Susquehanna River.[8]

If the authors of the Establishment Act thought that formal recognition would spur mass migration to Baltimore, they must have been disappointed. The high mountains, thick woods, barren spaces, and wild beasts that had disheartened Captain Smith in 1607 continued to drive people away fifty years later. No more than a handful of people had settled there before 1652. Although the Susquehannock treaty temporarily reduced the possibility of war with the greatest fighting force in the region, it has been estimated that only 300-400 settlers lived in Baltimore at the time of its establishment. Many years passed before the machinery of local government began to create a familiar sense of the ordered life left behind in the Old World. By 1667 the population had yet to reach 900. In 1675, a year after Baltimore lost its Eastern Shore territory, only 800 people were residing between the Patapsco and Susquehanna. During the next generation, the population continued to grow at a sluggish rate. Despite a short-lived demographic burst that brought the number of inhabitants to 1,700 at the end of the century, Baltimore remained one of the least desirable places in Maryland to live. It accounted for only one out of twenty colonists.[9]

Some Baltimoreans were inclined to blame their county's sputtering growth on human selfishness. In a spirited petition delivered to the governor in 1697, the grand jury drew attention to "Diverse Tracts of Land Appertaining to Severall Gentlemen not residing in this County who take noe Care to Seate the same." Not only did these absentee landowners discourage outsiders from taking up residence in the county, they forced hard-working residents to shoulder an unfair burden of the annual tax levy. Indeed, the petitioners claimed that Baltimore's per capita taxes exceeded those of any county in Maryland. The document, which undoubtedly reflected the sentiments of ordinary planters on the jury, concluded by entreating the government to enact legislation requiring absentee landowners to seat their tracts. In the event that these parasitic speculators continued to defy the common good, the petitioners exclaimed, honest men committed to Baltimore's development should be given a chance to make the land yield what everyone knew it could.[10]

It is no wonder that rich men were reluctant to settle in the county. For big planters, Baltimore was a dead end. A study of six Maryland counties between 1656 and 1719 has identified ninety-six individuals whose capital assets were appraised at more than £600 at their deaths. While Anne Arundel County had thirty-five rich planters, Baltimore accounted for a mere six. In fact, only undeveloped Somerset County on the Eastern Shore had fewer wealthy planters than did Baltimore. Because capital was scarce in newly settled regions, people with money frequently lent it to their neighbors. So it is not surprising that rich Baltimore planters invested more of their personal property in debts receivable and less in agricultural assets than did their counterparts elsewhere. Compared to Maryland counties whose economies rested on the twin pillars of tobacco production and plantation slavery, neither Baltimore nor Somerset "produced planters of the traditional stereotype, the squire who devoted his principal energies to farming and who invested heavily in slaves."[11]

Without a critical mass of slaveholding planters, Baltimore could not develop the kind of cohesive class structure that was taking shape in tidewater counties. Justices, sheriffs, constables, jurymen, and an array of petty officials provided only a show of legitimacy and stability, so long as the county lacked a core of leading families whose claim to power and respectability was accepted throughout the community. An analysis of the delegates who represented Baltimore in the assembly suggests the fragility and impermanence of the county elite. During the period from 1660 to 1700, the average Baltimore delegate served in only 1.6 assemblies. Compared to other counties, Baltimore failed to produce veteran politicians with extensive legislative experience. Four of six counties—Anne Arundel, Calvert, Charles, and St. Mary's—possessed a stable coterie of representatives who served in four or more assemblies. But in Baltimore and Kent counties, no one sat in more than three assemblies. Since Baltimore's politicians failed to make much of a mark at the provincial level, the assembly looked elsewhere for leadership. Not one of the nineteen speakers of the lower house before 1700 came from Baltimore. No Baltimoreans occupied influential positions in the proprietary establishment, and none of the twenty-seven men who served in the council between 1666 and 1689 made Baltimore his home.[12]

The absence of a cohesive county gentry also emerges from an examination of the local church. In 1689 disgruntled colonists calling themselves the Protestant Association overthrew the government of Catholic Lord Baltimore. Spurred by a desire to consolidate its own power and to institutionalize the revolution, the association set out to secure the establishment of the Church of England. Within three years it had achieved its goal. On the surface, the Establishment Act provided Baltimore with a much-needed infusion of institutional stability. Its essence was a poll tax of forty pounds of tobacco, levied on every able-bodied white man and every slave over the age of fifteen. Collected by county sheriffs, the tax generated clerical salaries that increased with the rise in population and in tobacco prices. The act also provided for the creation of a vestry in each parish, consisting of six men in addition to the rector. To ensure a proper rotation in office, the assembly ordered that on Easter Monday of every year the parish's freeholders should replace two vestrymen "by Majority of Voyces." The vestry was directed to meet on the first Tuesday of every month to conduct its principal business. At annual elections the parishoners also selected two church wardens whose reponsibilities included executing the directives of the vestry and collecting fines for moral transgressions that came to the attention of the lay leaders. The vestrymen and wardens were empowered to appoint a register who kept a record of births, marriages, deaths, and the vestry proceedings. Any parishioner who suspected misconduct on the part of the vestry could demand an inspection of the church records. If the matter could not be resolved locally, he could lodge a protest directly with the governor and council.[13]

It was decades before Baltimore's church began to look anything like the one so confidently delineated in the Establishment Act. The county was divided into three parishes: St. Paul's, between the Patapsco and Middle rivers; St. John's, between the Middle and Bush rivers; and St. George's, between the Bush and Susquehanna rivers. Drawing lines on a map was one thing; finding qualified ministers to serve as rectors, another. The parson who stayed at his post only long enough to find a more attractive incumbency elsewhere became a familiar figure in Baltimore, a far cry from the anchors of stability and authority envisioned by the authors of the Establishment Act. From

1692 to 1730 the average incumbency was a mere five years. Not until 1698 did St. Paul's secure a rector. St. John's had to do without one until 1696, and again between 1698 and 1702. St. George's did not get its own rector until 1718. In the 1670s a visiting English cleric who traveled through northern Maryland recoiled at what he called a "pesthouse of iniquity." It is doubtful that he would have found much improvement a generation later.[14]

In sum, as the process of social consolidation accelerated in the tidewater counties, Baltimore seemed to be sinking deeper and deeper into its backwater ways. The top rungs of society were occupied by small-time operators who lacked the economic base to transform themselves into a confident gentry class. Instead of a few families dominating the highest level of politics, a continual stream of new faces circulated into and out of the assembly. The other bastion of gentry rule, the Anglican church, rested on a shaky foundation so long as pastors refused to settle down to their posts. All together, a tidewater planter on a visit to Baltimore would have been struck by the absence of everything that made his life back home comfortable, convivial, and controllable.

He certainly would have noticed the absence of slaves. Long after tidewater planters began replacing indentured servants with African slaves, the Baltimore elite continued to rely on white laborers. The county work force included a large number of landless freemen who went from plantation to plantation in search of short-term employment. Although available sources do not permit us to reconstruct the precise conditions under which these freemen toiled, they leave little doubt that migrant workers constituted a central component of the laboring population. So as tidewater counties moved decisively toward slavery, Baltimore seemed to be heading in a different direction.

Slavery came late to Baltimore, as is evident in assessment and census records. An examination of three surviving assessment lists demonstrates that even at the end of the century Baltimoreans had few slaves and seemed little interested in acquiring more. Provincial authorities defined taxables as slaves over the age of fifteen and white males over the age of fifteen. Taxable slaves comprised only 10 percent of total taxables in 1692, 12 percent in 1694, and 9 percent in 1695. According to provincial censuses, slaves increased from 13 percent of the county's population in 1704 to 15 percent six years later. In both years, Baltimore had the sparsest black population anywhere on Maryland's Western Shore.[15]

Even rich planters with the most money to spend put off buying slaves. At no point during the seventeenth century did the county elite own more slaves than they did servants. As the new century opened, their commitment to indentured servitude seemed stronger than ever. Those who died between 1700 and 1709 had three times as many white as black workers. Not until the decade 1710-19 did slaves finally eclipse servants in the elite's inventories. Baltimore was running a decade or two behind southern Maryland, where large employers shifted to predominantly slave work forces as early as 1696.[16]

Freemen made up the backbone of the work force. They have left few traces in the records, and only by counting heads in the tax lists do we begin to appreciate their importance. In 1692, 467 white taxables lived in Baltimore. Of these, 258 consisted of either household heads or their kinsmen who lived under the same roof. That leaves 209 white men, called "inmates," who were working for the head of the household in which they resided. Who were these inmates? Overseers account for a small number of them and indentured servants for a somewhat larger one. But the majority of inmates seem to have been hired hands serving under short-term arrangements. A new tax list compiled two years later revealed that only 13 percent of the 209 inmates resided in the same household.[17]

Inmates usually moved out, not up. Relatively few succeeded in starting families and plantations of their own, at least not while they remained in Baltimore. Between 1692 and 1694 only 12 percent of the inmates had risen to become household heads in the county. Another 28 percent had taken up residence in another Baltimore household, where they continued the same round of seasonal labor under a different master. While some of these transients may have been indentured servants traded from hand to hand, it seems likely that most were freemen. We can only speculate about the remaining 47 percent of inmates whose names do not appear in the 1694 tax list. Bad water, disease, and the rigors of the work undoubtedly killed many of them. Survivors may have tried their luck in another part of Maryland or in newly opened Pennsylvania. A third tax list for 1695 indicates that laboring people continued to shift about in search of something better. After three years, 8 percent of 209 inmates remained in the same household, 13 percent had become household heads, 26 percent belonged to another household in the county, and 53 percent were simply gone.[18]

Even though landless men were on the move everywhere in the Chesapeake, Baltimore looks like a veritable revolving door for labor-

ers. The exceptional degree of mobility there may have reflected the
outbreak of King William's War (1689-97). Although the Chesapeake
colonies had entered a commercial downturn some years earlier, the
war deepened the depression. As sea lanes became infested with
French privateers waiting to carry off the annual fleets sent to the tobacco colonies, the economy spiraled downward: fewer ships arrived,
tobacco prices tumbled, insurance costs soared, freight rates increased, and imported goods disappeared. In earlier years planters
who faced falling tobacco prices had been able to maintain profit lev-
els by devising better ways to plant, harvest, cure, pack, and market
their crop. But now that they had mastered their business, productivity
gains could no longer shelter them against depressed tobacco prices.[19]

Many landless freemen hit the road, and provincial authorities
watched the unfolding exodus with alarm. The governors of Virginia
and Maryland warned their superiors about large numbers of laborers
fleeing to Pennsylvania, seduced by the promise of cheaper land,
lower taxes, and fewer grandees. Their complaints reached a crescendo
in the mid-1690s, which means that the Baltimore tax lists probably
captured this flood at its crest. Baltimore may have offered brighter
prospects to landless laborers than did tidewater counties whose economies were more closely tied to the depressed tobacco market. In Baltimore a man might find seasonal work before continuing his trek to
Pennsylvania. Since relatively few planters could afford slaves, migrant workers probably had no problem finding jobs.[20]

One look at this footloose work force is enough to show how far
Baltimore had diverged from the Tidewater. From the James River to
the Patuxent, planters were in the process of recruiting a new work
force of African slaves. But between the Patapsco River and the
Susquehanna, they seemed to be re-creating an old one of permanent
farm hands. For Englishmen who had left the mother country hoping
to escape the advancing tide of rural proletarianization but who now
found themselves going from job to job in Baltimore, the New World
must have seemed a lot like the Old.

A tidewater planter would have noticed something else missing in
Baltimore—prosperous local merchants. During the sixteenth and
seventeenth centuries the energies of countless Englishmen fused in an
explosion of economic enterprise that left few groups untouched. London's merchant princes wrested monopolies over the northern European cloth trade and the new markets of the Levant and India. Small
and middling merchants found unprecedented opportunities in the
North American fur, tobacco, and sugar trades. In tidewater counties,

the tobacco economy proved to be a boon for many small-time traders who possessed a little capital, a few contacts, and the shrewdness to turn them to advantage. But in Baltimore, it was a bust.[21]

From 1660 to 1690 ten men appeared in Baltimore calling themselves merchants. In any given year, their numbers ranged from two to eight (see appendix 2). Apart from a desire to make money fast, the only thing unifying this disparate collection of Quaker visionaries, Dutch refugees, and English transplants was frustration and disappointment. The most telling evidence of commercial failure comes from inventories. Only one of the seven merchants who died before 1690 and left an inventory ranked among the elite. Although the average appraisal of £180 placed merchants in the wealthiest 30 percent of probated decedents in Baltimore before 1699, the seven estates were heavily encumbered with debt. In three of four cases where administrative accounts survive, creditors completely wiped out the estate. And in the fourth case, they took over half of it.[22]

None of the merchants, not even a moderately successful one, could bequeath prosperity to the next generation or establish his children on a secure financial footing. It has been possible to identify the inventories of three sons of the ten first-generation merchants. Their estates were valued at an average of £65, a disappointing show compared to their fathers' £248. None of the sons chose the profession of his father but rather slipped into the ranks of simple planters.[23]

Bloodless statistics from probate records cannot convey the bitter experiences of merchants like Godfrey Harmer, who gambled and lost in Baltimore. Harmer was just a boy when he migrated from Germany to the tiny colony of New Sweden, but he soon became indispensable in the Indian trade through his mastery of the native languages of the region. No less a person than the colony's governor, Johan Printz, who hoped to attract the Great Lakes fur trade to the Delaware Valley by establishing commercial relations with the Susquehannocks, testified that Harmer "knows the savage languages and understands well how to carry on the trade." When in 1655 the Dutch conquered New Sweden, Harmer went to Maryland and soon acquired nearly a thousand acres of land on the Sassafras, Gunpowder, and Susquehanna rivers. These were ideal locations to continue his trade with the natives, especially with the Susquehannocks who controlled the fur supply of the upper Chesapeake. In 1661 Maryland authorities put his linguistic skills to good use by appointing him interpreter to the Susquehannocks, who were then at war with the Iroquois. In recognition of his public services, the assembly granted Harmer the full rights of a Maryland denizen and an English freeman.[24]

Yet even as this multilingual frontiersman received public honors, he was sinking in a financial morass. In 1659 the Dutch emissary from New Netherlands, hoping to negotiate disputed claims to the Delaware Valley, accused Harmer of "enticing and transporting" runaway servants from New Amstel to Maryland. Harmer, he alleged, was selling fugitives to eager planters on the Severn River. Nothing apparently came of the charge, but a decade later the fur trader's fortunes hit bottom when he was forced to sell nearly all of his land. By his death in 1673 Harmer had apparently withdrawn from the Indian trade, since he left behind a small supply of "Indian trading stuff" valued at five shillings and not a single fur. Appraisors found his small plantation neglected and run down, with many livestock roaming freely "in the woods." To each of his three daughters, Harmer could bequeath nothing more than a cow and calf. What property remained went to his widow Mary, who described the estate as "Very Small and many Debts due to be paid."[25]

Edward Gunnell took a different path to disaster by attempting to parlay his position as a British factor into commercial independence. In the 1670s he arrived in Maryland as an agent of the prominent London partnership of Edward Bleeke, Micajah Perry, and Thomas Lane. Although Gunnell acquired 300 acres of land by his death in 1679, he never bought the tools, servants, or slaves necessary to develop them. Indeed, he never bothered to buy a bed. Because Gunnell lacked capital to strike out on his own, he formed a partnership with Joseph Sayres, a recent English immigrant who also had commercial dealings with Bleeke and Company. In 1676 the two partners rented a room in a private home with the intention of converting it into a store. Their landlord agreed to supply "dyet washing & lodging" at the rate of 1,500 pounds of tobacco for the first two months and 1,000 pounds thereafter. He also rented the merchants a boat since the "Small old Suncke Sloope" Gunnell owned was useless.[26]

But everything went wrong. By the end of six months Gunnell and Sayres had not only run up a bill of 7,000 pounds for back rent but kept the boat a full year without making payment. Their exasperated landlord had little choice but to sue. Then in 1677 Sayres died and left Gunnell with the task of sorting out their tangled finances, including debts they had accrued in importing several shipments of goods from Bleeke and Company. With the English firm claiming that the partnership refused to make a "reasonable accompt." of the goods, Gunnell was dragged into court again, this time facing a huge suit of £700 sterling. In the midst of the legal battle Gunnell died, and the disposition of his estate brought a fitting end to the career of this embattled merchant. Edward's brother, George, who was appointed estate administrator, embezzled as much property as he could and fled the colony. In 1685 he was rumored to be in Gloucester County, Virginia, and a year later in Allemack County, Carolina. George had run about as far as he could.[27]

John Gilbert, who arrived in the province in the 1660s, also fell victim to his own ambitions. He may have first tried his luck in England's newly conquered colony of Jamaica, for Gilbert not only served as an agent of a Jamaican merchant but also named his 300-acre tract on the Sassafras River "Jamaica." Like Gunnell, Gilbert had little interest in improving the land he patented. Rather, he hoped to establish an independent trading operation on the basis of a partnership with Philip Shapleigh of St. Mary's County. In return for a 20-percent commission, Shapleigh agreed to sell English merchandise that Gilbert imported and to collect debts that local planters owned him. Neither the partnership nor much else worked. Within five years of the agreement Gilbert was suing Shapleigh to recover £70 assigned to him. Gilbert was not above a swindle reminiscent of Harmer, for in 1670 a local sheriff arrested him on suspicion of selling a freeman as an indentured servant. When Gilbert died seven years later, one of his suppliers, Peter Quodman, stood at the front of a long line of anxious creditors, claiming that Gilbert owed him £83 for a cargo of goods shipped in 1669. The court named Quodman's attorney as administrator of the estate, which was completely consumed by outstanding debts.[28]

In contrast with these dismal stories of law suits and bankruptcy, Thomas Todd defied the odds and broke into the ranks of the county elite. Born in the English town of Denton, Todd probably migrated to Virginia sometime around 1651, the year he patented a 600-acre tract in Gloucester County called Toddsbury. He and his wife Ann put down roots in Gloucester and raised a large family there. But thirteen years later they began a new plantation, Todd's Range, on the Patapsco River. Unlike Gunnell and Gilbert who reached Baltimore with connections but without capital, the wealthy Todd imported thirty-eight people into the province. Before long he had transformed the 1,500-acre Todd's Range into one of the premier plantations in Baltimore, the only one Augustine Hermann singled out by name in his 1673 map of the Chesapeake. By contrast with the merchants who went under, Todd built his commercial interests on the solid foundation of a thriving plantation. At his death he had invested 65 percent of his personal assets in livestock and labor, compared to only 21 percent for Harmer and Gunnell.[29]

In uprooting his family and building a new plantation in Baltimore, Todd seems to have envisioned a family enterprise spanning the Chesapeake. He and Ann settled in Baltimore with their five youngest children. Their first son, Thomas Jr., stayed behind and quickly doubled his Virginia landholdings. In 1676 Todd wrote his son a letter from which we infer that Todd's Range and Toddsbury were being managed as a joint enterprise. The old man was preparing to board the ship *Virginia* bound for London. Sick and fearing the worst, Todd asked his son to send him "some good Syder" that might "keepe mee alive" during the voyage. It is possible that the mature apple orchards of Toddsbury produced cider for both branches of the family. If so, Todd may have marketed Virginia cider among his Patapsco neighbors whose plantations were still undeveloped and whose fruit trees were still saplings. This kind of exchange might explain why Todd owned two small boats outfitted with sails, the kind of craft used in the coastal trade. The Todds also shifted laborers back and forth between the two plantations. "I looked long for you to bring up the Negroes," Todd informed his son, "which I shall loose my Crop for want off them." That a delay in getting the slaves from Toddsbury to Todd's Range could jeopardize the entire harvest underscores how interdependent the operations had become.[30]

The family also seems to have worked out a joint arrangement for marketing tobacco produced at Toddsbury and Todd's Range. In an effort to assemble a shipment of tobacco for sale when he reached London, Todd urged his son to "send me what tobaccoes you Can." He died at sea as he had feared, but not before drawing up a will that was eventually recorded in London. In one of its provisions, Todd directed his London executors to sell eighty-seven hogsheads of tobacco in his possession and to divide the proceeds among his daughters. This tobacco probably had been shipped aboard the *Virginia*. Since the family's Virginia and Maryland plantations could not have produced a crop of this size, the Todds may have bought tobacco from their Gloucester and Baltimore neighbors. That Todd owned the hogsheads outright indicates that he was not an agent for a London merchant house who bought tobacco on commission from local planters. Rather, he was an independent merchant who financed the entire operation on

his own. To represent his interests in the metropolis, Todd could have
called on his brother who resided in England and who received an un-
usually generous bequest in the will.[31]

Being a merchant in the war-torn seventeenth century always carried risks, but in Baltimore the risks seemed fatally high. In the tidewater counties, where large-scale tobacco production developed in
tandem with local commercial networks, prosperous merchants were
as recognizable a part of the social landscape as planters, yeomen, and
slaves. The first families of Virginia might not broadcast their commercial ancestry, but at the base of their family trees one was likely to
find a merchant. In Baltimore, by contrast, trade was rarely the path
to family fortune. For every Thomas Todd, one could count a dozen
Godfrey Harmers.[32]

All in all, the prospects for political stability in Baltimore were not
good. The scarcity of good farm land and navigable rivers, the sluggish rate of population growth, the small number of slaveholding
planters, the tenuous position of the established church, the transi-
tional nature of the labor system, the dismal record of local merchants,
and the absence of a cohesive gentry class—these did not portend
peace and quiet. But it took an outside event, the Glorious Revolution,
to expose the volatile character of Baltimore's political life and the
fragile authority of its leading families.

The Calverts were wrong if they thought the Restoration would
bring an end to their troubles or restore peace to their colony. Although the violence and plundering that had disrupted Maryland for
almost two decades subsided, forces were gathering for yet another explosion. By the 1680s Calvert and the assembly were deadlocked over
a number of perennial issues: taxes, Indians, and depressed tobacco
prices. We need not disentangle the specific legal and constitutional
questions to see that at the heart of the impasse was the delegates'
insistence on a greater voice in provincial affairs. At ordinary times,
these skirmishes would have fallen within the accepted limits of political discord. But now religion began to transform arcane points of
law into deadly matters of principle.[33]

The overwhelmingly Protestant colonists watched with growing
suspicion as Charles Calvert, who became resident governor in 1661
and third Lord Baltimore fourteen years later, showered proprietary
offices on his fellow Catholics. That the Calverts favored their kinsmen and coreligionists was nothing new. But now they faced a new,
powerful adversary to challenge their patronage practices. For several
decades younger sons of English gentry families had been arriving in

Maryland, expecting to advance their fortunes faster and further than they could at home. Excluded from proprietary favor, these men accused Lord Baltimore of conspiring with both Indians and French to destroy the Protestant colonists. They rejoiced in 1689 upon receiving word that William and Mary had driven James II from the throne and had declared war on France. With the Catholic king on the run, the Catholic proprietor seemed defenseless. A newly formed Protestant Association promptly toppled the proprietary government and assembled a convention of delegates from across the colony. The Convention ruled until 1692, when Gov. Lionel Copley took his seat in Maryland and initiated a period of royal government that lasted twenty-three years.[34]

What happened in Baltimore between 1689 and 1692? Maryland escaped the fate of Virginia thirteen years earlier, when Nathaniel Bacon plunged the colony into full-scale civil war. But it would be wrong to underestimate the revolutionary character of events in Maryland. A few shreds of evidence suggest that in Baltimore the Associator's revolution shattered an already fragile leadership. If a political oligarchy existed in Baltimore, George Wells and Miles Gibson were its two pillars. Ranking among the county's richest men, no one else in Baltimore could match their long years of service in the provincial assembly and county court. Proprietary stalwarts, Wells and Gibson fell from power under the Convention. When in 1689 the association issued new lists of county justices, their names were conspicuously absent.[35]

Old names were giving way to new ones. The first elections to the Convention were held in August 1689. Baltimore voters chose four delegates with virtually no experience in local or provinical office. Throughout the colony, the Convention elevated many men to political prominence for the first time, but no county so completely repudiated its old guard. Only one of Baltimore's representatives had ever sat in the assembly before, and none had served as a justice, militia officer, or sheriff. By contrast, the forty-one delegates who came from other counties included twenty-two justices, ten militia officers, thirteen assemblymen, and four sheriffs. The sudden shift in political leadership split the county into antagonistic factions, although it is impossible to gauge their respective size, organization, and agenda. Residents who remained loyal to the old regime sent a petition to the king defending the proprietor and blasting the new government. Only two other counties followed Baltimore's lead, while five counties submitted petitions in support of the Convention.[36]

Thomas Thurston's was one of the new names. Elected to the Convention in 1689, his tempestuous career illustrates how the Associator's revolution temporarily opened an unobstructed path to a new, militant breed of politician. Indeed, it is impossible to imagine Thurston coming to power by any path other than revolution. Born in a village near Bristol, a hotbed of early Quakerism, George Fox made a fiery convert of Thurston, although he probably lived to regret it. In 1656, aged thirty-four, Thurston set out for Massachusetts with a band of Quaker missionaries, only to have Puritan authorities ship him back to England. A year later Thurston renewed his missionary work in the Chesapeake colonies, with no greater success. This time he was exiled from both Virginia and Maryland. Undeterred, Thurston walked 300 miles to New Amsterdam, where he landed in a Dutch jail. He eventually pushed on to New England, and after another short stay returned to Maryland. The provincial authorities, who continued to see the unrepentant Thurston as a threat to social order, banished him again. During the next five years Thurston's proselytizing activities carried him to England, Virginia, Maryland, and the West Indies. Finally, in 1664 he settled in Anne Arundel County and later moved to Baltimore County, where he continued to reside until his death at the age of seventy-one.[37]

Thurston was a shrewd businessman as well as a religious visionary. In 1664 he imported twenty indentured servants into Maryland, thereby earning a claim to 1,200 acres of land. Within three years he had patented nearly all of them. But Thurston did not intend to become a planter. A shoemaker by trade, he purchased a tract called "The Tanyard," where he seems to have produced finished leather for boots and shoes. To obtain raw hides for the operation, he plunged into the Indian trade, perhaps taking advantage of contacts he had made with natives during his trek to New Amsterdam. The 2,500 acres he eventually acquired in Baltimore were located at the mouths of the Bush and Susquehanna rivers, long-established gathering points for the fur trade. Not surprisingly, one of his tracts had been owned previously by another Indian trader.[38]

In backwater Baltimore, rich men frequently acquired their fortunes in unconventional ways, but few were as unconventional as Thurston. Amid the unbroken forests of the northern Chesapeake, he made his living with hammer and awl, not with hoe and axe. In 1693 the appraisors of his estate found a full range of craftsman's tools, but not a single piece of plantation equipment. Thurston also owned a valuable cache of pelts that included raccoon, fox, deer, bear, wild cat, beaver, otter, wolf, elk, and mink, which were worth 6 percent of his total personal property. "Trading Indian Shirts," "Trading Linen," "Small Trading Kettles," and "Indian Ropes" all testify to Thurston's continued interest in the Indian trade. Shoemaking and fur trading were profitable for Thurston. At his death he ranked in the top 15 percent of probated decedents and owned over 2,000 acres.[39]

Thurston was also an unconventional Quaker. The Society of Friends, which knew something about defying convention, simply could not contain Thurston or his anarchic impulses. He eventually succumbed to the antinomianism that ran so close to the surface of early Quakerism. By the 1660s Thurston had embraced the teachings of Quaker rebel John Perrot, who condemned the emptiness of religious form. His list of objectionable forms included the Quaker customs of removing the hat during prayer, of shaking hands at the end of service, and of holding meetings for worship at regular times rather than when the spirit moved the congregation. By tarring so many conventional behaviors with the brush of "form," Perrot threatened to undermine the institutional foundation of the church George Fox was laboring to construct. In 1675 Fox himself persuaded Thurston to renounce his errors and welcomed him back into the fold, but the rapprochement did not last long. Soon, local congregations in Baltimore were complaining that Thurston disrupted their proceedings, created dissension among the members, and poured abuse on everyone who disagreed with him.[40]

If Thurston's combative spirit alarmed the Quaker authorities, it made him a natural leader in the struggle against Lord Baltimore. He burst on to the scene in 1686, when Baltimore voters elected him to the last proprietary assembly. Three years later Thurston was sitting in the Convention. But feeling more comfortable on the battlefield than in the assembly hall, he managed to secure an appointment as the "principal Military Officer in Baltimore." Thurston inevitably made enemies as he climbed to power, and they dragged him before the council in 1692 on charges of "unruly and disorderly actions." As the imperial government tightened its reigns on Maryland, radicals like Thurston felt the squeeze. One of his enemies, Capt. Thomas Richardson, testified that Thurston refused to turn over to him possession of the county magazine as the assembly had directed. Thurston responded by taking a verbal shot at his very round antagonist. Richardson was only "half a Colonel," he exclaimed, although "big enough to make two if he were split in two." Such humor smacked of insolence, and Thurston was removed from office. It would be wrong to cast this militant

associator as a spokesman for democracy, but like Nathaniel Bacon of
Virginia and Jacob Leisler of New York, he certainly knew what ordinary planters feared most. Predicting that county taxes would increase now that proprietary favorites had wormed their way back into
power, Thurston declared, "there is fine times now, none but linsey
Woolsey fellows and Papists rules." He died a few months later, de-
fiant to the end.[41]

That a fire-breather like Thomas Thurston was able to storm past
George Wells and Miles Gibson, win election to the Convention, and
secure control over the county's military establishment suggests the
revolutionary character of the events of 1689-92. It also says a great
deal about the kind of society that had evolved in seventeenth-century
Baltimore. This was a society without great slaveholders, prosperous
merchants, or dignified clergymen. This was a society without men
who believed they had a right to rule and who had the economic and
political resources to make others believe it. This was a society without a gentry.

2

The Open Elite

From 1700 to 1760 Baltimore County came of age. As centripetal forces steadily leveled the disparities between the northern periphery and tidewater core of Chesapeake society, a recognizably uniform pattern of life spread from the James River to the Susquehanna River. At last Baltimore found a place in the social order of what might be called the Greater Tidewater. At the highest level of county society, this process of convergence took the form of gentrification. Thomas Todd, George Wells, and Thomas Thurston were hard-handed frontiersmen whose scramble to the top of the economic pyramid epitomized the rough-hewn world in which they lived. But a generation later their successors exhibited a patina of politeness and polish altogether absent in the seventeenth century. In short, the foremost families of Baltimore were beginning to look, act, think, and spend like a real gentry.

Yet Baltimore confronted a stubborn legacy of backwardness. At no point before the imperial crisis of the 1760s did it develop a "provincial gentry" of the kind to be found in the tidewater heartland of Virginia or Maryland. The great planter-merchants who comprised this tightly knit group each owned tens of thousands of acres, employed scores of slaves, dominated the county courts and parish vestries, and sat year after year—indeed generation after generation—in the assembly. In Baltimore, by contrast, a man counted himself rich and powerful if he possessed a thousand acres and a dozen slaves, served a year or two on the county bench, and won a single election to the assembly. He and his kind made up the "county gentry." Although county gentries constituted the backbone of the upper class throughout the colonial Chesapeake, historians have understandably been drawn to such towering figures as Landon Carter, William Byrd, and Daniel Dulany. Based largely on the experiences of these provincial giants, they have concluded that stability, cohesiveness, and continuity were hallmarks of the Chesapeake upper class. But the picture becomes more complex if we shift the focus from the provincial to the county gentry. The economic elite of Baltimore inhabited a world that the

Tidewater's patricians would have found both unfamiliar and uninviting, a world characterized by a remarkable degree of openness, fluidity, and impermanence.

During the first half of the eighteenth century, Baltimore looked more like a tidewater county than at any other time in its history. One reason was population growth. As new settlers occupied the shoreline and fanned out along the main rivers and tributaries, Baltimore began to shed its frontier roughness. By 1712 a small-scale demographic explosion had pushed the county's population to nearly 3,000, an increase of 69 percent over the previous twelve years, or twice the provincial growth rate. The county that had perennially trailed behind lower Maryland could now hold its own in open competition for settlers. Indeed it was starting to outdraw some of the longer-settled counties. Whereas in 1700 Baltimore contained only 5 percent of the provincial population, two decades later the figure had reached 7 percent. That the upward demographic trajectory held steady through the depression of Queen Anne's War (1702-13) and the economic recovery that followed suggests it was sustained by internal forces largely independent of the tobacco economy. Between 1720 and 1737 the number of inhabitants more than doubled from 4,100 to 9,100.[1]

Another process that swept Baltimore into Greater Tidewater society was the emergence of slavery. As we have seen, at the end of the seventeenth century landless freemen drifting from plantation to plantation in search of seasonal employment seemed on the threshold of becoming a permanent work force. But a generation later African slaves were supplanting migrant workers in the tobacco and corn fields. In 1737 about a third of the county's 1,113 households included one or more adult slaves. At the head of the master class stood eleven men who owned more than ten adult slaves. Baltimore never had as many slaves or slaveholders as tidewater counties, but by the second quarter of the century it had enough of both to qualify as a slave society.[2]

The trend toward occupational differentiation also helped narrow the gap between Baltimore and the Tidewater. Throughout Maryland and Virginia most white men called themselves planters, but the number who did not was large and probably getting larger. Carpenters, blacksmiths, merchants, physicians, and dozens of other specialists transformed a relatively simple export-economy into one of the most dynamic and diversified regions in British North America. During the 1730s the clerk of the county court recorded the occupations of 717

Table 1. Distribution of Occupations in Baltimore County: 1729-39

Occupation	% of All Occupations	Occupation	% of All Occupations
Planter	66	Innkeeper	2
Craftsman	17	Laborer	2
Gentleman	6	Mariner	1
Merchant	3	TOTAL	100
Professional	3		

SOURCES: This table covers all individuals whose occupations were recorded in the Baltimore County Land Records, Maryland State Archives; Baltimore County Court Proceedings, Maryland State Archives.

NOTES: The data have two flaws. First, they are biased against lower-ranking occupations less likely to appear in court buying and selling land. Second, they create a false impression of functional specialization because forty-seven individuals (chiefly planter-craftsmen) listed more than one occupation.

Baltimore residents (see table 1). One of three said he was something other than a planter. Nearly one of five said he was a craftsman, although he may have raised a crop and livestock on the side. The growing number of specialists who made a living outside agriculture demonstrated that the tobacco colonies were experiencing qualitative economic development alongside quantitative economic growth.[3]

The same institutions that gave meaning and order to people's lives in tidewater counties were sinking deeper roots in Baltimore. And no institution touched as many lives as the county court. Although its origins reached back to the establishment of Baltimore, not until the early eighteenth century did the court move squarely to the center of community activities. One crucial factor enhancing the status of the court was its location. For decades Baltimoreans had wrangled inconclusively over where to put their courthouse, selecting first a spot on the Bush River and then various sites along the Gunpowder River. Finally, in 1712 the assembly called for the construction of a new courthouse at Joppa Town on the Gunpowder, where the county seat remained for fifty-six years.[4]

At quarterly sessions of the court, the entire gamut of Baltimore society paraded through Joppa Town. Grave men in black robes and powdered wigs took their seats on the bench; planters and merchants huddled over important business deals; yeomen drafted for jury duty smoked pipes and killed time outside the courthouse; plaintiffs and defendants got last-minute advice from their attorneys; the laboring poor awaited criminal prosecution for everything from fornication to running away; slaves worked in the stables, waited on tables, and ran errands for their masters. The court brought out people like Bridget Ward, who received permission to hawk "liquor cakes" in the streets to support her needy family. The establishment of a permanent county seat gave this swirling social activity a patterned, predictable, almost theatrical quality. Four times a year Joppa Town became the stage on which the great and humble acted out roles assigned them in the social hierarchy.[5]

A second reason why the court came to throw a larger shadow over county life stemmed from its own internal evolution. As judges and juries accumulated a larger pool of experience and confidence, they took steps to formalize practices that had grown up haphazardly over the years. Judges insisted on a strict observance of correct procedure and proper decorum, not just because they wanted to escape their hot robes and stuffy courtrooms as soon as possible, but because they wanted to impress upon everyone the solemnity of the proceedings and the majesty of their own persons. So in 1721 a new list of rules was issued codifying court procedures and instituting heavy fines for violators. All court officers who failed to appear by noon had to pay a fine; the sheriff had to call the petite juries once a day to check attendance; deputy sheriffs who failed to administer corporal punishment as directed faced a fine; and most ominously, the sheriff was required to "provide A Sufficient Catt of Nine tailes Which the first Day of Each Respective Court he shall produce to the Courts View and Lay the Same on the Table Within the Barr." With this instrument of bloody terror separating judges and judged, who could doubt that the court meant business?[6]

If judges commanded reverence, juries insisted on respect. In selecting men for jury service, sheriffs usually cajoled and conscripted middling planters considered to be of good character and sound judgment. This recruitment practice had far-reaching political significance, for it provided ordinary planters with a singular opportunity to speak with a collective voice. As early as 1697 a particularly bold grand jury fired a petition to the governor, claiming to be the "Representative body of Baltomore [sic] County." But not until the next generation did grand juries regularly act as such, calling for the appointment of officials who enjoyed the support of "Freeholders" and protesting against measures that threatened their interests. However inadequately and irregularly, the court offered a forum where Baltimoreans could map the boundaries of the rulers' prerogatives and the people's rights. By dulling the edge of class conflict and fortifying the coalition between gentlemen and yeomen, the court exerted the same stabilizing influence in Baltimore that it did in tidewater counties.[7]

As the court gained power, prestige, and permanence, so did the other mainstay of institutional life—the church. In 1742 the growing number of Anglican families in the upper reaches of the Patapsco and Gunpowder rivers necessitated the addition of a new parish, St. Thomas's. With church membership on the rise, clergymen who had once seen Baltimore as a mere stepping-stone to better jobs elsewhere began to give it a second look. From 1730 to 1776 rectors stayed at their posts an average of eleven years, twice as long as their predecessors. By the last generation of the colonial period each parish was under the care of a venerable rector who personified spiritual continuity and institutional stability: Thomas Chase of St. Paul's (1745-79), Hugh Deans of St. John's (1742-77), Andrew Lendrum of St. George's (1749-69), and Thomas Cradock of St. Thomas's (1745-70).[8]

As ministers moved into their parishes, they moved up the economic ladder. Of seven clergymen who died before 1776 and left an inventory, two ranked in the top 7 percent of probated decedents and six in the top 17 percent. Maryland clerics made good livings by standards of the day, but few of them got rich on their salaries alone. In the everything-has-its-price milieu of eighteenth-century Maryland, no social stigma attached to earning something on the side, so most ministers combined preaching, planting, and trading. At his death in 1738 Reverend William Cawthren owned four slaves and two servants who had recently brought in a valuable harvest of 6,000 pounds of tobacco. And he was not the only planter. Except for Evan Evans, every minister who left an inventory owned unfree laborers: Andrew Lendrum had twenty-six slaves; Benedict Bourdillon, six slaves and two servants; William Tibbs, six slaves; Joseph Hooper, two slaves and four servants; and Hugh Carlisle, one servant. As a profit-maximizing entrepreneur, no one could match the Reverend Tibbs who supplied the material as well as spiritual cravings of his flock by offering a full line of dry goods at his well-stocked store. Clergymen who stayed in Baltimore the longest were most likely to acquire land in addition to their other assets. Those who purchased land had an average tenure of seventeen years, compared to four years for nonlandholders. The average estate was about 500 acres, putting ministers in the top quarter of Baltimore's landed population. In addition, two ministers bought lots in Baltimore Town.[9]

Parish life settled into the same familiar routines found in any tide-water county. In 1724 Reverend Tibbs of St. Paul's sent a report to his superiors on the state of his parish. Although clearly a piece of self-promotion, the document opens a small window onto parish affairs. With 363 families under his guidance, Tibbs claimed to offer services every Sunday and on "some Holidays," and he could usually count on a "full congregation." Communion was administered three times a year to a few dozen men and women. In addition, the rector provided catechism to youngsters during the six weeks of Lent and tutored children whose parents were willing to pay a little extra. The conservative Tibbs could not help but grumble at the absence of a parish library, school, surplice, pulpit cloth, cushion, silver chalice, and other High Church trappings. But if he is to be believed, St. Paul's was success-fully meeting the religious needs of his parishioners as well as the in-stitutional needs of the county.[10]

As the process of social and institutional development brought Baltimore into line with tidewater counties, the local elite began to resemble a real gentry. Simply put, the rich were getting richer. In practically every decade between 1660 and 1760, the Baltimore elite made significant additions to its stock of personal property (see appendix 1, table 17). Whereas a person who died before 1690 had to own an estate worth £133 to rank in the elite, seventy years later nothing less than £603 would suffice. Of nearly two hundred Balti-moreans whose estates passed through probate during the seventeenth century, only one would have cracked into the elite in the 1750s. At his death in 1689, James Phillips owned an estate appraised at £860, the largest his generation had ever seen. But it would have been possible to fit nine such estates into the one Nicholas Rogers left behind in 1758.[11]

The elite owned more of the things that symbolized gentility. The eighteenth century witnessed a revolution in consumer behavior throughout the Anglo-American world, as the well-to-do began stuff-ing their houses with things their parents and grandparents would never have dreamed of. Niceties replaced necessities. From British workshops came a flood of consumer goods—china settings, silver tea sets, floor carpets, great clocks, fine furniture, fancy clothes, leather-bound books—all of which found eager buyers among the Bal-timore elite. This is not to say that the proportion of elite property made up of consumer goods increased. On the contrary, throughout the colonial period elite spending habits remained remarkably stable (see table 2). In any given decade after 1690, household goods made

Table 2. Composition of Elite Estates: 1660-1776

	-1690	1690-1699	1700-1709	1710-1719	1720-1729	1730-1739	1740-1749	1750-1759	1760-1769	1770-1776
Household	17%	11%	13%	12%	12%	13%	10%	7%	10%	11%
Livestock	31	23	22	24	18	19	10	7	11	10
Labor	16	12	24	35	30	34	24	26	35	29
Capital	3	3	3	3	4	4	5	6	9	15
Crops	2	4	6	4	4	8	4	4	7	8
Merchandise	1	2	7	6	10	6	21	20	9	5
Cash	1	2	4	3	2	4	3	4	4	3
Debts	29	43	21	13	20	12	23	26	15	19
TOTAL	100%	100%	100%	100%	100%	100%	100%	100%	100%	100%

SOURCE: Inventories; Inventories & Accounts; Baltimore County Inventories, Maryland State Archives.

up between 7 percent and 13 percent of elite estates, without any long-term tendency up or down. But in assessing how the furnishings of elite homes actually changed, the relative value of such goods is less important than their absolute value, which increased steadily from an average of £52 per estate before 1690 to £140 in the 1740s.[12]

The gentrification of the elite is illustrated by the cases of Miles Gibson and William Young. We have already met Gibson in the rough-and-tumble of the Glorious Revolution. When in 1689 the Protestant Association destroyed the proprietary regime, he was probably in his early forties, having reached Maryland as an indentured servant some twenty years before. Starting at the bottom of white society, Gibson pushed himself to the top. By the 1660s he was a freeman buying land near the Bush River; by the 1670s he was calling himself a gentleman; and by the 1680s he was serving in the assembly and as county sheriff. At his death in 1692 Gibson owned about 2,500 acres of land and a personal estate appraised at £605, the third largest of the 1690s.[13]

But Gibson did not live in luxury, at least not by later standards. Much of the space in his home was taken up by beds, with every room probably containing at least one. Gibson owned a total of eight and presumably slept in the most expensive one equipped with two sets of curtains and a counterpane. Even more ubiquitous were tables and chairs. Twelve "old" leather chairs flanked the main dining table, but fifteen additional wooden ones along with assorted stools and trunks provided extra seating for guests. Few items indicate that Gibson cared much about cultivating or displaying genteel tastes. His china collection consisted of one cup. The walls were bare except for three looking glasses (one was cracked). Only one floor was covered by a carpet described as "old." When Gibson wanted to look the gentleman, he could pull out his castor hat, "plush" breeches, silk jacket, quilted waistcoat, "old" long coat, gold ring, and periwig. But this was a threadbare wardrobe. Save for a pair of leather breeches, some stockings, five "old" shirts, and two pairs of "old" shoes, Gibson did not have anything else to wear.[14]

The path William Young took to the top was strewn with fewer obstacles. In 1743, when his name first appeared in county records, he already occupied a prestigious position on the vestry of St. John's Parish. Two years later "Captain" Young was serving as deputy ranger and as overseer of the roads on the Great Falls of the Gunpowder River. For a time during the 1750s he held the post of county sheriff, making him the equal of any man in Baltimore. From that point until his death in 1773, Young was invariably referred to either as "Colonel" or "Gentleman." These titles of distinction rested on a personal estate worth £1,710, the sixth largest of the 240 inventoried between 1770 and 1776.[15]

If Gibson had been a guest in Young's home, he would have been struck by a combination of familiar and unfamiliar sights. The large number of beds would not have seemed strange, but their location would have. Most of the twelve beds seem to have been squeezed upstairs into the "green" and "blue" rooms. The emergence of separate sleeping chambers reflected not only the functional specialization of interior space as upper-class homes became larger, but perhaps a new feeling that the family's private activities should be physically screened from public ones in the parlor and hall. A heightened desire to partition private from public spheres might explain why Young owned chamber pots and Gibson did not. One could find plenty of places to sit in both houses, since a gentleman was expected to entertain friends, neighbors, clients, and strangers. But the quality of the furniture differed markedly between the two. The rough-hewn chairs, backless stools, and sealskin trunks of Gibson's day had been replaced by expensive pieces of craftsmanship. The thirty-eight chairs scattered through Young's house included six of mahogany, twelve of walnut, and six leather armchairs. Each one was worth no less than ten shillings.[16]

What might have impressed Gibson most was not any single item but the overall sensation of glitter, sparkle, and gleam. A costly china set was displayed in the cupboard, and an even more valuable collection of silver was probably on the teaboard and tea table. A great clock rang out the time. Curtains hung in the windows. Carpets covered the floors. Several writing desks, including one of fine mahogany, were in various rooms. On the shelves of three bookcases stood one of the county's largest libraries. The walls were festooned with forty "framed gilt prints," four "India prints," eleven "pictures," and four "framed pictures." A backgammon board and violin set the tone of sociability. Appraisors did not itemize Young's wardrobe, but it alone was worth a small fortune of £49.[17]

If Gibson could manage nothing better than a grubby gentility, Colonel Young cut an impressive figure with his "cane washed with gold," silver spurs, and silver shoe buckles. This was the way a flashing gentleman was supposed to look. The stark contrast between the two suggests that by the mid-eighteenth century a recognizable gentry class had emerged from the obscure small-timers of Gibson's generation.

Even so, Colonel Young and his peers would have been overshadowed alongside the provinical gentry of the Chesapeake Tidewater. Having established themselves in the latter half of the seventeenth century, the first families of eastern Virginia and lower Maryland spent the rest of the colonial period consolidating their hegemony and defending it against ambitious outsiders. In all of British North America it would be hard to find a more solidly entrenched ruling class. By contrast, the richest men of Baltimore rarely approached the economic stature of tidewater gentlemen and never succeeded in shutting the door on outsiders who arrived without familial and political connections.[18]

The openness of the county elite becomes apparent in the process of land acquisition. Like all Chesapeake counties, by the mid-eighteenth century Baltimore harbored vast disparities in the distribution of its economic resources, land above all. A few dozen families sat securely atop the pyramid of landed wealth. How much they owned emerges from an examination of debt books compiled annually between 1754 and 1771. In these books proprietary officials were supposed to list every landowner in the county along with each tract of land in his possession. The purpose of the exercise was to compute the quitrent owed to the lord proprietor. The 1754 debt book reveals that the top tenth of Baltimore landowners accounted for 56 percent of

Table 3. Distribution of Land in Baltimore County: 1754

Decile	Acres	% of Total Acres
Top 10%	794+	56
2nd	793-480	13
3rd	479-319	9
4th	318-230	6
5th	229-190	5
6th	189-134	4
7th	133-100	3
8th	100-88	2
9th	87-50	1
Bottom 10%	50-0	1
TOTAL		100

SOURCES: Baltimore Debt Book 1754, Maryland State Archives.

NOTES: A total of 470,910 acres was recorded in the debt book. Lots in Baltimore Town and Joppa Town were recorded as one acre each.

the privately-owned acres in the county; the bottom half, only 11 percent (see table 3). An estate of 794 acres put one at the pinnacle of landed society.[19]

A landowner did not get to the top by relying solely, or even primarily, on his patrimony. Consider the fifty-four members of the elite who appear in county debt books and who owned a total of 85,374 acres. In 1754 the average elite estate of 1,581 acres would have ranked in the top 3 percent of landholdings. The key point is that most of the this land had *not* been inherited. Of the 85,374 acres, three-fifths had been purchased by the elite landowner either from the proprietor or in the private market. The remaining two-fifths, which cannot be located in the patent records or county deeds where purchases were recorded, had presumably been acquired through inheritance or marriage. In sum, almost 1,000 of the 1,581 acres comprising the average elite estate represented the fruits of individual initiative, not the blessings of family privilege.

In-migrants and immigrants are the key to understanding why most elite land was purchased rather than inherited. Notwithstanding the widely held view that by the second quarter of the eighteenth century most Chesapeake gentlemen were second- and third-generation natives who owed their high status to inherited wealth, the Baltimore elite continued to receive a steady infusion of new blood from the outside throughout the colonial period. There is perhaps no clearer sign of the openness of the county gentry than the large number of in-migrants and immigrants who rose to the top without the benefit of a landed patrimony in Baltimore. It has been possible to identify the birthplaces of forty-two of the fifty-four members of the elite who appear in the debt books. Of these forty-two, twenty-two were not born in Baltimore. Fifteen of them were in-migrants who came from other Maryland counties: six from Anne Arundel, five from Calvert, two from Cecil, and one each from Prince George's and Kent. The British Isles contributed six immigrants, while only one member of the elite traced his family history back to another mainland colony, Pennsylvania.[20]

Ambitious immigrants had no choice but to throw themselves into the private land market. The twenty-two outsiders purchased at least 75 percent of the land they owned as recorded in debt books. This pattern held true even for in-migrants from nearby counties, whose fathers were in a position to purchase land in Baltimore with the intention of settling their sons on it. Only two of the fifteen Maryland-born in-migrants received Baltimore land in their fathers' wills: Ephraim Gover of Anne Arundel County inherited 487 acres along the Susquehanna River and James Heath of Cecil County got 650 acres on Bynum's Run.[21]

That in-migrants and immigrants arrived without land does not mean they arrived penniless, for many of them seem to have brought start-up capital or well-placed connections, or both. A few of the British immigrants had commercial links to London merchant houses, which they turned to advantage in Baltimore. Likewise, Maryland-born in-migrants came from families best described as middling to upper-middling. Of the fifteen, twelve had fathers who left inventories. The average personal estate, appraised at £796, would have ranked in the top 10 percent of Baltimore decedents at any point during the colonial period. But from the perspective of a hopeful heir, the total value of the estate was less important than what remained after creditors had finished with it. In ten cases where accounts are available, the average net worth of the estates fell to £280. Of the fifteen, only two were clearly born to the manor. James Heath of Cecil County and John Addison Smith of Calvert County both had extremely powerful fathers who each left personal estates approaching £3,000, which only a handful of men in all of Virginia and Maryland could match. All in all, it appears that the typical Maryland-born in-migrant who attained elite status in Baltimore could count on financial support from his family, although not nearly enough to buy a full-fledged gentleman's estate.[22]

The case of William Govane sheds light on why a man would leave his birthplace to make a new life in the northern Chesapeake. Born in Anne Arundel County in 1717, Govane knew from an early age that he would have to earn his fortune himself. Although his father had influential family ties and called himself a gentleman, he amassed no more than 300 acres on the Severn River, all of which had to be sold off before William came of age. When William's father died in 1739, creditors took his entire personal estate, a modest one appraised at £150. Undismayed, the ambitious twenty-two-year-old decided to apply "himself to Trade and Merchandize to Advance himself and Fortune." The young merchant's prospects brightened a year later when he married Anne Homewood, widow of the wealthy Thomas Homewood, who brought to her new husband a dower of £700 and a one-third interest in the Homewood landed estate, later estimated to be worth £50 current per year.[23]

Things went smoothly for almost a decade, but in 1749 the marriage began to crumble amid accusations of unfaithfulness on both sides. In the spring of 1750, while on a voyage to the West Indies, William decided that he and his wife should make a fresh start in Rhode Island, where they might salvage their marriage and profit from the colony's commercial expansion. Some people who knew William suspected him of scheming to separate Anne from her father so that he might enjoy a free hand in disposing of her dower. The dispute ended up in the courts, exposing the couple to two years of public humiliation. Finally, in 1752 the chancery court ordered William to relinquish his control over the Homewood estate and to pay Anne £20 a year for her maintenance while they remained separated. With little holding him in Anne Arundel, William crossed the Patapsco into Baltimore, where by 1760 he had purchased 1,120 acres on the Back and Gunpowder rivers. At his death nine years later William left his estate to his two children by Mary Salisbury, a Baltimore woman he never married.[24]

If in-migrants and immigrants bought most of their land, natives inherited most of theirs. Remember that twenty of the forty-two members of the elite whose origins could be identified were born in Baltimore. For natives, some of whose families had been in the county three or four generations, inheritance played an indispensable role in amassing an estate. Considering that the twenty natives purchased only 41 percent of the land registered in debt books, 34 percent less than immigrants, it is safe to say that most of their land had been inherited. For twelve of the twenty natives whose fathers left wills specifying landed bequests, it is possible to say exactly how much was inherited: 845 acres. Without adding a single acre to his patrimony, the typical native ranked in the top tenth of the landed population.[25]

A few examples illustrate the range of possibilities available to native members of the elite. James Phillips and John Paca exemplify the classic tidewater pattern in which family wealth, accumulated over several generations, was transmitted largely intact to the male heir. They led the list of heirs with inheritances of 3,490 acres and 2,456 acres, respectively. Both were third-generation Baltimoreans; both inherited land originally patented or purchased by their grandfathers; and both had the good luck to be only sons, making them virtually sole heirs to the family's landholdings.[26]

Joshua Bond did not receive nearly as much as Phillips and Paca, but he provides a more typical example of land accumulation among the native elite. The Bonds had been settled in Baltimore for several generations, producing an extensive clan of kinsmen in the region of the Bush and Gunpowder rivers. Although Joshua's first purchase of land in 1747 was a modest tract of forty acres, he hoped for bigger things to come. A year earlier his father had begun distributing property to his five sons through deeds of gift. Joshua received his portion in 1752, a 500-acre tract named Poplar Neck, although he had enjoyed de facto possession of the land for years and had already built his dwelling plantation there. When Joshua's father died four years later, he confirmed the earlier gifts to his sons and provided that each of them receive equal shares of whatever real and personal estate remained. The brothers drew lots for the residual property, and Joshua won a one-third share of a water mill together with 286 acres of adjoining land. Another windfall came in 1765 when Joshua gained 241 acres in a resurvey. He died four years later in possession of four tracts of land totaling 976 acres, 695 of which he had received from his father through either gift or will.[27]

The top ranks of Baltimore society, compared to the provincial gentry, remained remarkably accessible throughout the colonial era. Immigrants right off the boat from England and Scotland used their overseas connections to break into the county elite. From other parts of Maryland came sons of middling and upper-middling planters no less determined to make their mark. Make no mistake, these men did not rise from rags to riches, as did Miles Gibson in the seventeenth century. Still, the large number of outsiders who succeeded did so without the advantage of a landed inheritance. Indeed, the immigrants and in-migrants in the debt books ended up with an average of 200 acres more than the natives. If the very lack of an inheritance gave immigrants an extra psychological spur to accumulate property as quickly as possible, it would not be the first or last time in American history.

It was a steep climb to elite status. For everyone who scaled the slope, another lost his footing and tumbled back down. Downward intergenerational mobility was the corollary of upward intragenerational mobility, and both processes reveal the open character of the Baltimore elite. Those heading down included the elite's own children. Reared amid servants, slaves, and the glistening products of the consumer revolution, these sons and daughters discovered in adulthood that they would have to settle for a lot less than their parents had accumulated. Few of them, if any at all, ended up in the bottom ranks of tenant farmers or landless laborers. Even so, their experiences belied any complacent assumption that elite status could be counted on as an automatic birthright. The large number of elite children who skidded down the social scale each generation guaranteed that at no time during the eighteenth century would Baltimore develop the kind of stable family lineages that characterized the provincial gentry of tidewater Virginia and lower Maryland.[28]

What was the fate of elite sons? In theory, it should be possible to gauge how well daughters did by measuring the economic status of the men they married. In reality, even if daughters who married local men could be traced in the spotty parish records, most of those who took husbands outside the county would remain beyond our reach. So we are left with their brothers, not because men are more important than women, but because they are less elusive in the records. Also it should be stressed that the analysis is by no means definitive, since rather than following the individual careers of the elite sons, it measures their economic performance at several points in time. Of the 181 members of the county elite, 114 recorded a will in the probate courts. The following examination of the 209 sons mentioned in those wills concludes that most elite sons did well, but not as well as their parents.

One source shedding light on the economic status of elite sons is a 1773 tax list. It contains the names of all white taxables and the number of adult slaves belonging to each household. Unfortunately, the list is flawed because assessors failed to distinguish between white and black inmates in Baltimore Town and because they omitted people who lived north of the Gunpowder River. Nevertheless, it has been possible to identify forty-five elite sons in the list. A large proportion of them (thirty-eight of forty-five) had taken the crucial step toward establishing their economic independence by forming separate households. The remaining dependents seem to have been minors under the care of relatives, like Benjamin Boyce and James Bond, both of whom resided with their mothers. The vast majority of elite sons had also made a decisive move into the upper ranks of householders through their acquisition of slaves. At a time when only 23 percent of county households contained an adult slave, 79 percent of the thirty-eight sons owned at least one.[29]

If the relatively large number of slaveholding household heads suggests that elite sons kept a grip on their parents' economic status, other evidence points in the opposite direction. Elite sons owned an average of only 3.6 slaves, not many compared to their parents. And if we omit the three largest holdings—Archibald Buchanan's twelve, William Lux's twelve, and James Govane's ten—the average falls to 2.0. Only three elite sons were listed as owning outlying quarters in addition to their home plantations, an indication that their estates did not sprawl across the county. Finally, few elite sons seemed ready to seize the teeming opportunities for personal enrichment in booming Baltimore Town, even though by the 1760s it was already clear that in the future the greatest commercial fortunes would be linked to urban development. Only seven of the forty-five sons were townsmen, including merchants Richard Moale, William Buchanan, Philip Rogers, and Gerrard Hopkins, who opened stores, invested in urban property, and emerged from the revolutionary war with considerable fortunes. The overwhelming majority of elite sons preferred the sluggish rhythms of their rural estates to the freewheeling pace of urban life.[30]

Another source illuminating the economic status of elite sons is debt books. It has been possible to identify fifty-six sons in the debt books between 1754 and 1771. Without doubt, they owned a lot of land. The average estate equaled 905 acres, which at mid-century would have ranked in the top tenth of Baltimore landholders. But the average conceals great variation. Half of the sons owned less than 500 acres. More important, the landed estates that elite sons aggrandized paled next to those on which they had been raised. Remember that those members of the elite who could be identified in debt books owned an average of nearly 1,600 acres. By the 1770s hundreds of investors, large and small, had jumped into the great real estate boom in Baltimore Town, but few elite sons jumped with them. Only five of the fifty-six owned town lots.[31]

Inventories provide a third source of information on the economic standing of elite sons. The estates of forty sons passed through probate courts before 1776. In terms of the personal wealth they had accumulated by the time of their deaths, most sons did not measure up to their fathers. Only three out of ten maintained their elite ranking in the top 10 percent of probated decedents. Practically all of the remaining sons were scattered in the middling to upper-middling wealth range. Eight of ten fell in the top 50 percent of decedents.[32]

As the eighteenth century advanced, the sight of elite sons losing their grip and slipping from the top rung became increasingly commonplace. Of those whose estates were inventoried before 1729, 40 percent fell in the wealthiest tenth of decedents and therefore maintained elite status. But the figure dropped to 31 percent between 1730 and 1759, and again to 22 percent between 1760 and 1776. Another sixteen sons appeared in probate records between 1776 and 1798. Only four of them had estates appraised at £612 or more, the cut-off point for elite status during the final six years of the colonial period. That all four were urban merchants confirms the general impression that after the revolutionary war the path to riches led increasingly through the counting houses of Baltimore Town.[33]

In sum, fragmentary evidence combed from tax, land, and probate records suggests that elite sons did well measured against virtually any standard, except the one set by their parents. While a minority of them clung fast to the economic standing they had enjoyed as childen, the majority dropped into the broad ranks of middling and upper-middling planters. This pattern of downward intergenerational mobility contrasts sharply with the situation in tidewater Virginia and lower Maryland where, generation after generation, the same family names dominated economic and political life. Such continuity was impossible in Baltimore. Given the periodic reshuffling of economic fortunes that occurred each generation, few elite families were able to preserve their place at the top over more than a lifetime.

The openness, fluidity, and impermanence that distinguished the Baltimore elite left an unmistakable imprint on political life. In a society where power and wealth were considered inseparable, sons who failed to inherit their parents' economic position would not expect to advance their political careers as far as their fathers had. And conversely, newcomers who climbed into the elite would expect to rise in politics as far as their wealth allowed. Throughout the eighteenth century a constant stream of new people circulated into and out of the county court and provincial assembly, the only indispensable prerequisite for officeholding being wealth. The accessibility of local political office to men of wealth, irrespective of family background, set Baltimore apart from Chesapeake counties dominated by the provincial gentry. The handful of families who in tidewater counties monopolized local office and who constituted, in the words of one historian, an "almost hereditary caste" had no real counterpart in Baltimore.[34]

The place to begin is the county court. Lists of Baltimore judges survive for thirty-four of the forty-two years between 1722 and 1763. An examination of the sixty-three justices who attended quarterly sessions reveals that only the very rich secured a spot on the bench. Of the thirty-eight justices who died before 1776 and left inventories, sixteen fell in the top 5 percent of probated decedents, twenty-five in the top 10 percent, and thirty-two in the top 20 percent. Only one justice failed to reach the top half of the wealth hierarchy, but he was a young man who died shortly after his appointment to the bench. Had he lived longer, he undoubtedly would have risen higher.[35]

If only rich men sat on the bench, they did not sit there long. The sixty-three justices had an average tenure of 5.8 years. No one served more than twenty years. One way to appreciate the high degree of turnover is by freezing the court in a typical year. In 1746, of the twelve men who sat on the bench, only three had eight or more years of judicial experience. By contrast, five of the twelve judges had served no more than two years. Although a few individuals carved out lengthy careers on the county bench and undoubtedly provided a living source of continuity and leadership, the graybeards were always outnumbered by unseasoned newcomers still feeling their way through the labyrinth of court politics.[36]

Political endogamy was much less pronounced in Baltimore than in tidewater counties. That forty-six surnames were represented among the sixty-three justices does not evoke an image of well-entrenched magistrates passing down their offices to sons, grandsons, and nephews. Admittedly, the Hall family of northern Baltimore, which supplied five justices between 1722 and 1763, illustrates the enormous influence that certain clans could exert in local politics. But the Halls were not typical. Before 1763 only six justices had sons who also served on the bench.[37]

The next step up the political ladder led to the assembly. Baltimore sent four delegates to Annapolis. In the increasingly intense
competition for these scarce seats, it helped to have experience on the
court, and the more experience, the better. Of the sixty-three justices,
twenty went to the assembly before 1773. These twenty had an average
of 8.8 years of court service, compared to 4.4 years for the forty-three
judges who were not elected to the assembly. Stated differently, of
twelve justices who sat on the bench ten or more years, nine moved up
to the assembly. While a political apprenticeship on the bench stength-
ened the hand of an aspiring assemblyman, some men were able to
leapfrog the court altogether. Between 1722 and 1773 nineteen of
thirty-nine men who served as delegates from Baltimore County had
no experience in the court at the time of their first election. Another
six assemblymen received court appointments either at their election
or afterwards, making it unclear whether a justiceship was a reward
for legislative service or vice versa.[38]

The county delegation was not a closed political elite in the tidewater mold. Given that the average age of assemblymen at their first
election was only 38.9 years, it seems unlikely that impatient young
men were clamoring to dislodge the old guard. Most assemblymen left
the assembly after a brief stint to make room for fresh delegates who
wished to try their hand at provincial politics. Between 1722 and 1773
twenty assemblies were elected, about one every two or three years.
Only three of the thirty-nine delegates managed to win election seven
or more times. These old hands steered unseasoned delegates around
Annapolis, introduced them to the unfamiliar haunts where so much
politicking took place, and furnished valuable personal contacts. Yet
they were exceptions to the rule. Delegates served in an average of
only 2.4 assemblies.[39]

Family connections facilitated but did not guarantee election to
the assembly. That the fathers of fifteen of the thirty-nine delegates
also served in the legislature proves that a well-known family name
carried weight. But the remaining twenty-four delegates, including
six immigrants and in-migrants, managed to break into the assembly
without this pedigree. Hence a big name was not indispensable.
Counting the number of delegates whose sons became assemblymen
leads to a similar conclusion. Of the thirty-nine representatives,
twenty-seven had sons who were old enough to sit in the legislature
before 1776. In only eleven cases did sons succeed their fathers in
the assembly.[40]

With or without a prominent name, only rich men went to the assembly. All sixteen of the thirty-nine delegates who left inventories before 1776 ranked in the top 20 percent of decedents, thirteen in the top 10 percent, and nine in the top 5 percent. The average landed estate for thirty-four assemblymen who can be identified exceeded 2,000 acres. It was wealth, not family connections, that enabled a man to take a seat in the assembly without first serving the customary probationary period as a justice of the peace. Of the five probated assemblymen who had not served on the county court at the time of their first election, four ranked in the top 5 percent of the wealth hierarchy. By contrast, only five of the eleven assemblymen who began their careers as justices of the peace belonged to the top 5 percent.[41]

The term *open plutocracy* fits the style of political officeholding that took shape in Baltimore. It was a plutocracy because *only* wealthy men could participate; it was open because *all* wealthy men could participate, whether or not they came from long-established families. The overall conditions of openness, fluidity, and impermanence that prevailed at the highest level of white society assured that Baltimore did not develop the closed political dynasties of tidewater Virginia and lower Maryland. In short, plutocracy did not become oligarchy.

By the mid-eighteenth century an unremarkable, backwater county at the northern extremity of Chesapeake society had been pulled into the mainstream of tidewater development. In Baltimore, the changes were obvious and dramatic: population was growing faster than ever, slavery had superseded migratory labor, specialized occupations were proliferating, court and church had extended their influence, rich people were becoming conspicuously richer. Yet even as the process of social and institutional development ground down the historic differences between Chesapeake core and Chesapeake periphery, fundamental disparities remained deeply rooted at the highest level of white society. The facility with which individuals rose to the top of society and the frequency with which they fell back down imparted to upper-class life a quality of impermanence and uncertainty unknown among the provincial gentry. They combined to produce a remarkably open elite.

3

The Work Force

From the Coastal Plain to the Piedmont Plateau, from the James River to the Susquehanna, the Chesapeake gentry built its class hegemony on slavery. The transition from servitude to slavery did not occur everywhere at the same time or in the same way. But whenever and however it occurred, the emergence of slavery in the colonial Chesapeake gave masters unprecedented personal control over their work force. It blunted class conflict by committing all segments of white society to a regime of racial supremacy that some scholars have termed *herrenvolk democracy*. It reduced the economic breathing space of nonslaveholders by concentrating capital and credit in the hands of fewer and fewer families. It also strengthened the slaveholders' grip on the public sphere by freeing them from the backbreaking physical labor of plantation agriculture to pursue their political careers and promote their political ambitions. [1]

Yet Chesapeake slavery was not monolithic. If by the second quarter of the eighteenth century the enduring features of plantation slavery were already in evidence on the greatest tidewater estates owned and managed by the provincial gentry, flexibility and fluidity continued to characterize labor practices among the county gentry of Baltimore. Slavery, which came late to Baltimore, never eclipsed other kinds of labor as completely as in the prime tobacco-producing counties of Virginia and Maryland. The small-scale nature of the institution put a premium on improvisation. In an impressive display of resourcefulness and innovation, elite planters blended slaves, servants, and freemen into a hybrid work force flexible enough to accommodate the needs of a developing economy. But the social costs of these eclectic labor practices were staggering, for they eviscerated the collective potential of Africans and their offspring who endeavored to maintain a viable family and community life within the confines of slavery. Ironically, the same qualities of openness, fluidity, and impermanence that permeated elite life in Baltimore were mirrored among the people whose labor made that life possible.

Someone surveying the state of labor in the upper Chesapeake at the turn of the century could have made a good case that migrant free workers were destined to supersede both servants and slaves. But he would have been wrong—Baltimore did not reproduce the labor practices characteristic of the English countryside, where a landless proletariat was harnessed to meet the heavy demand for agricultural labor. On the contrary, by the second quarter of the eighteenth century the county had evolved into a genuine slave society, although admittedly on a more modest scale than elsewhere in the Chesapeake.

The transformation of the labor system during this formative period can be traced through tax lists for the years 1692 and 1737. The first and most obvious change that emerges from the lists was rapid growth in the relative number of slaves. During these forty-five years, adult slaves rose from 10 percent of the taxable population to 36 percent. If we accept the proposition that genuine slave societies—as distinct from societies with slaves—must have "reasonably large" numbers of unfree people, which have historically ranged from 30 to 35 percent of the total population, then Baltimore could have claimed to be a slave society by the second quarter of the century. Virtually all other counties in Maryland and Virginia experienced increases of similar magnitude, although they usually began and ended with higher black ratios. Thus a general survey of the Chesapeake population around 1750 shows that of the sixty-four counties into which Maryland and Virginia were divided, only four had smaller proportions of slaves than Baltimore. Not surprisingly, these four were located in either traditional backwaters like the lower Eastern Shore or the newly opened regions of western Maryland.[2]

A second indication of the emergence of slave society was the general diffusion of slaveholding throughout the white population. From 1692 to 1737 the proportion of Baltimore households containing at least one adult slave jumped from 10 percent to 32 percent (see table 4). The growing ubiquity of slaves signified that Baltimore was evolving along regional lines, even though it lagged somewhat behind the richest tobacco-producing counties in southern Maryland and tidewater Virginia. To cite but one example for comparison, in 1733 the proportion of slaveholding households in Calvert County, Maryland, which contained some of the best farmland along the Potomac River, amounted to 45 percent, considerably above the level in Baltimore.[3]

The third change reflecting the consolidation of slavery was the trend toward an even geographical distribution of the black population. The early settlement of Baltimore unfolded in a pincerlike

Table 4. Distribution of Taxable Slaves in Baltimore County: 1692, 1737, 1773

N of Slaves Per Household	1692		1737		1773	
	% of Households (N = 173)	% of Slaves (N = 48)	% of Households (N = 1,113)	% of Slaves (N = 1,063)	% of Households (N = 2,334)	% of Slaves (N = 1,808)
0	90		68		77	
1–2	5	23	18	25	12	22
3–4	4	44	8	30	5	21
5–6	1	33	3	15	2	16
7–10			2	16	2	16
11+			1	14	1	25
TOTAL	100%	100%	100%	100%	100%	100%

SOURCES: Wilkins, comp., "Maryland Genealogical Notes"; Wilkins, comp., "Baltimore County Court Records, Joppa, Maryland"; Wilkins, comp., "Baltimore County Tax List, 1773" Maryland State Archives.

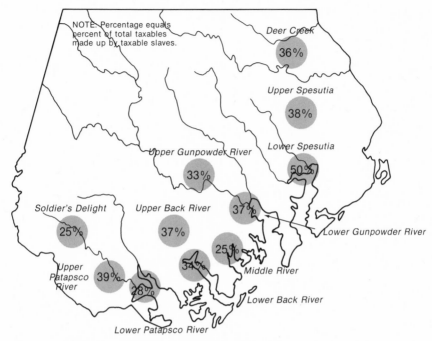

NOTE: Percentage equals percent of total taxables made up by taxable slaves.

Deer Creek 36%

Upper Spesutia 38%

Lower Spesutia 50%

Upper Gunpowder River 33%

Lower Gunpowder River

Soldier's Delight 25%

Upper Back River 37%

37%

25%

34%

Upper Patapsco River 39%

28%

Middle River

Lower Back River

Lower Patapsco River

Map 2. Distribution of Slaves by Hundred, Baltimore County: 1737

SOURCES: Wilkins, comp., "Baltimore County Court Records, Joppa, Maryland," Maryland State Archives

movement. One group of pioneering planters pushed northward from the Patapsco River, while another crossed the Susquehanna and then headed south toward the Bush River. The result in 1692 was two clusters of slaves, the first at the southern end of the county in St. Paul's Parish, the second at the northern end encompassed by St. George's Parish. These two parishes together contained 77 percent of the county's taxables but 94 percent of the slaves. By contrast, St. John's Parish between the Bush and Middle rivers could claim only 6 percent of the county's working-age slaves, even though it had 23 percent of the county's taxables. By 1737 this local white belt had all but disappeared as larger numbers of slaveholders, attracted to the lands around the Gunpowder River, began to occupy St. John's Parish (see map 2). In the late seventeenth century only a few slaveholding pockets existed within an overwhelmingly white county; two generations later blacks were literally everywhere.[4]

The final testimony to the triumph of slavery comes from an analysis of the inventories of the county elite. Judging from these records,

Table 5. Number of Servants and Slaves Owned by Baltimore Elite: 1660-1776

Years	Mean Number of Servants	Mean Number of Slaves
-1690	2.6	2.3
1690-1699	2.8	3.1
1700-1709	5.6	1.8
1710-1719	.6	10.1
1720-1729	1.3	11.4
1730-1739	.9	17.2
1740-1749	1.1	16.2
1750-1759	1.9	18.3
1760-1769	.2	15.3
1770-1776	2.5	14.8

SOURCES: Inventories; Inventories & Accounts; Baltimore County Inventories, Maryland State Archives.

the wealthiest families did not begin the transition from using indentured servants to using slaves until the first decades of the eighteenth century (see table 5). The process of consolidation unfolded rapidly, however, and was nearly finished by 1730s. Indeed, the next forty-six years saw relatively little variation in the average number of slaves—a range of fifteen to eighteen—per elite decedent. Once the Baltimore elite made a commitment to plantation slavery, the institution reached its fully developed form in little more than a generation.

Directly and indirectly, slavery touched every aspect of county life. It was the economic base upon which members of the county gentry built their fortunes. To the extent that this emergent class of slaveholders solidified its power and legitimacy in the public arenas of the assembly, court, and church, the new labor system played an indispensable role in the institutional maturation of the county. The steady consolidation of slavery during the first decades of the eighteenth century sent an unmistakable signal that Baltimore now belonged to the social order of the Greater Tidewater.

At the bottom of that social order were slaves. Although recent historians have justifiably questioned the older emphasis on the psychological demoralization and cultural devastation suffered by Africans and African-Americans under slavery, it is essential not to lose sight of the tremendous odds slaves faced as they struggled to construct collective lifeways. Students of eighteenth-century slavery, in particular, should take care not to underestimate the rawness of the system during its early phase of development. While the evidence for vigorous social networks among antebellum slaves is indisputable, projecting it automatically into the colonial period would be a mistake. In Maryland and Virginia, the "domestication of slavery" was a complex process that remained incomplete until the great cotton boom of the nineteenth century. It was especially complex and incomplete in places like Baltimore where the classic pattern of great planters, large work forces, and sprawling estates failed to develop.[5]

Baltimore's slaves confronted many obstacles to stable family and community life. The first stemmed from the comparatively small-scale nature of slaveholding in the county. It is not surprising that in 1692, several decades before Baltimore had undergone full-scale conversion to slavery, no household had more than six adult slaves (see table 4). Yet slavery remained on a modest scale throughout the colonial period, for as late as 1773 only 3 percent of households had more than ten slaves. If we adopt the perspective of slaves themselves, the same picture emerges. In 1737 only 14 percent of adult slaves lived in households containing over ten slaves, and in 1773 only 25 percent. Slaveholding patterns in Baltimore increasingly diverged from the Chesapeake norm of larger work forces, as illustrated by the piedmont counties of Amelia and Prince Edward, Virginia, where the proportion of adult slaves who resided in households of ten or more slaves increased from 35 percent to 59 percent between 1737 and 1767. Likewise, in Lunenburg, Charlotte, and Mecklenberg counties, it rose from 36 percent in 1750 to 49 percent in 1764.[6]

The small size of plantation work forces imposed real limits on the intensity of slave social interaction. Smaller holdings reduced the prospect of finding a spouse at home and increased the likelihood of children being separated from parents and spouses from each other. In such circumstances, any kind of extensive social life depended on interaction between plantations. While these lines of communication crisscrossed the county and hummed with activity most of the time—slaves visited with one another after sundown, on Saturday afternoons, on Sundays, or during occasional holidays—edgy authorities could shut them down without warning, disrupting the daily ebb and flow of human relationships on the plantations. Even if actual crackdowns occurred infrequently, the ever-present threat of such preemptory action must have had a chastening effect on slave social life.[7]

The second impediment to family life was the *quarter* system. The largest slaveholders of Maryland and Virginia did not concentrate all of their slaves in one place but divided them between their "home plantations" and outlying quarters. Unfortunately, it is difficult to determine exactly where slaves lived. When tax assessors compiled their lists, they simply wrote down the total number of slaves under the authority of the household head whose actual landholdings might have been widely scattered. More helpful are inventories, since they occasionally specify slaves' residence. These records indicate that the quarter system operated extensively on the estates of the Baltimore elite, with the result that slaves frequently found themselves isolated in small work groups. In nine of the 181 elite inventories, appraisors designated the residence of the slaves. Of 169 slaves included in these inventories, 60 percent lived at the home plantation while the rest were scattered among outlying quarters in small work groups. For the elite's slaves physical dispersal was the norm.[8]

It is impossible to determine kinship relationships among slaves at any particular quarter, but the overall sex and age profile suggests that relatively few of these work crews were complete, nuclear families. Possible exceptions included the quarters owned by Richard Colegate, which were occupied by men, women, and children who conceivably constituted a family. When Colegate died in 1722, his Patapsco quarter contained ten slaves who may have formed a three-generation family: one old man, two adult males, two adult females, three children, and two females of unspecified age. But most of the work gangs were smaller than Colegate's—units of four or five individuals were most common—and consisted of an assortment of adults and children, men and women, males and females, that defies any simple pattern. Consider the case of Brian Philpot who at his death in 1768 bequeathed to his heirs nineteen slaves at four different places. At his home in Baltimore Town lived three women, one girl, and one boy; at the "old" quarter, five men and one woman; at "stanford" quarter, two women, two girls, one man, and one boy; and at "bidlys" quarter, two men. It does not belittle the accomplishment of quarter slaves who struggled to preserve ties with kinfolk at the home plantation or at other quarters to acknowledge that physical isolation could disrupt the formation of stable kinship groups.[9]

The third challenge to slave family life arose out of the local iron industry. The greatest slaveholders of Baltimore included a large number of iron manufacturers, probably larger in both absolute and relative terms than in any other Chesapeake county. An abundance of easily mined ore, readily available firewood, and fast-moving streams provided the essential ingredients of a thriving local industry. Beginning with the establishment of the Baltimore Company, iron furnaces and forges sprang up throughout the county under the ownership of prominent Maryland families and British investors. With the exception of Northampton Furnace, which Col. Charles Ridgely established in 1762 in partnership with his two sons and which employed a large number of convict servants imported from Great Britain, these enterprises recruited heavily from among the local slave population. The appraisors of a 1773 assessment list for Baltimore reported eight ironworks in the county, with slaves making up 52 percent of the total work force of 432 men and women. These enterprises owned an average of twenty-eight slaves, a vast labor force by the standards of the northern Chesapeake. Indeed, they accounted for the six largest slaveholdings in the county, led by Nottingham Forge with forty-eight slaves. It would be a serious distortion to consider the iron industry a relatively minor activity in an overwhelmingly plantation economy, for the furnaces and forges possessed a total of 225 black workers, or 12 percent of the entire adult slave population.[10]

The overwhelming preponderance of males at the forges and furnaces must have made family life exceedingly difficult to maintain. It is possible to identify the sex of slave ironworkers at seven of the eight establishments, and in every case males outnumbered females—25:3 at Middle River Forge, 42:6 at Nottingham Forge, 24:5 at Kingsbury Furnace, and 8:1 at Northampton Furnace. Taken together, ironworks employed 171 males and 41 females. Of course, male ironworkers who failed to find a spouse where they worked might look someplace else, but the large number of unattached men concentrated in a few locations must have quickly exhausted the pool of marriagable women in the immediate vicinity, forcing many ironworkers to seek mates further away and others to abandon the search altogether.[11]

The fourth factor militating against the formation of stable black families appears in the demographic profile of the elite's slaves. It has been argued that after 1740 the natural reproduction of the Chesapeake slave population led to balanced sex ratios, especially on the largest plantations, which in turn multiplied the opportunities for stable family and community life. In this respect, Baltimore presents a mixed picture. On the one hand, the gentry's slaveholdings displayed the overall Chesapeake trend toward a balanced sex ratio (see table 6).

Table 6. Demographic Profile of Slaves Owned by Baltimore Elite: 1660-1776

	1690-1699	1700-1709	1710-1719	1720-1729	1730-1739	1740-1749	1750-1759	1760-1769	1770-1776
Sex Ratio	1.10	1.51	1.10	1.24	1.43	1.20	1.46	1.04	1.14
Males									
-5				15%	18%	17%	15%	20%	21%
6-15				14	19	31	22	22	25
16-44				50	41	36	50	46	37
45+				21	22	16	13	12	17
TOTAL				100%	100%	100%	100%	100%	100%
Mean age				25.7	25.8	21.2	24.2	22.4	21.8
Females									
-5				11%	22%	30%	18%	22%	22%
6-15				16	28	20	26	28	23
16-44				60	43	42	25	41	42
45+				13	7	8	11	9	13
TOTAL				100%	100%	100%	100%	100%	100%
Mean Age				25.0	18.9	17.4	20.2	16.7	19.4

SOURCES: Inventories; Inventories & Accounts; Baltimore County Inventories, Maryland State Archives.

NOTES: A total of 2,321 slaves were listed in the gentry inventories that passed through the probate courts after 1690. The data on sex ratios are based on an analysis of 2,236 slaves (96 percent of the total) who could be identified by sex. The age breakdown is for 1,539 slaves (66 percent) whose age was given by the appraisors. Figures on sex ratios before 1690 and age composition before 1720 are omitted because the samples were too small to be meaningful.

The preponderance of males was to be expected during the seventeenth century when planters were assembling their work forces through the acquisition of adult male field hands. After 1700 the formation of slave families and effects of natural reproduction tended to redress the imbalance between males and females. Although the sex ratio among slaves owned by the Baltimore gentry fluctuated from decade to decade, perhaps due to the continued importation of Africans during the eighteenth century, by 1760 pronounced imbalances were a thing of the past.[12]

On the other hand, the contrasting age structure of the males and females must have exerted a negative effect on family formation. For every period that can be documented the mean age of male slaves owned by the Baltimore elite was greater than that of females, and in some decades the differential amounted to as many as six or seven years (see table 6). The data from the inventories suggest that males were older than females because relatively few black women lived beyond the age of forty-five. From 1720 to 1776 these "old" women ranged from 7 percent of the gentry's female slaves to 13 percent, whereas men in the same age group made up between 13 and 22 percent of the male slave population. The most likely explanation for this divergence is that rigors of successive childbirths took a tremendous toll among black mothers and left relatively few of them to enjoy the physical rest brought by menopause. Given the inevitable matriarchal tone of kinship networks in the slave quarters, the absence of older women must have had a demoralizing impact on family life by depriving men of wives, children of mothers and grandmothers, and the entire community of female elders.

The fifth factor disrupting family life was the narrowness of the occupational spectrum among slaves. The provincial gentry of Maryland and Virginia assembled remarkably diverse work forces. For example, it has been estimated that one-fifth of the male slaves on the estates of Thomas Jefferson, George Washington, Robert Carter of Nomini Hall, and Charles Carroll of Carrollton were skilled artisans. But these estates, which had well over one hundred slaves each, eclipsed any in Baltimore. If the degree of occupational specialization was directly related to the size of the plantation work force, the elite's slaveholdings were probably too small to support a sizable number of specialists. As a result, practically all the slaves owned by the county gentry worked in the fields. Of over two thousand slaves who appeared in the elite's inventories, only twenty-two were listed with a skill: four carpenters, four blacksmiths, three coopers, three hammermen, two sawyers, two carters, two founders, one ship carpenter, and one plowman. Although appraisors in a hurry to finish their work must have passed over many slave artisans without comment, their inventories furnish little evidence that the elite's work forces included significant numbers of skilled slaves.[13]

The relative absence of an occupational elite must have distorted family and community life. In eighteenth-century Virginia, highly acculturated skilled workers formed the natural leadership of the slave population, both by mediating between the worlds of whites and blacks and by orchestrating resistance against the institution. Further, slave artisans are known to have trained their own sons as apprentices, a practice which not only transmitted prized skills from one generation to the next but bolstered the authority of the artisan in his role as father. To the extent that black artisans were able to market their skills beyond the plantation and earn something for the support of their families, they enjoyed a privileged position as both husbands and breadwinners. The point here is not to glorify the slave artisan or to sanitize the conditions under which he worked, since for every advantage he enjoyed, there was a debt to be paid. As go-between for the slave quarters and the plantation house, he walked the precipice of psychic marginalization; as the obvious leader of resistance, he became the obvious victim of repression; as a man who possessed a valuable skill in great demand, he was simultaneously a valuable commodity liable to be sold away from his home and family. These liabilities notwithstanding, the slave artisan remained a potential source of stability anchoring the slave community, and his absence in Baltimore must have had a debilitating effect on all dimensions of social life.[14]

To reconstruct the quality of slave life from fragments of evidence that appear in tax and probate records is obviously a dangerous undertaking. The quantifiable nature of this material can easily create an impression of precision and comprehensiveness, when in truth the vital human relationships that breathed life into the institution fail to emerge from the records. Even so, given the economic and demographic realities of slavery, it is impossible to avoid the conclusion that the small and mixed work forces assembled by the county gentry vitiated the efforts of slaves to create viable structures of community life.

Nonslave laborers are the invisible people of the eighteenth-century Chesapeake. Every county had hundreds of indentured servants, skilled craftsmen, long-term contractual laborers, tenants, and casual laborers who found work on the large plantations in their neighborhoods. Far from constituting two self-contained systems, free and unfree labor interlocked at many points, especially in counties like Baltimore where the small-scale nature of slavery undermined any tendency toward plantation autarky. It is probably safe to say that the county gentry of Baltimore was more dependent on nonslave workers than the Tidewater's provincial gentry was, chiefly because its own

Table 7. Demographic Profile of Servants Owned by Baltimore Elite: 1660-1776

	1660-1699 (N = 56)	1700-1719 (N = 29)	1720-1749 (N = 68)	1750-1776 (N = 82)	Total (N = 235)
Males					
Men	25%	59%	49%	37%	40%
Boys	20	14	1	13	12
Age Unknown	7	3	22	22	16
Females					
Women	20%	21%	18%	6%	14%
Girls	5	3	7	9	7
Age Unknown	23		3	13	11
TOTAL	100%	100%	100%	100%	100%

SOURCES: Inventories; Inventories & Accounts; Baltimore County Inventories, Maryland State Archives.

NOTES: In the vast majority of cases appraisors did not give a specific age for a servant, but only a general description like "man servant" or "boy servant." Thus it was necessary to construct the broad age categories in the table. Servants who were listed as age sixteen or under were placed under either the boy or girl heading. The data in the table do not include twenty-six servants whose sex could not be identified.

comparatively unspecialized slave work forces could not furnish many of the skills needed on the plantation. As a result, the people who worked on elite plantations were a kaleidoscopic mix of slaves and servants, free and unfree, black and white.

Of the various categories of nonslave workers employed by the Baltimore elite, indentured servants are the easiest to identify. During the eighteenth century, indentured servitude underwent several changes. The first was that fewer servants were reported in the inventories (see table 5). While the elite continued to rely heavily on servants until about 1710, thereafter the average decedent's estate had no more than one or two. The increase in servants on the eve of independence reflected the activities of Col. Charles Ridgely and his son John, whose twenty-four servants were employed at the family's ironworks. Excluding their holdings, the average number of servants for the 1770s fell to the level of earlier decades. Second, male servants came to comprise a larger percentage of the elite's servant work force (see table 7). During the seventeenth century, the elite owned roughly the same number of male and female servants, but after 1700 males came to constitute between two-thirds and three-fourths of the servants.

The third change was that adults constituted an increasingly larger proportion of male servants. The magnitude of the increase cannot be measured precisely because appraisors did not identify the age of a sizable minority of the male servants. Yet even assuming that all those male servants whose age could not be determined before 1700 were adults and all those after 1700 were youngsters, the proportion of men servants climbed from 32 percent to 44 percent (see table 7). Finally, servants who reached Baltimore during the eighteenth century advanced up the occupational hierarchy from ordinary field hands to skilled workmen. While this last point is difficult to document quantitatively because appraisors did not systematically record whether or not a servant possessed a special skill, the gentry's inventories contained references to four blacksmiths, two shoemakers, two schoolmasters, one carpenter, one cooper, and one tailor—and all of these skilled workmen appeared in estates appraised after 1720. In sum, the data from the inventories support the contention of one historian that during the eighteenth century indentured servants were employed by large planters not as common field hands but rather as craftsmen, teachers, and overseers.[15]

The second group of nonslave workers were freemen. Of all the people who worked on elite plantations, free laborers are the most elusive because they do not appear in inventories, wills, or the other sources from which recent historians have been reconstructing the social landscape of the tobacco colonies. Yet an analysis of assessment lists casts a few rays of light on these men and suggests they comprised a significant component of the elite's work force. In the 1737 tax list, households owning eleven or more taxable slaves included an average of almost nine white males over the age of fifteen (excluding the household head) (see table 8). Taken together, white "inmates" made up about one-third of the members in the greatest slaveholding households. By 1773 the white ratio had dropped to a fourth, but even so, the largest slaveholding households had an average of about seven white men.

Who were the white inmates? Not every white taxable was a free laborer, for servants and kinsmen of the household head undoubtedly accounted for some of the inmates. Yet even when due allowance is made for these groups, the relatively large number of white men residing in the largest slaveholding households suggests that throughout

Table 8. White Inmates in Slaveholding Households in Baltimore
County: 1737, 1773

Number of Slaves per Household	White Taxables per Household		Proportion of White Taxables	
	1737	1773	1737	1773
1-5	1.9	1.8	47%	44%
6-10	2.0	3.9	22%	35%
11-20	4.3	3.8	27%	21%
11+	8.6	6.7	35%	25%

SOURCES: Inventories; Inventories & Accounts; Baltimore County Inventories, Maryland State Archives.

the eighteenth century the Baltimore elite continued to recruit free laborers to supplement their black work force, much as their predecessors had done in the 1690s.[16]

The third group of nonslave workers were tenants who, in addition to farming their own leaseholds, often supplied their landlords with occasional labor. Recent historians have demonstrated that tenancy was more widespread in early America than we have traditionally believed, but most efforts at quantitative measurement founder on the fact that landlords and tenants often dispensed with a legal agreement recorded at the local court. The informality of a simple handshake was especially common in the case of the tenants-at-will who were most likely to seek part-time employment. Even so, an examination of the conveyances, leases, assignments, and mortgages recorded at the county court during the colonial period indicates that many members of the elite had tenants. Leases of rural property and assignments of leases comprised 5 percent of the elite's 869 legal transactions. About one out of four gentlemen recorded a lease or assignment at the court. These leaseholds could not have provided more than a fraction of the elite's income, since the average tenement of ninety acres was hardly enough for a family farm. Landlords who collected their rent in current money usually received about £7 per year, while those who took theirs in tobacco got 650 pounds. These sums were equivalent to a decent horse or a few head of cattle.[17]

Leases of rural tracts conformed to a common pattern. Although the longest one spanned the lifetime of the tenant and his wife, twelve of the sixteen that specified the duration ranged from ten to twenty-one years. In an effort to protect his property, the landlord often inserted a provision into the lease prohibiting his tenants from cutting timber on the property unless for firewood, but he might relax the restrictions when the tenement included a dwelling house and outbuildings. For example, in 1748 Stephen Onion granted his tenant the right to cut timber for "Necessary repairs" to keep "the houses & Plantation in good order." Protecting woodlands seems to have been the chief concern, but landlords like Samuel Owings also worried about soil exhaustion. In 1767 he stipulated that his tenant William Cheetam could "not employ in the Cultivation and tending of said Land and premises more than himself his Wife and Children." Perhaps the most attractive aspect of leasing was that it enabled a landlord to improve his property without tying up any of his own money, and thus a common provision required the tenant to plant an orchard of fifty or sixty apple trees. A few landlords expected more costly improvements, but no one was as demanding as James Phillips, who in 1763 gave detailed instructions to his tenants on the kind of dwelling house and tobacco house they were to construct.[18]

It is doubtful whether Baltimore's leading families could have operated their plantations as smoothly as they did without supplementing their slave work force with indentured servants, free workers, and tenant farmers. By the eighteenth century many servants and artisans possessed specialized skills in great demand on the elite's plantations, whereas tenants not only added value to the property of their landlord but also furnished a source of short-term labor. It was this constantly changing mix of slaves, servants, artisans, and tenants that characterized labor practices in Baltimore and distinguished the work forces of the county gentry from those of the provincial gentry.

How did the county gentry manage to transform this most disparate collection of laborers into productive work units? To answer this question we must turn from tax lists, probate records, and land deeds to private plantation accounts. Although only one collection of family business papers has come down to us largely intact, it opens a large window onto the inner workings of an eighteenth-century Baltimore plantation. Housed at the Maryland Historical Society, the Ridgely papers contain over one hundred boxes of daybooks, ledgers, accounts, and correspondence. As practical men of affairs, Col. Charles Ridgely and his descendents compiled these records to keep track of their money, not to document the lives of their workers. Despite this, the meticulous accounts they left behind introduce us to some of the principal characters and characteristics of slave society in colonial Baltimore.[19]

The Maryland branch of the Ridgely family was established by the colonel's grandfather, Robert, who probably reached the province in the 1660s. Ambitious and hard-driving, Robert spurred his political career from the assembly to the council, became one of the three or four best-paid lawyers in Maryland, and plowed his money into land and labor. At his death in 1681 he owned an estate exceeding five thousand acres, which was divided among his wife and three sons. The second-born child, the colonel's father and the first in a long line of Charles Ridgelys, received one thousand acres at the head of the Patuxent River, which he transformed into a profitable tobacco plantation before an early death in 1705. He left behind a young widow and three orphans, including his two-year-old namesake.[20]

The colonel never really knew his father, but this was a common fact of life in the malarial environment of the early Chesapeake. During his youth, he dropped out of the records except for a brief appearance in 1721 on the occasion of his marriage to Rachel Howard. This was a good match, bringing together two prominent families. We pick up his track again in 1726 when the colonel, looking like a typical young planter, bought his first tract of land, a few hundred acres on the Middle Branch of the Patapsco River, less than a mile from the future site of Baltimore Town. This was just the beginning. By the early 1730s the colonel had pieced together an estate of over one thousand acres in Upper Patapsco Hundred, centered on the home plantation optimistically named "Ridgely's Delight." Then, from 1731 to 1745, he stopped buying land, opened a store, and joined a handful of merchants trading on the Patapsco River. At the same time he and Rachel raised two sons and three daughters, all of whom expected to receive a sizable financial stake once they became adults and set out on their own. How seriously Charles and Rachel took their parental obligations became clear in 1748 when the eldest of their children, John, was deeded in entail the dwelling plantation and surrounding lands of Ridgely's Delight.[21]

Even though the colonel was no longer a young man, he was starting a new life. Several years before turning over the Patapsco estate to his son, he mobilized every resource at his command to launch a new estate on the Gunpowder River, about ten miles north of Ridgely's Delight. Beginning in 1745 with the purchase of "Northampton," a tract of 1,500 acres, he grabbed up land at a frenzied pace, almost all of it in northern Baltimore. In the first two years alone, the colonel spent

£2,500 current on land purchases, an extraordinary sum roughly equal to a full year's receipts at his store. In 1757, when the buying spree was largely over, he was paying quitrent on thirty-five tracts of land containing over ten thousand acres, in addition to five lots in Baltimore Town. The dream of building a New World barony in the forests of Baltimore continued to consume the colonel's time and money until his death in 1772 at the age of sixty-nine.[22]

It also consumed the working lives of several scores of men and women. From the Ridgelys' account books we catch frequent glimpses of these people going about their daily routines, but amid such sharply focused details it is easy to lose sight of the larger labor system that framed their lives. When we step back and view Northampton from a respectful distance, three things stand out. First, slaves formed the backbone of the work force. In each of his successive incarnations— as the young planter of Ridgely's Delight, as the established merchant of Upper Patapsco, and as the aging patriarch of Northampton—the colonel ranked among the county's largest slaveholders. Second, slavery coexisted with other forms of labor. The colonel relied not only on indentured and convict servants but also on a variety of free laborers: overseers who received a share of the crop, long-term contractual laborers, free artisans who provided a variety of special skills, day workers, and tenants-at-will. Third, these diverse ingredients were blended into a responsive productive unit that accommodated the jagged rhythms of the marketplace. In addition to the traditional staple, tobacco, Northampton workers produced vast quantities of grain and lumber for the market.

Many images of the colonel's work force are frozen in the surviving records, but the earliest one comes from 1737. Ridgely was then the thirty-five-year-old owner of a thriving plantation and busy store. When William Hughes, the local constable, drew up his assessment list for Upper Patapsco Hundred where the colonel lived, he began by writing down the names of the most prominent heads of household. Ridgely must have been an important man—his name was fifth from the top. According to the list, his household contained five adult slaves and four white men.[23]

Thanks to Constable Hughes, we know something about the colonel's work force eight years before the move to Northampton. It was clearly a large one by standards of the day, consisting of blacks and whites. To own a single slave was a mark of distinction where the colonel lived, since two-thirds of the 117 households in Upper Patapsco Hundred had none. To own five slaves brought membership in the most exclusive group of all. If we omit a pair of ironworks, which had a combined slave work force of thirty-seven, and three absentee landowners who operated quarters in Upper Patapsco, the colonel ranked as the fourth largest slaveholder in his hundred.[24]

The four white men under his authority were probably free workers. Three of them had the same last name, Okeson. Since servants almost always migrated to the Chesapeake as individuals rather than in family units, it seems safe to assume that the Okesons were employed by the colonel either as overseers, long-term contractual laborers, or tenants-at-will. This assumption is born out by the colonel's willingness to extend the Okesons credit at his store. In 1735 Isaiah Okeson's account was £40 in arrears, the largest single debt in the store ledger for that year. Even if the colonel was willing to open an account with an ordinary servant (a possibility since slaves like "Negro Jack" appear in the ledgers), it is hard to believe he would have allowed him to fall so hopelessly behind. The fourth of the white taxables was John Arnall, who ran up a debt of £5 at the store. Of all the accounts in the ledger, Arnall's was the only one recorded in both current money and the tobacco equivalent. Overseers were usually paid a share of the tobacco harvest, so the colonel may have kept the account in tobacco in order to deduct the expenditures from Arnall's final pay. There were several other Arnalls in the neighborhood who traded at the store, none of whom was a slaveholder, indicating that John came from one of the local yeoman families who frequently supplied overseers for gentlemen's estates.[25]

The assessment list tells us nothing about white women, who were not defined as taxables, but the colonel may have had at least one female indentured servant—Elizabeth Mounseir. In 1739, two years after Constable Hughes's visit, she was dragged into court for having given birth to a bastard child. Servant women in such circumstances could expect little mercy, and Mounseir received none. With the official cat-of-nine-tails laid out on the table before him, the judge pronounced the sentence: "Whipping on the Bare back with fifteen lashes well Laid on till the blood doth Appear." Mounseir's crime went beyond bastardy, for she had disgraced the household of one of Baltimore's up-and-coming gentlemen.[26]

So it seems that when the colonel purchased Northampton in 1745, he had already assembled a mixed work force of blacks and whites, slaves and freemen, males and females. No sooner was the deed signed and sealed than he ordered several of his workers to begin clearing the heavily wooded lands. One of them, a slave named Savee,

who may have been among the slaves at Ridgely's Delight eight years
before, seems to have been in charge of the crew engaged in this hard
work. In October 1745 the colonel, issuing commands from his Patapsco plantation, packed together an assortment of tools and sent them
up to Savee. Part of the inventory is torn away, but from the remaining
fragment Savee and his companions emerge as quintessential American frontiersmen, their days an unremitting round of felling trees,
splitting logs, making staves, clearing fields, and planting a crop. The
tool kit included three grubbing hoes, three narrow axes, two augers,
two chisels, a gouge, a lathing hammer, a handsaw, and a cooper's
axe. Assuming that each hand got a grubbing hoe and a narrow axe,
the colonel had a total of three workmen on the job. Within a few
years the slave crew had grown to at least a dozen. In January 1748 the
colonel shipped another parcel of "good axes" to Savee and twelve
other workers. By this time he had placed a white overseer in charge
of the operation, although Savee may have continued as de facto overseer, since slaves seldom worked in groups of more than five or six.[27]

For Savee and his black companions—Pompey, Harry, Jack,
Clapham, Wapon—the purchase of Northampton was a stinging re-
minder of the arbitrary, unpredictable, and capricious nature of life as
a slave. The ten-mile trek from Ridgely's Delight to Northampton,
across numerous creeks and falls and through dense woods, made
daily visits back home impossible and weekend trips difficult. All of
the Northampton slaves were forced to abandon the relative material
comforts of an established plantation; some of them left behind
spouses, children, and loved ones as well. For slaves the unfolding crisis of forced separation was all too familiar but no less painful, with
anxious whispers about the rumored purchase, cries of frustration
when rumor became reality, and final words of comfort and resigna-
tion as Savee and his men set out for Northampton. Whether from a
genuine sense of compassion for his slaves or from a cold-blooded re-
alization that sullen workers were unproductive workers, the colonel
seems to have shifted his slaves back and forth between the Gunpowder and Patapsco estates. In late 1747, as winter approached, the colonel dispatched a parcel of "coarse Kersey" jackets to his men at
Northampton. Of the eighteen men who weathered the winter in their
new jackets, the thirteen listed by their first names were probably
slaves. Only four of the thirteen were still at Northampton a few
months later when the colonel sent up a batch of axes. The rest had
probably been sent back to Ridgely's Delight to enjoy a welcomed re-
spite from the raw isolation of the forest.[28]

Not all of the workers were slaves. Four of the eighteen workers who received jackets were referred to by their last names, and a fifth appeared simply as "Dutchman." If this group consisted of indentured servants (on the assumption that freemen would be expected to provide their own clothing), then bonded white laborers constituted between one-third and one-fourth of the colonel's work force. A few of them may have been convict servants. One of the colonel's day books contains several copies of the standard contract used for English convicts, in which it is stated that servants arriving in October 1747 aboard the ship *Mediterranean* were bound out for seven years. It does not seem farfetched to suppose that some of these convicts found their way to Northampton.[29]

From the colonel's perspective, the biggest problem with the servants was that they ran away. On July 10, 1747, Richard Cook made a break for freedom. It was an unsuccessful one as it turned out, for six weeks later the colonel sent a man to Annapolis to get Cook out of jail and bring him home. On top of the prison fees, the runaway was charged for the advertisements the colonel placed in the provincial newspapers and several other expenses he had incurred in hunting Cook down. Cook may have joined forces with another servant, Darby Mahoney, who also was charged with runaway expenses. In one case, the colonel seems to have unknowingly abetted a runaway. On November 2, 1747, he sold servant Joseph Smith a black gelding for £5. Smith gave his new horse a good ride, but the colonel's men caught up with him five days later and brought him back in chains. Female servants also fled when they had the chance, but none was more determined than Hannah Richardson, who ran away four times during the winter of 1747-48.[30]

By 1748 the colonel could probably see in the roughhewn skeleton of his three-year-old plantation the body of a great estate. An inventory of tools drawn up in 1748 suggests how much progress had been made (see table 9). In the three years since Savee and his men had cut down the first trees, the Northampton estate had evolved into a complex of five separate quarters. Each had a plow and accessories for two plow horses, except for Peach's quarter whose equipment may have been on loan to the crew at Haile's quarter. The large number of carpentry and coopering tools at Peterson's quarter suggests that it was the most developed operation, whereas the scarcity of such tools at Peach's quarter probably reflected its newness. In addition, the quarters were equipped with axes, broad hoes, narrow hoes, and grubbing axes—the indispensable tools for cultivating tobacco. If, as seems

Table 9. Distribution of Tools at Northampton Quarters: 1748

	Boreing's Quarter	Merryman's Quarter	Peterson's Quarter	Haile's Quarter	Peach's Quarter
Plows and Accessories					
Plow	1	1	1	2	
Collar-Harness	2	2	2	2	2
Blind Bridle	2	2	2	2	
Trusses	2	2	2	2	2
Back Bands	2	2	2	2	2
Cart Bridle					2
Field Tools					
Narrow Ax	5	5	8	6	3
Broad Hoe	5	4	7	6	3
Grubbing Ax	5	5	10	6	3
Narrow Hoe	6	5	10	6	3
Wedge	4	4	8	4	3
Carpentry Tools					
Augor	2		2	2	
Chissel	2		2	2	
Gouge	1		1	1	
Mould Rings	2	2	3	2	1
Drawknife	1	1	1	1	
Adz			1		
Handsaw			1		
Cooper Ax			1		
Crosscut Saw			2		

SOURCES: Forest Daybook 1748, box 1, Feb. 1748, MS. 691, Ridgely Account Books, Maryland Historical Society.

likely, the colonel assigned to each laborer a set of tools, he had a crew of five or six men at Boreing's quarter, four or five at Merryman's, seven to ten at Peterson's, six at Haile's, and three at Peach's. Thus the Gunpowder estate had a total work force of between twenty-five and thirty hands.[31]

As befitted a mature plantation complex, each quarter was headed by a white overseer. In the colonial Chesapeake, an employer and overseer usually sealed their agreement with nothing more formal than a handshake, but in one case the colonel recorded the contract in a memorandum. On January 13, 1748, he hired Anthony Musgrove, Jr., to oversee Haile's quarter. For his part, Musgrove agreed to "completely finish the crop," raise the foals on the plantation, and produce fifteen bushels of oats. Musgrove was a married man, an important asset from the colonel's point of view, since his wife added one more hand to the work force. Mrs. Musgrove's specific assignment was to "do all the spinning knitting sewing that she possibly can." In return, the colonel furnished the Musgroves with a dwelling place, two plow horses, working tools, one-fourth of all the tobacco harvested, and one-fifth of the wheat and corn. The contract mentioned three other individuals at the plantation: Clapham, Wapon, and Elizabeth Mudgett. The first two were probably slaves, having appeared on the list of workmen who received axes in 1748, while Mudgett may have been an indentured servant. The contract followed the common pattern in which the employer's share of the tobacco crop equaled the number of workers under the direction of the overseer—in this case, three-fourths. An overseer might also receive his payment in money, as when in 1747 the colonel paid Richard Cross £5/10 "for wages when overseer at my quarter."[32]

The agreement between Colonel Ridgely and overseer Musgrove captures their relationship at one dramatic moment, leaving the impression of a modern-day contract between two free agents. But any resemblance to an impersonal market transaction is misleading, for this relationship was buried beneath many layers of clientage that had accumulated over the years. This was true for practically all of the colonel's overseers. His day books for 1748 contain references to two overseers in addition to Musgrove: Thomas Hamilton at Merryman's quarter and James Roose at Boreing's quarter. Isaiah Okeson and John Musgrove, Anthony's son, were probably in charge of the two remaining quarters, since in 1747 the colonel assumed the employer's obligation of paying the annual county levies for Okeson, Hamilton, and the two Musgroves. Most of these men had been attached to the Ridgely household for years. Constable Hughes, it will be recalled, reported Okeson as a member of the colonel's household in 1737, and for the next eleven years he kept an account at the store. Both Musgroves had strong ties to Ridgely—three generations of the family surface in the colonel's day books between 1741 and 1756. Hamilton's account ran from 1746 through 1748, probably the years he served as overseer. Only Roose seems to have left the colonel's employ after a year. Whether the arrangments at Northampton were typical of other large plantations is an unanswered question, but they confirm the conclusion of one historian that overseers in colonial Maryland were from "the best of the landless class" and were regarded as "respected members of the community."[33]

Overseers were not the only local men who appeared at the colonel's door looking for work. Many yeomen farmers and landless whites hired on at Northampton, and though the job might be for a day, a week, or a month, they constituted an indispensable part of the colonel's work force. Consider the case of artisans. Among the first substantial improvements the colonel made at Northampton were the construction of tobacco houses, which were frequently more substantial than ordinary dwellings. While Savee and his fellow slaves were expected to furnish the basic labor, the colonel looked elsewhere for high-level carpentry skills. In February 1748 he contracted with two local artisans, William Warford and John Robinson, to build four tobacco houses, each forty feet by forty feet, the standard dimensions of the time. The colonel undertook responsibility for "falling and sawing and nailing the Board timber," leaving Warford and Robinson to oversee the project and do the finish work. They agreed to complete the job by the first of September, at which time they would receive 7,500 pounds of tobacco. A year earlier one of the colonel's former overseers, Richard Cross, had received £6 for helping to construct a tobacco house at Boreing's quarter, and another £14 for two more at Peterson's quarter. Thus in arranging for the construction of tobacco houses on his five quarters, the colonel was forced to call upon the skills of his neighbors.[34]

Not all of Northampton's free workers had special skills. Many men and women in the neighborhood looked to the colonel for short-term employment. That these individual transactions recorded in the account books rarely involved more than ten shillings should not obscure their importance to ordinary planters who needed cash or a line of credit. During the years from 1745 to 1748, Ridgely kept accounts with dozens of people who did odd jobs, like William Page who sawed walnut plank and Jonathan Munn who cleaned "the clock." The great demand at Northampton for cloth and clothing also meant jobs for John Cooper who weaved seventy-one yards of cloth, Jonathan Hanson who fulled seventeen yards, and William Ferguson who made the colonel a coat. John Roberson, William Warford, James Bryan, and Gale Frizel were only a few of the men who earned a bit of cash packing Ridgely's tobacco into hogsheads and rolling them to the landings.[35]

Tenants are the most difficult component of the Northampton work force to document. The annual quitrent collected by the lord proprietor was designed in part to discourage large landowners like the colonel from sitting on their property in expectation of escalating land values. One way of meeting the proprietary exactions was by renting out the land. How much the colonel actually leased is unknown, but it could have been considerable. If each of the five quarters contained between 100 and 150 acres, about average for the time, then he was directly cultivating no more than 7 percent of the 10,300 acres he owned in 1757. Eight leases are referred to in the colonel's day books and in county court records, and they yielded an average annual rent of 600-800 pounds of tobacco. The size of the leaseholds was never specified but probably ranged from 100 to 150 acres. Most of these were long-term leases, but Northampton estate also attracted an unknown number of tenants-at-will who may have furnished seasonal labor. For example, in 1745 Ridgely charged William Towson £2 (equivalent to 240 pounds of tobacco) for "1 years rent of a cornfield on Northampton." In 1748 Henry Oram, whom the colonel had hired a year before as a common laborer, rented a plantation for 600 pounds. Living in the shadows of the colonel's plantation, Towson and Oram resembled the cottage workers of southeastern Pennsylvania, who found jobs with large farmers during harvest season when the demand labor was especially intense.[36]

In 1755 the colonel could look with satisfaction at his Northampton estate. He now required a small fleet of wagons, driven by slave teamsters, to carry plantation goods from Northampton to the growing market of Baltimore Town. During that year Ridgely's wagons delivered at least forty-five hogsheads of tobacco, 869 bushels of corn, 3,830 staves, and 2,390 heading. At going prices, the colonel could expect to get £225 for his tobacco, £109 for his corn, and another substantial sum for the lumber that was in great demand in England and the Caribbean. Northampton had become a great estate on the basis of a work force that embraced slaves and freemen, unskilled and skilled, blacks and whites.[37]

Of the vast changes Chesapeake society underwent during the eighteenth century, no two were as important as the emergence of slavery and the rise of the gentry. And no two were more inextricably linked. Every step to extend the institution of slavery into new areas or to consolidate it in old ones strengthened the power, prestige, and pretentions of the gentry. Yet the small-scale nature of slavery in Baltimore placed the county gentry under greater pressures than the Tidewater's provincial gentry to find other sources of labor. The resulting work force was an ever-changing mosaic of unfree and free laborers. One might argue that success came to those gentlemen who exhibited a spirit of flexibility, improvisation, and innovation in recruiting and managing their plantation work forces. But such open labor practices came at the price of a slave population whose potential for collective action was severely limited.

4

The Landed Estate

The Chesapeake gentry was a class of landholders as well as slave-holders. Although the corrosive forces of commercialization were clearly gathering strength as market relations began to entwine all realms of eighteenth-century life, land itself continued to carry a heavy load of traditional obligations and to occupy an anomalous position in the world of pure-and-simple commodities. Land represented the ultimate source of power, prestige, and privilege. It served as the most reliable means of bequeathing social status from parents to children. It also furnished the vital nexus between the members of a lineage, past, present, and future. It might be said that land was not owned in any absolute sense but held in trusteeship for future generations. This delicate blending of proprietorship and stewardship defined the relationship of gentlemen to their landed estates.

The principal characteristics of elite life in Baltimore—openness, fluidity, and impermanence—were closely connected to the ways in which land was acquired by one generation and transmitted to the next. In contrast with the provincial gentry of tidewater Virginia, for whom land speculation was an avenue to wealth and power, the Baltimore elite generally shunned large-scale wheeling and dealing in the marketplace. Of course, all large landholders dedicated themselves to expanding the boundaries of their estates wherever and whenever possible, but in Baltimore they did so with studied caution. This conservative pattern of slow and steady accumulation has to be understood in the larger context of inheritance strategies. By eschewing risky ventures that might backfire and plunge the entire estate in ruinous debt, elite landowners demonstrated their desire to provide at least a basic level of economic independence for their wives and children. In wills, deeds of gift, and informal exchanges, they rejected the notion of maintaining the estate largely intact through some form of primogeniture, preferring instead to spread the wealth in a remarkably equitable fashion among all members of the immediate family. This pattern of partible inheritance brought about a radical redistribution of wealth each generation and virtually guaranteed that many sons and daughters would lose their grip on elite status. It helped keep the doors to elite status open.

Securing a landed estate was the dream of every gentleman. Despite a significant trend toward economic diversification during the eighteenth century, the fact remained that wealth, power, and prestige ultimately flowed from the number of acres a man owned. Like every landed class, the leading families of Baltimore knew that bold ventures in the land market might bring windfall gains of hundreds of acres and lay the foundation of a proud estate. But they also knew that a single bad judgment could mire an estate in debt and jeopardize a lifetime of careful investment. To shield themselves against the vagaries of the marketplace, the Baltimore elite adopted a strategy designed to minimize risks. It might be called a *strategy of conservation*.

The conservative instincts of the elite can be seen in an examination of county debt books. The forty-nine members of the elite who appeared in two or more debt books between 1754 and 1771 increased their average holding by relatively modest increments from year to year. Taken together, their estates gained an annual average of only thirty acres. Needless to say, some estates grew significantly during the careers of their owners, since even small annual additions could mount over a number of years. The twenty-six estates that could be traced through at least thirteen debt books grew by an average of 562 acres. Put differently, all of the estates that gained more than one thousand acres appeared in at least fifteen of the eighteen years covered by the debt books.[1]

The strategy of carefully managed growth reflected a strong aversion to selling land. It seems reasonable to suppose that if landowners had pushed their finances to the limit of solvency in pursuit of high-risk ventures, the result would have been a rash of business failures and estate liquidations once the economy entered one of its periodic downturns. But the process of estate formation does not show this boom-bust pattern. Only four of the forty-nine estates that appeared in more than one debt book declined in size between the first entry and the last, and the average drop was a mere fifty-one acres. Even the handful of unlucky individuals forced by circumstances to put large parcels of land on the market lost no time in recouping their losses. For example, in 1758 William Dallam sold almost half of his 1,349 acres, but by his death two years later he had managed to restore the estate to its original size. Likewise, although on two occasions during the 1750s John Hall of Swan Town was obliged to sell a 700-acre tract, his holdings were back at their original level of 4,164 acres a few years before his death. Whatever drove Dallam and Hall to the extremity of temporarily dismembering their estates did not affect the vast majority of the elite, who seemed absolutely determined to hang on to every last acre they owned.[2]

The conservative behavior of elite landowners surfaces no less clearly in hundreds of conveyances, mortgages, leases, and assignments recorded at the county court. The mammoth land schemes of tidewater aristocrats like the Carters, Byrds, Carrolls, and Dulanys have been carefully documented, but no one in Baltimore operated on such a scale. Indeed, the elite transacted amazingly little business at the court. During the colonial period the elite registered a total of 869 conveyances, leases, assignments, and mortgages at court, an average of only 4.8 transactions per individual. Yet even this figure exaggerates the scope of the land market because almost one-third of the elite never appeared in the land deeds at all, and another quarter of them made just one or two deals during their lifetimes. Conversely, large-scale operators always constituted a small proportion of the whole: only 14 percent of the elite had over ten transactions and only 6 percent over twenty.[3]

Even at the close of the colonial era, when the land market stood on a firmer institutional and economic base, big-time operators remained the exception. The average number of transactions for members of the elite who died before 1690 was 3.3. For the period 1690-1719 it dropped to 1.5, perhaps because the prolonged depression in the tobacco market associated with the Anglo-French wars dampened the demand for land. The downturn in the land market proved temporary, with the average rising to 4.8 in 1720-49, and again to 7.4 in 1750-76. Yet even those members of the elite who died on the eve of the Revolution made relatively few appearances at the court; over half of those whose estates were appraised in the 1770s registered fewer than four deeds during their lifetimes.[4]

Another indication of the elite's underlying conservatism regarding land is the small number of acres that exchanged hands in these transactions. An examination of 662 conveyances of rural tracts in which the elite appeared as either buyers or sellers shows that conveyances consistently involved relatively small parcels of between 100 and 200 acres, equivalent to a family plantation or outlying quarter (see table 10). Only once or twice each generation did a member of the elite buy or sell one thousand acres, while the largest conveyance ever

Table 10. Size of Rural Tracts Bought and Sold by Baltimore Elite: 1660-1776

Years	Median Acreage per Tract		Acreage of Largest Tract	
	Sales	Purchases	Sales	Purchases
-1690	180	219	640	1200
1690s	238	140	500	400
1700s	175	122	1000	700
1710s	200	200	500	1200
1720s	100	200	500	526
1730s	170	100	919	990
1740s	137	135	1000	1600
1750s	101	100	1600	500
1760s	100	100	500	950
1770s	200	140	1200	551

SOURCES: Baltimore County Land Records, Maryland State Archives.

recorded amounted to sixteen hundred acres. Once again, it is difficult to escape the conclusion that elite landowners pursued a prudent strategy of land acquisition and steered clear of excessive risk-taking. Their occasional forays into the marketplace did not involve grandiose schemes of aggrandizement, but rather reflected such limited objectives as opening a new quarter, restocking timber reserves, or connecting scattered holdings.

Relatively little money was involved in these transactions, at least from the elite's perspective. In the typical conveyance of rural land, between £20 and £40 changed hands (see table 11). Although this sum was beyond the reach of many small landholders (not to mention tenants, overseers, and propertyless laborers), an expenditure of £20-£40 could not have placed a severe financial strain on the wealthiest families in the county. For example, at mid-century £30 was the price of a working-age male slave or seventeen cows with calves. Prices remained relatively stable except during two inflationary periods. The first came in the 1690s, perhaps because by that decade the most desirable and accessible land had been patented, forcing newcomers to enter the private market to obtain choice tracts. The second coincided with the tremendous expansion of Baltimore Town during the 1760s,

Table 11. Price of Rural Tracts Bought and Sold by Baltimore Elite: 1660-1776

	Price per Tract		Median Price per Acre	
Years	Sales	Purchases	Sales	Purchases
-1690	£10.4	£30.4	1s 9d	1s 4d
1690s	£40.9	£23.4	5s 6d	3s 10d
1700s	£49.17	£26.3	4s 8d	3s 10d
1710s	£35.18	£43.10	7s 11d	4s 1d
1720s	£22.5	£42.11	4s 1d	4s 2d
1730s	£31.19	£22.11	4s	4s 2d
1740s	£36.1	£31.4	6s 7d	4s 11d
1750s	£38.19	£17.2	7s 1d	5s 9d
1760s	£39.2	£72.19	10s 11d	10s 2d
1770s	£388.2	£23.16	21s 1d	10s 3d

Sources: Baltimore County Land Records, Maryland State Archives.

which increased demand not only for urban property but also for rural land surrounding the port.

The elite operated within a highly localized and personalized land market. Large landowners preferred to do business within a few miles of their home plantations and rarely ventured beyond the familiar confines of their neighborhood. Before the growth of Baltimore Town caused the population to shift to the southern end of the county, most members of the elite tended to cluster around either the Patapsco River or the Bush River. For example, two out of every five members of the elite whose residence can be identified in the 1737 tax list lived in either Upper Patapsco Hundred or Lower Spesutia Hundred. That members of the elite stayed close to their plantations when buying and selling land is suggested by the fact that 34 percent of the land conveyances were located on the Patapsco River and 26 percent on the Bush River. By contrast, the Susquehanna and Gunpowder rivers, which attracted relatively few elite residences, together accounted for only 39 percent of the transactions. The percentages fluctuated within a narrow range from one decade to the next, but the Patapsco and Bush always attracted the greatest number of elite buyers and sellers.[5]

An exchange of land brought together friends, neighbors, and acquaintances who probably knew exactly what a given tract of land was
worth from years of first-hand experience and observation. Indeed, it
might be misleading to speak of a single land market in the county, for
buying and selling usually took place within small settlements that
clustered on the major rivers, thus creating a series of localized markets. The residence of the other party in the transaction was listed in
391 of the 662 conveyances of rural land. During the entire colonial
period 84 percent of the people with whom the elite did business came
from Baltimore, and this figure did not change much from one decade
to the next. The second most frequently listed residence was neighboring Anne Arundel County, making up 7 percent of the transactions.
Only 3 percent of the conveyances involved parties outside the province, most of whom came from Pennsylvania.[6]

The parties in the transactions often lived next door to one another. The 1737 tax list provides an opportunity to examine minutely
the people with whom the elite did business because it arranges taxables according to the hundred in which they lived. There were eleven
districts in all, each with a radius of a mile or two. The residence of
the other party was identified in eighty-four of the 125 transactions
registered in the 1730s. In 39 percent of the cases, the two parties
came from the same hundred, while in another 44 percent they lived in
adjoining hundreds. Stated differently, in three out of four transactions
the elite did business with someone who lived within five miles. Nowhere was the market more localized than in elite-dominated Lower
Spesutia Hundred, where twelve of the seventeen transactions involved parties from the same hundred.[7]

Because the elite landholders were intent on building up their estates gradually and prudently through the purchase of relatively small
tracts from neighbors and friends, land speculation held little appeal.
During the colonial period purchases of rural tracts outnumbered sales
431 to 231, compelling evidence that most elite bought land with the
intention of keeping it. The most notable exception was Isaac Webster.
In 1733 Webster formed a partnership with fellow merchant Jacob
Giles, and together they bought thousands of acres at the northern
edge of the county in the vicinity of Deer Creek and the Susquehanna
River. The elite almost always avoided partnerships in their land deals,
but Webster probably had no choice but to pool his capital with someone else, since the purchase price of £1,500 was a huge sum for even
the biggest investor, much less a young man in his late twenties or
early thirties who had not yet received his inheritance. Combining re-

sources with Giles must have seemed a logical step, as both men came from Quaker families that had been intermarried for years. During the first five years of the partnership, Webster and Giles sold thirty-two separate tracts to small farmers and tradesmen from Maryland and Pennsylvania, although a few prominent individuals also made purchases. The average tract was 193 acres, and none exceeded 418 acres. By the time the partnership dissolved fifteen years later, Webster and Giles had sold more than 7,000 acres in northern Baltimore. Yet what is striking about this profitable enterprise is how few of the elite followed Webster's lead and speculated for themselves.[8]

The strategy of conservation outlined here does not square easily with the view of the Chesapeake gentry as modern profit-maximizers who felt fully at home in the marketplace. It is undeniable that the eighteenth-century Chesapeake witnessed the advance of market relations, the spread of a commercial mentality, and the onset of a consumer revolution. Yet in Baltimore the emergent economic order met pockets of stubborn resistance that continued to hold out against the commodification of life. In a world of simple commodities freely bought and freely sold, the landed estate retained a distinctive identity as something that possessed a core value beyond the forces of the marketplace.[9]

Why did elite landholders cling so tenaciously to their estates? None of them responded directly to this question in the surviving records, probably because the answer seemed all too obvious. Although admittedly circumstantial, evidence from wills suggests that large landholders adhered to their strategy of conservation out of a profound sense of obligation to the members of their immediate family—widows, sons, and daughters—each of whom had a legitimate claim to the estate. The freewheeling landowner who gambled for big stakes in the market, with the attendant risk of losing everything, closed his eyes to these claims and placed his own interests above those of the lineage. By contrast, the cautious landowner who shepherded his holdings with an eye to posterity fulfilled his duties as a gentleman, husband, and father. Thus, when elite landowners sat down to write their final wills, their guiding principle was to provide as equitably as circumstances would permit for their widows, sons, and daughters, notwithstanding that partible inheritance tore to pieces an estate that took a lifetime to build. They gladly paid this price to see their own children settled in the shadows of the home plantation, where another generation would renew the cycle on land encrusted in family tradition.[10]

A man composing his will walked a narrow line between two competing priorities. On the one hand, he wanted at least one of his heirs to receive a bequest large enough to keep the family name at the pinnacle of society. Primogeniture was the obvious way to achieve this goal. On the other hand, many considerations argued for partible inheritance. No man relished the idea of condemning his younger children to a life of penury, even to ensure the perpetuation of the family fortune. The expectation that sons and daughters should marry within their own class often required fathers to make substantial dowry payments at the time of the wedding, which reduced the portion available to the eldest son. And besides, it was only prudent to spread property among several heirs in the hope that at least one would make something of himself. If the eldest son turned out to be a spendthrift or a fool, he could easily squander his patrimony and undo the careful planning of his father. Worse, he could die unexpectedly without having prepared a will—an ever-present possibility in the colonial Chesapeake—causing the estate to become mired in the probate courts, where impatient creditors, dubious kinsmen, and a long line of fee-takers threatened to ravage a lifetime of work.

Members of the elite were constrained by the laws of England and Maryland, which favored the eldest son at the expense of his younger brothers, sisters, and mother. In the event that an individual died intestate, the law applied two general principles for settling the estate: primogeniture for realty and partibility for personalty. According to intestacy law, land that had not been devised by will devolved on the first-born son and his heirs, whereas personal property was distributed equally among the widow and children. This division was made after the widow collected her dower claims—a kind of "widow's old age pension"—to one-third of the personal property and a life interest in one-third of the real property. The objective underlying these legal prescriptions was to award as much of the estate as possible to the eldest son, consistent with the need to provide other members of the immediate family with a sufficient maintenance so that they did not become economic burdens on the community.[11]

Inheritance strategies obeyed demographic as well as legal dictates, since the size and composition of families played a large role in defining the options available to testators. Of 181 members of the elite, 114 left wills. These documents indicate that mortality rates were declining in eighteenth-century Baltimore, certainly for children and probably for adults, with the result that stable nuclear units eclipsed the assortment of kinsmen and acquaintances that made up earlier households. One piece of evidence is the increasing number of children mentioned in the wills. The thirty-two elite who died between 1676 and 1720 listed a total of seventy-three children, or 2.3 per testator. This figure suddenly jumped to 5.7 in the 1720s, and never dropped below 3.2 in any decade before the Revolution. During the entire period 1720 to 1776, 376 children appeared in eighty-two wills, an average of 4.6 per testator, twice the level of the earlier years.[12]

A second indication of falling mortality rates is the relative number of testators who died with mature children. Before 1720, 43 percent of testators (N = 23) with offspring whose ages can be identified had at least one child who was married, over the age of twenty, or named executor of the estate. The 1720s again represented a demographic watershed, for six of the seven elite wills in that decade referred to mature children. Between 1720 and 1776, 74 percent of the wills (N = 53) contained references to adult children, and in only one decade during that period did testators with minors outnumber those with older sons and daughters.

As the eighteenth century unfolded, more and more members of the elite sought to balance the competing demands of their wives, sons, and daughters for a share of the estate. Although they usually owned enough real and personal property to whet the appetite of every potential heir, the most coveted prize was the "dwelling plantation." In everyday use this term included not only the main house and its outbuildings but adjoining fields, meadows, and woodlands that together could amount to a sizable landed estate. In nine wills that described the land attached to the dwelling plantation, the average holding was 361 acres, with a range of 150 to 600 acres. It is possible to identify the recipient of the dwelling plantation in eighty-seven of the 114 wills. The following analysis focuses on seventy wills in which testators were married and had at least one child, for in these cases gentlemen confronted the difficult task of reconciling the claims of rival heirs within their own families.

With few exceptions gentlemen gave the heart of their landed estate to male heirs. The dwelling plantation went to sons fifty-six times, daughters ten times, and grandsons four times. Yet the assumption that male heirs should succeed to the home estate upon their fathers' death ran deeper than even these figures suggest, for eight of the ten daughters who inherited the dwelling plantation did not have brothers. In other words, daughters could expect to inherit the plantation only when there was no son available, and sometimes not even then. Sons kept a steady—even tightening—grip on the dwelling plantation throughout the colonial period. Before 1720, 63 percent of the testators (N = 19) gave the plantation to their sons, but during the next fifty-six years the proportion increased to 86 percent (N = 51).

If the son normally succeeded his father as master of the dwelling plantation, he did not automatically receive the key to the front door the moment the estate completed its journey through the probate courts. Half of the sons who inherited the house did so with a limiting condition: sixteen could not assume legal possession until the death of their mothers, and another twelve gained ownership at the age of twenty-one or when their mothers remarried. Younger sons had a better chance of getting an unencumbered plantation than did their older brothers. Of twenty-four heirs who could be identified as minors, 46 percent received the dwelling plantation without encumbrances, compared to only 31 percent of the sixteen adults. We can only speculate about the motives underlying this behavior. Given the attractiveness of a rich widow in the marriage market, a testator could be reasonably sure that his wife would remarry and transfer control over the estate to another man. To have required a minor heir to wait until his mother's death before gaining full possession of the plantation would have increased the risks of embezzlement by a scheming stepfather. By contrast, the father of an adult heir had less cause for concern, since his older son was presumably in a better position to protect the estate against the depredations of his mother's new husband.[13]

Despite the deepest cultural traditions proclaiming the preeminence of the first-born, elite fathers seemed determined to invest each of their sons with an equal stake, as is suggested by an analysis of forty-seven testators who had more than one son. Twelve of them found the notion of setting one son above the others so troubling that they bequeathed the dwelling plantation to two or more sons as joint owners, and in another fourteen cases where the ages of the male heirs could be identified, younger sons received the plantation nine times, compared to only five for eldest sons. In short, relatively few members of the elite practiced primogeniture with respect to the dwelling plantation. The majority chose instead to bequeath the heart of the estate to a younger son or to several sons in joint ownership.[14]

The dwelling plantation was the main prize but not the only one. Beyond the immediate vicinity of the home fields stretched additional acres cutting across parishes and even spilling over county lines. The largest estates were like a microcosm of the local economy, with rough-hewn farms producing corn and tobacco, outlying quarters containing a few cleared fields, and forest tracts awaiting axe and hoe. In addition to the land not attached to the dwelling plantation, elite estates included slaves, livestock, household goods, and other types of personal property. There was much here to entice a hopeful heir. To inherit a quarter, slaves, cattle, and domestic property transformed overnight the prospects facing a young man or woman. For the son who dreamed of becoming a full-fledged planter or for the daughter seeking an advantageous marriage, what remained of the estate after the dwelling plantation was devised promised to bring independence and respectability.

Elite fathers faced a familiar dilemma. Should they keep their estates (minus the dwelling plantation) largely intact by leaving everything to one or two heirs, or should they break up their holdings and distribute the pieces in a more equitable fashion? Most members of the elite chose the second course. A total of 209 sons appeared in the 114 wills recorded by the elite, 203 (97 percent) of whom received a landed bequest in the will or at some earlier date. Extenuating circumstances probably explain why six sons did not receive land. At least one of them had a physical or mental disability, forcing the father to leave his entire estate to a younger son on the condition that he care for his needy brother. Another father did not explicitly set aside land for his youngest child, but he directed his wife to "provide for him as to make him equal in fortune with the rest of my Children." To elite fathers and their sons, land seems to have been viewed as an unquestioned birthright.[15]

Daughters did not inherit land automatically as did their brothers, but the remarkably large number of them who claimed a share of their fathers' real estate demonstrates that the pattern of partibility was not limited to sons. The wealthy testator who endowed his sons with substantial tracts of land while giving his daughters nothing more than a cash payment or a family heirloom was conspicuously absent in colonial Baltimore. Indeed, of the 196 daughters mentioned in the wills, eighty-eight (45 percent) got land at their fathers' death or earlier. A daughter who was an only child or had only sisters could count on a bequest of land as a virtual certainty, and even married women had a one in three chance of getting land in the wills, even though they had probably received some form of dowry payment on their wedding day. Occasional references in the wills to the size of landed bequests leave little doubt that male heirs obtained more than their sisters. Judging from five wills that specified the acreage of the landed legacies for both daughters and sons, female heirs received between one-third and one-half what males were bequeathed. It would be a mistake, however, to assume that daughters were saddled with a few stone-filled acres no one else wanted. On the contrary, in the five wills where testators listed the size of the landed bequests, daughters received an average of 414 acres, a handsome inheritance by any standard.[16]

Daughters who did not get land got something else. Of the 107 daughters who did not obtain a landed legacy, ninety-five (89 percent) received personal property of some type. That left twelve daughters who went away empty-handed or with only a few shillings to buy a mourning ring. But eleven of them were married women whose portion had most likely been awarded years before on their wedding day. A bequest of land did not prevent a daughter from receiving additional personal property. All but two of the daughters who received land also inherited cash, slaves, or moveables—usually in the form of a share of what remained of the estate after the legacies and debts had been paid off. Elite testators did not list the value of their bequests, so it is impossible to measure quantitatively how daughters did compared to sons. Yet, on the whole, daughters did well in the face of the most stubborn social and legal traditions consigning them to subordinate status.

Their mothers also received remarkably equitable treatment. By entitling widows to dower rights of one-third of the estate's personal property outright and one-third of the real property during her lifetime, the law guaranteed that no widow would be turned out into the cold. Nothing prevented elite testators from giving more than the law required, and most of them did. Of the eighty-three widows with children, fifty-six (67 percent) received property in excess of their dower rights. The prospects of packing up her belongings and finding another place to live must have frightened every wife, and most husbands did what they could to ease the transition to widowhood. Of the eighty-three widows, twenty-nine were vested with a life estate in the dwelling plantation, and another thirteen were given occupancy rights until they remarried or the principal heir became an adult.[17]

Widows also fared well in the area of estate administration. A testator might insert into his will a thousand contingency provisions and last-minute codicils, but the truth was that the document was only as good as the exeuctor named to enforce it. An executor had to combine sound judgment and good faith, so that the spirit of the will prevailed in the event of unforseen circumstances. To shoulder this solemn trust, most men looked no further than their wives. The widow was appointed as sole executrix by 58 percent of the men (N = 12) who died without children, and by 42 percent (N = 83) with children. Although after 1720 the proportion of sole executrices declined in elite wills, it would be wrong to infer that widows were suffering an erosion of status or losing the confidence of their husbands. The eighteenth century witnessed a drop in mortality rates, leading to an increase in the number of mature sons old enough to administer the estate, with the result that fathers shifted more and more responsibility onto the shoulders of their adult sons. Yet even when the firstborn son was named as executor, he usually shared the duty with his mother. Testators with children made their widows sole executrices or co-executrices in 70 percent of the wills before 1720 and in 65 percent afterward, indicating that throughout the eighteenth century widows continued to play a key role in estate management.

Husbands also gave their widows a free hand in raising the children. Only a handful of wills included specific provisions regarding the upbringing of sons and daughters, usually reflecting the testator's suspicion that a crafty stepfather might destroy the children's legacies before the heirs reached maturity. The wills furnish little evidence that husbands feared that their wives might neglect the children in a new marriage. For example, in 1694 George Goldsmith stated that if his wife remarried and his sons and daughters "thereby should suffer," then his wife's brother was to take the children "unto his care and Tuition, and to see them carefully Educated." Twenty-four years later Nicholas Dorsey directed the county court to appoint new guardians for his children in the event that his wife's remarriage resulted in "waste or Imbezzlement" of the estate. The case of Roger Boyce also suggests that testators intended to protect both the widow and children against an unscrupulous interloper. If a new husband caused "the interruption of my wife's freedom of action," Boyce declared in a telling phrase, then his brother-in-law should take her place as executor. The only testator who seemed worried about his wife's loyalty was Aquilla Paca, who in 1721 ordered two fellow Quakers to raise and educate his children should his wife refuse to bring them up in the Society of Friends. Little trace of Paca's religious zeal can be found in other wills, for in only five cases did the testator appoint a guardian other than his wife for one or more of his children.[18]

The egalitarian theme that continually surfaces in the wills reached a culmination of sorts in the independence struggle. Only four testators who had wives and children divided their estates evenly among their sons and daughters, and all of them died in the decade before 1776. David McCulloch was the first. In 1766 he ordered his executors to liquidate his entire estate within seven years, including two lots in Joppa Town where his "dwelling House" was located. The proceeds from the sale were then to be divided equally among his wife, son, and two daughters. McCulloch added that if his wife was pregnant at the time of his death and gave birth afterward, then this child too could claim a share. By the 1770s this type of will was becoming commonplace. Of nine wills recorded between 1700 and 1776, three called for a measure of equality in the distribution of legacies among heirs. Like McCulloch, William Cockey directed that his house in Baltimore Town be sold for the payment of debts, while the residue of his land was to go to his wife, son, and daughter. Barnet Holtzinger also ordered his executors to sell everything and pay each of his children £200, except for a married daughter who was to receive only £20 because she had presumably been given her portion earlier. Samuel Owings did not go quite this far, but he too provided that upon remarriage of his widow, his dwelling plantation was to be divided evenly among his five sons and four daughters.[19]

What motives lay behind these bequests? The uncertainties of the independence struggle may have prompted some testators to liquidate their assets in the face of an imperial crisis that promised to bring a profound economic dislocation. But the egalitarian rhetoric of these years also played a vital, if unquantifiable, role in transforming testamentary practices. Perhaps we catch a glimpse of the interplay between ideology and inheritance in the will of Roger Boyce who, four years before the colonies declared their independence, asked his executors to avoid "ostentation" at his funeral and to "have the good sense and discernment to prefer the American new way of mourning." In dealing with his own heirs on a basis of equality, this republican was literally putting his money where his mouth was.[20]

The wills tell only part of the story of how wealth was transferred from one generation to the next. Long before a father considered making a final testament he might lay out a plantation for his son or provide a wedding gift for his daughter. A number of these "tokens of love and esteem" were formally recorded at the county court, but it was more common for the exchange to occur gradually and without legal fanfare as the son steadily assumed more responsibility around the plantation. Examining the transmission of property between generations from the perspective of wills easily creates the impression that parents retained control over their property until their deaths. This was emphatically not the case among the Baltimore elite. Wealthy parents seemed almost anxious to turn over de facto, if not de jure, possession of their estates to their children as soon as possible. They did not use inheritance to prop up paternal authority. On the contrary, elite parents seem to have felt deeply that economically independent sons and financially secure daughters should, at the earliest possible age, take their places in the world of adults.

The wills themselves contain numerous allusions to these gifts. Of the forty-two testators who could be identified as having at least one adult child, twenty indicated in their wills that one or more sons had already received their portion. The actual number was undoubtedly greater, since an unknown number of testators used their wills to confirm gifts that had been in the son's possession for years.

In making these gifts, elite fathers acted on the belief that their sons should assume the independence and responsibilities of manhood as soon as possible. At least a few sons had already obtained their entire portion before the will was drawn up, as in the case of Edward Norwood, who in 1772 explained that his son Nicholas was getting just one shilling because he had "received his full share of my Estate already." Other testators also revealed that they had already established their sons on plantations. For example, in 1766 Thomas Stansbury granted his son Dickson 268 acres and the plantation house he "lives upon," while nine years later John Chamberlain willed his son Samuel all the land "whereon he now lives." No one showed a greater determination to make his sons full-fledged planters than Benjamin Wheeler, Sr., who in 1770 bequeathed to his eldest boy two tracts of land "adjoining the Plantation where he now lives on Together with what I already possessed him with," and to his second son 100 acres next to the plantation "where he now lives." Having already taken care of his two older sons, Wheeler willed his own dwelling plantation to his two youngest sons as joint owners.[21]

Admittedly, a few gentlemen who conveyed property by means of these informal gifts kept the purse strings firmly in hand, perhaps fearing that sons who enjoyed a measure of economic independence might challenge the authority of their parents. For these patriarchs a policy of gradual emancipation seemed appropriate. At his death in 1757 Samuel Wallice was probably employing his son John to manage one of the family's plantations, but he never permitted him to advance much beyond the rank of a glorified overseer. Samuel paid his son a hogshead of tobacco, "being my promise to him made for his Incouragement." Nor was John the only son earning his independence one step at a time. When in 1726 John Giles drew up his will, his son Jacob was already living on a plantation that he had probably been given years earlier. Yet the gift had a price, for Jacob had to pay his father half of the tobacco and corn produced on the plantation, the kind of bargain that might have been struck with an ordinary tenant. The cases of James Maxwell and William Grafton clearly illustrate that a few fathers retained authority even after they had given their sons land. Maxwell had a son by his first wife, to whom he gave land without a formal deed. When both the son and mother died, Maxwell remarried and in 1720 bequeathed to a son by the second marriage the very tract his first son had "seated and improved." In a similar case forty-eight years later, William Grafton gave to his eldest son the "use of dwelling house whereon he now lives with that part of the Land he has Inclosed in fence Joining the said house," but he stipulated that at his son's death the property was to be divided evenly among his grandchildren.[22]

In addition to wills, deeds of gift registered at the county court indicate that for most members of the elite, independent sons seated on their own plantations were a source of pride, the crowning proof that a family had achieved wealth, prestige, and the respect of its neighbors. During the entire colonial period, about one out of five members of the elite recorded a deed of gift at the court. Not surprisingly, the seventeenth century witnessed very few instances of gift giving, in large part because parents died before their children had reached an age when they needed a stake to launch their careers. But with the general drop in mortality rates during the eighteenth century, more and more mature sons had to have land to start plantations, while their marriageable sisters required dowries to attract suitable husbands.

The pattern of gift giving can be followed in the court records. While only 11 percent of the elite who died before 1700 recorded a deed of gift, the figure rose to 19 percent for the period 1700 to 1720, and reached a peak of 26 percent between 1730 and 1759. Then the trend broke off, with gift giving falling to 15 percent between 1760 and 1776. One possible explanation of the reversal was the movement away from dowry payments, a change that historians have associated with the rise of what has been called the "closed domesticated nuclear family." Marriages were increasingly seen as a union of two people based on love, not an alliance of two families consolidated through an exchange of property. The elite made a total of eight gifts to their sons-in-law exclusively or to their sons-in-law and daughters jointly, but all of these dowry payments came before 1760.[23]

The elite's largess rarely extended beyond the circle of immediate kinsmen, especially during the eighteenth century when the average number of children and grandchildren per family rose. Not surprisingly, sons hauled in more gifts and bigger gifts than everyone else. Of the sixty-five gifts recorded before 1776, thirty-six went to sons. Three sons got what every young man hoped for, a fully developed plantation and a slave work force. In 1749 George Buchanan gave his son Lloyd a plantation with livestock, tools, plows, and fifty barrels of Indian corn to feed his animals. The gift also included a slave family of one man, one woman, and two boys for bringing in a harvest of about 5,000 pounds of tobacco per year as well as providing a source of future workers. The plantation had at least one barn, for Buchanan said he intended to keep the tobacco hanging in it. Although the tract itself contained only 150 acres, Lloyd undoubtedly knew that it was part of a larger estate that his father planned to give him. When Buchanan died a year after making the gift, he left a will bequeathing Lloyd an additional 579 acres, two slaves, and a lot in Baltimore Town. At his mother's death in 1758 Lloyd acquired possession of the main dwelling plantation that his father had built decades before.[24]

Even if most elite sons did not do as well as Lloyd Buchanan, they did well enough. Of the thirty-six sons who received gifts, twenty-two got land without the capital to develop it, although they could probably borrow tools and workers from their fathers' estates, usually a short distance away. For ordinary planters even a few dozen acres would have been a windfall, but elite sons needed much more to maintain the social position they had inherited. And their fathers did not disappoint them. Of the twenty-one deeds that stipulated the number of acres, the mean gift equaled 505 acres, and half of the sons received more than 300 acres. The average size of these gifts remained stable at about 300 acres throughout the colonial period, more than enough for a self-supporting plantation and several outlying quarters. Landed gifts averaged 277 acres before 1709 and 272 between 1710 and 1759. Although the figure jumped to 963 acres between 1760 and 1776, that increase resulted from two enormous gifts of over 2,000 acres each. Putting aside these exceptional cases, the average dropped to 270 acres and fell in line with the earlier period. That these gifts were considerable is suggested by the fact that nineteen of the twenty-two elite sons got enough land to put them in the top half of the county's landholders at mid-century. Whether they would make it to the very top depended on careful management of their property, prudent investment, and a bit of luck—but certainly their fathers had pointed them in the right direction.

Sons who did not get gifts of land could always hope for slaves. Of the thirty-six sons in the deeds of gift, eleven received slaves. As many as half of these slaves had been singled out as personal servants. In five cases the father picked a black youth who was roughly the same age as his son, perhaps hoping to groom a lifelong companion and trusted servant. Since these young slaves had to learn how white people of the plantation house spoke, dressed, and thought, elite fathers believed their training must begin at an early age. The domestic slaves averaged six years of age, and one was only ten months old. Whatever the intent of their fathers, elite sons with personal slaves were learning from an early age what it meant to belong to the ruling race. The remaining six sons received adult slaves destined for the tobacco fields. In four cases, the fathers gave their sons a black man and woman who were intended to become the source of a self-sustaining work force.[25]

Although most sons got their land and slaves in fee simple, fifteen of the thirty-six gifts contained a provision stipulating specific conditions under which the son could take possession of the property. Only one father, Luke Ravens, Sr., insisted on retaining the right to alter or revoke the deed in whole or in part at any time, a provision he placed in six deeds of gift made to his children during the 1720s and 1730s. In addition, Ravens prohibited his children from taking possession of their gifts until his death, a stipulation that only one other father made. Three members of the elite resorted to a sharing arrangement like that of Thomas Wheeler, Sr., who in 1766 gave his son Benjamin a tract of land while retaining the right to plant crops and cut timber during his lifetime. Elite sons could generally do whatever they wished with the property they had been given, but three fathers left careful instructions on what should happen to the gift at the son's death. No one was more preoccupied with keeping land in the family's hands than Thomas Tolley, Sr., who in 1731 gave his son Thomas, Jr., 300 acres called Cullen's Lot at the head of the Gunpowder River. According to the deed, at Thomas, Jr.'s, death the land would descend to one of his lawfully begotten children, and afterwards to one of his or her children, and so on forever. If Thomas, Jr., died without sons or daughters, then the land would pass to his younger brother, Walter, and his lawful children; and if the same thing happened to Walter, the tract went to a third son, James. The man who so carefully spelled out this entail did everything to ensure that all future owners of Cullen's Lot would represent "the Blood & name of Tolley," but few gentlemen felt the need to impose such restrictions on their sons' freedom of action by making them life tenants of the property.[26]

Daughters were not entirely left out of the gifts, but the ten who did receive something had to settle for far less than their brothers.

Only three of them got land, although the average gift of 507 acres was equivalent to what sons received. The other seven daughters were given slaves or a combination of slaves and chattel, which from the perspective of a young woman seeking a husband might actually have been more desirable than land. If the newly married couple did not live in the vicinity of the wife's father, a gift of a distant tract of land under the supervision of unchecked overseers might have seemed more trouble than it was worth. Some of the gifts were outright dowry payments. Of the five sons-in-law who received gifts, three got land in the county and one in Baltimore Town. The average size of rural tracts was only 149 acres, less than one-third of what elite sons and daughters received, but still a valuable addition to a young man's estate. Likewise, in the three cases where elite fathers gave land jointly to their sons-in-law and daughters, the gift averaged only 157 acres.[27]

If elite fathers generally assumed that sons should enjoy a free hand in disposing of their property, the same was not always true for daughters. Fathers dictated the line of descent in three of seven cases where a daughter received land either on her own or jointly with her husband, an assertion of parental authority designed to protect daughters from husbands who might turn out to be incompetent or devious. In Baltimore as elsewhere such separate estates were created to ensure that the land would go to an heir of the daughter, thus preventing the son-in-law from selling or bequeathing the property to someone unrelated to his wife. For example, in 1725 John Stokes presented several hundred acres to his daughter Francis and her husband Aquilla Paca, stipulating that the land was for the use of the couple until Francis died, at which point it would descend to her heirs. Stokes also provided that if his daughter died without heirs, then the land would return to him.[28]

The final group of recipients included distant kinsmen and friends. The relatively small number of people outside the orbit of immediate family who were named in deeds of gift indicates that the elite's notion of kinship, at least with respect to property, did not extend far beyond the household. Only five relatives who fell outside the immediate nuclear family received gifts, ranging from a 260-acre tract to a slave girl. Another five people described simply as "friends" also benefited from the elite's generosity, but these "tokens of esteem" were not especially impressive compared to what gentry children received. The only friend to receive a tract of land got a mere 120 acres, while the rest had to content themselves with livestock, usually a cow and calf. Nor is it strange that no friends received gifts after 1718, for by then almost all members of the elite had kinsmen somewhere in the province, and competition among immediate family members for a share of the estate intensified.[29]

The case of Col. Charles Ridgely underlines the lengths to which some gentlemen would go to provide independence for their sons and security for their daughters. Recall that in 1721, at the age of eighteen, Ridgely married Rachel Howard, and together the couple raised a family of two sons and three daughters. By the late 1740s the colonel had amassed an estate of approximately 7,000 acres and began distributing parts of it in deeds of gift to his children. The first gift went to his eldest son, John, then in his mid-twenties: a life estate in 260 acres on the Patapsco River that included the family plantation Ridgely had spent two decades building. The deed stipulated that at John's death the plantation would descend to his son Charles. But this grant was just the beginning, for twenty-two years later Ridgely added between 2,000 and 3,000 acres to John's estate.

The colonel did not stop with John. Next came his recently married daughter Achsah, who in 1753 received almost 1,000 acres between the Patapsco and Gunpowder rivers. That same year Ridgely gave a life estate in 300 acres to his second daughter, Pleasance, on the condition that it go to her daughter, Elizabeth Goodwin, at her death; and another gift of over 600 acres that would pass to her other daughter, Rachel Llyde Goodwin, when Pleasance and her husband died. Pleasance also had a son, William Goodwin, who in 1770 received 260 acres in fee simple from his grandfather. By 1760 Ridgely's second son, Charles, Jr., who was twenty-seven years old, took possession of 2,000 acres on the upper reaches of the Gunpowder. Now only one child remained, the youngest daughter, Rachel, and in 1767 she and her husband received 433 acres on the condition that it go to their son, William Lux, at their deaths. All in all, the colonel seemed driven by a desire to surround himself with children and grandchildren securely established on their own estates. To achieve this goal, he gave away between 6,000 and 7,000 acres, naming as the beneficiaries a total of five children and five grandchildren.[30]

In striving for stability, Baltimore's foremost landowners promoted mobility. Their tendency to invest modest sums of money in the land market, their determination to prevent even a single acre from slipping out of their grasp, their reluctance to engage in land speculation—these do not support the view of the elite as profit-maximizing entrepreneurs who regarded land as just another commodity to be bought and sold. But the conservative values of stewardship that fostered this pattern of economic behavior contributed paradoxically to the open, fluid, and dynamic quality of elite life, because they led elite landowners to break up their landholdings and distribute them in a remarkably equitable manner within the circle of immediate family members. Partible inheritance guaranteed that Baltimore would have few family dynasties.

5

The Merchant Community

In an agricultural society dominated by planters and slaves, where urban functions and commercial networks were highly decentralized, merchants seem strangely out of place. Yet it would be a mistake to overlook a group whose influence by the mid-eighteenth century had seeped into every corner of Chesapeake life. Merchants were the human links between countless plantations—large and small—and the Atlantic economy. The steady flow of credit, capital, and connections supplied by merchants fueled the region's economic growth and buttressed the gentry's economic hegemony. With the massive expansion of British credit to the Chesapeake colonies in the decades following Queen Anne's War, merchants came to occupy an increasingly prominent position in the local economy. The credit networks radiating out from their stores entangled entire communities and represented an immense source of economic power.[1]

The permeability of social barriers in Baltimore seems to have offered merchants a unique set of commercial and social opportunities. It is probably safe to say that by the third quarter of the eighteenth century Baltimore had a larger concentration of merchants, in both absolute and relative terms, than most tidewater and piedmont counties. Each generation brought a new contingent of British traders to the county, many of whom arrived with the kind of insider contacts to London commercial houses that were difficult for natives to acquire in out-of-the-way Baltimore. At the same time, native families whose economic fortunes had been traditionally tied to plantation agriculture began to steer their sons toward commercial careers. Whether immigrants or natives, Baltimore's merchants specialized in trade to a greater extent than did "planter-merchants" who comprised the provincial gentry of the Chesapeake. Indeed, it may have been the very absence of a provincial gentry of slaveholding planter-merchants ready and able to defend its class privileges that explains the dramatic rise of Baltimore's merchants.[2]

During the late seventeenth and early eighteenth centuries the North Atlantic trade basin was transformed into a theater of war, and the shock waves produced by fighting between the major European powers reached places as remote as Baltimore. In the colonies, the principal phases of the struggle went by the names King William's War (1689-97) and Queen Anne's War (1702-13). As merchant ships became fair prizes, freight and insurance rates shot up, long-standing marketing arrangements were disrupted, and the Chesapeake tobacco trade entered a prolonged malaise. The sinking fortunes of tobacco affected different groups of traders in distinct ways. Even at the best of times, merchants who lacked a sufficient supply of capital and connections tottered at the edge of insolvency. So it is no surprise that in the uncertain conditions of the Anglo-French conflict, many of these small-timers went under. By contrast, merchants with the right combination of economic resources and overseas contacts were able to absorb momentary losses and ride out the periodic slumps of the tobacco trade. As the new century opened, a handful of men were not only consolidating their position in the commercial life of Baltimore but climbing to the top of the wealth and power hierarchies.[3]

This new generation of merchants differed from its predecessors in several ways. The number of men calling themselves merchants in court records increased steadily between 1690 and 1730, so that by the end of the period about twenty merchants were actively trading in Baltimore (see appendix 2, figure 5). Further, the new merchants were richer than the hapless collection of traders who reached Baltimore before 1690. Of ten merchants whose estates were appraised between 1690 and 1730, five owned enough property at their deaths to rank among the economic elite. Their average personal estate was appraised at £685, almost a four-fold increase over their predecessors'. The top merchant was nearly ten times richer than his first-generation counterpart. And while 86 percent of the assets of the first generation went to retire estate debts, the figure was only 13 percent for the second generation.[4]

The merchants who established themselves after 1690 specialized in trade to a greater degree than their predecessors did. To chart the merchants' investment strategies over time an *index of commercialization* has been constructed. This index is defined as the percentage of a decedent's inventoried property that was made up of commercial assets: merchandise, money, and debts receivable (see figure 1). For the purpose of this analysis the 181 individuals who

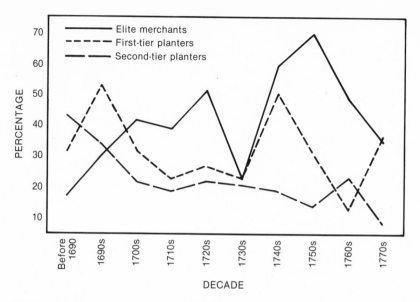

Figure 1. Index of Commercialization for Economic Elite: 1690-1776

SOURCES: Inventories; Inventories & Accounts; Baltimore County Inventories, Maryland State Archives

comprised the county elite have been divided into three groups: Thirty-three individuals who called themselves merchants in court records, sixty-three "first-tier" planters who fell in the top 5 percent of inventoried decedents, and eighty-five "second-tier" planters who ranked in the top 6-10 percent.

The period 1670-99 marked the heyday of the planter-merchants. During the seventeenth century the index of commercialization was 44 percent for the first- and second-tier planters, but only 17 percent for merchants. These numbers suggest that local traders had not yet carved out a well-defined niche for themselves in the local economy— as the unhappy experiences of Godfrey Harmer, Edward Gunnell, and John Gilbert amply attest—perhaps because the county was too sparsely inhabited to support a specialized trading class. Planters, not merchants, played the indispensable role as money lenders at a time when the establishment of new plantations generated a great demand for credit.

The period 1700-1739, however, witnessed a dramatic shift. The steep fall in the commercial index for both first- and second-tier planters suggests that they were withdrawing from the commercial activities characteristic of the frontier phase of development. As elite planters concentrated on their plantations, merchants moved into the commercial vacuum by plowing more of their assets into trade, at least until the 1730s when their commercial index dropped abruptly. This temporary break in the trend may have reflected the fact that some elite merchants who died during the 1730s had already retired from active trading and settled their outstanding accounts, thus reducing the debts-receivable component of the commercial index. The relative prosperity of the 1730s may also explain the declining index. The gradual increase in tobacco prices conceivably enabled greater numbers of small planters to avoid purchasing goods from local merchants on credit, which would have translated into fewer debts receivable in merchant inventories. Looking at the long-term pattern, it is clear that the first decades of the century witnessed the emergence of functionally specialized merchants.

Who were they? Almost all were English immigrants who reached the northern Chesapeake as factors of large London commercial houses. Indeed, it is no exaggeration to call this period "the age of the London agent." Richard Colegate, the preeminent figure of his generation, appeared in 1698 as a factor for the London partnership of Michael Yoakley and John Pettit. Four years later William Talbot registered a letter of attorney at the county court as a factor of London merchants George Purthas and Company. In 1705 both John Israel and James Crooke were described as factors. Edward Stevenson came as a "factor & Agent" of Peter Paggan and Company of London. When in 1698 Mark Swift first surfaced in the records, he was a factor of London merchant John Sheiffield "to Dispose of a Cargoe of Barbadoes and Other European Goods." Roger Newman certainly brought metropolitan connections, for as late as 1689 he was described as a "merchant of London." Like Thomas Bale, who a few years after his arrival testified to being aged forty-four "or thereabouts," most of these agents probably came as mature men. Only Thomas Hedge, Jr., reached Maryland as a youth, but within twenty-five years he was serving as a factor of Richard Bell and Company. Only William Marshall from Ireland's County Downe clearly fell outside the English fold.[5]

The merchant-factors represented the interests of their London employers, but they nonetheless aspired to commercial independence. For example, in 1708, after a decade of managing the Maryland business affairs of Yoakley and Pettit, Colegate took control of the company he had helped to create by paying £130 sterling for the legal rights to the company's Maryland debts. In addition to their work as commission agents, most local merchants probably undertook ventures on their own as well as entering into partnerships with other local merchants. When Colegate died in 1722, appraisors found £260 in merchandise in his store that he owned outright. Further, he had just received a spring shipment of goods on his own account invoiced at £161 and another in partnership with his neighbor and fellow merchant, John Israel, worth £241. These cargos overshadowed any that the first generation had imported.[6]

In contrast to the first-generation merchants, who exhibited little, if any, awareness of shared interests and who were scattered throughout the county, the London factors formed a compact community at the southern end of Baltimore. The residences of eight merchants have been identified: seven resided on the Patapsco River and one on the nearby Back River. If some of these neighbors knew each other from London, it would help to explain the rapidity with which merchants developed bonds of friendship and mutuality along the Patapsco. When in 1713 William Talbot drew up his final will, he appointed two friends and neighbors, merchants Richard Colegate and Edward Stevenson, as executors of his estate. In another gesture of trust and affection, Stevenson and his wife named one of their sons after merchant Richard King.[7]

Patapsco merchants invested less of their wealth in livestock and labor than elite planters did, but they nevertheless carefully tended their plantations. They did not repeat the mistake of first-generation merchants who pinned all their hopes on trade alone. Of the ten probated merchants active in the first decades of the eighteenth century, seven owned over 700 acres, and four over 1,000 acres. To work their fields, they assembled some of the largest slaveholdings in the county. In contrast with first-generation merchants who owned an average of only one servant and one slave, Patapsco merchants held one servant and eight slaves. The success of their agricultural endeavors became apparent in their growing herds of livestock, for the average merchant estate included fifty-eight cattle, forty-three hogs, twenty-eight sheep, and eight horses. Take the example of Richard Colegate, whose estate of over 5,000 acres was centered on his "home plantation" where he and his wife Rebecca raised their six children. In addition, Colegate carved out four outlying quarters that contained nineteen of his thirty-two slaves and two-thirds of his livestock. Equipped with the barest essentials—working tools, "Negro bedding," a few pots and pans, a parcel of earthware, perhaps a kettle or a candlestick—the slaves who occupied these primitive work camps seem to have been largely on their own, for at only one site did Colegate supply a flock bed for the white overseer.[8]

Yet one fact marred the economic success of Colegate and his peers. Only four of the eleven left behind male heirs, none of whom had reached the age of twenty-one when his father died. Like their predecessors, merchants grappled with high death rates that interrupted generational continuity and undermined the smooth transition of wealth. Growing up in the homes of stepfathers, uncles, cousins, godfathers, and guardians, fatherless boys in the tobacco colonies frequently lost their inheritances through deliberate embezzlement or inept management. Consider the case of Richard Colegate's four sons. As the wealthiest merchant of his generation and the political spokesmen for his neighborhood, Colegate undoubtedly expected to bequeath each of his children a sizable estate and a secure future. What he did not count on was an early grave. He had not been dead more than a few years when Richard, Jr., entered the home of his second guardian and Benjamin his third. How this shifting about from place to place affected their patrimonies is unknown, but none of the Colegate boys measured up to the economic attainments of their father. All of them became planters; none served on the court or in the assembly; only one adopted the honorific "Gent." The only son to leave an inventory was Benjamin, whose estate was worth about one-twentieth of his father's.[9]

In life as in death, Richard Colegate epitomized his generation. As an agent for a London merchant house, he reached Baltimore at the end of King William's War with capital and connections of the sort his predecessors could only dream about. He used these resources to weather the commercial dislocations of Queen Anne's War and build one of the greatest fortunes Baltimoreans had ever seen. That fortune was tangible evidence of how the determinants of individual success, even in remote Baltimore, were being increasingly defined by the larger world of the Atlantic economy.

But for many Baltimoreans that larger world was a threatening place. The appearance of the London agents injected a disruptive element into local political life just as Baltimore was recovering from the storm of the Glorious Revolution. At the turn of the century cohesive political elites were emerging throughout the colonial Chesapeake, and Baltimore was no exception to the regional trend. In contrast to the fragile political situation of the seventeenth century, a stable core of leadership now closed ranks in both the provincial assembly and the county court. It was this homegrown leadership that viewed the London agents with alarm.[10]

Baltimore voters elected four men to the assembly, and their representatives invariably included a few experienced politicians. In seven of eight assemblies convened between 1701 and 1722, at least half of the county's representatives had served in the previous legislature. Four representatives won election to four or more assemblies and thereby succeeded in carving out an enduring political niche at the provincial level.[11]

The same process of political consolidation was evident in the county court. From 1708 through 1720 twenty justices sat on the bench an average of 5.3 years. While the court was always receiving fresh infusions of new blood, five seasoned magistrates served for ten or more years and exerted a powerful influence on all of the court's proceedings. Not surprisingly, the same men who year after year took their places on the bench also dominated the assembly delegation.[12]

Aquilla Paca typified the two-fisted planter elite that dominated Baltimore during the first decades of the eighteenth century. His father, Robert, had started at the bottom as an indentured servant of John Hall of Anne Arundel County. When Hall died soon after his arrival in Maryland, Robert promptly married his widow and began building an estate. By his death in 1681 Paca had accumulated over 800 acres, of which 300 were bequeathed to his only son, Aquilla. The family then moved north to Baltimore County and settled on the Bush River, where by 1695 Aquilla was purchasing land and putting together an estate of his own. Four years later he married the daughter of planter James Phillips, a future colleague on the court, and received a substantial dowry that further consolidated his position at the pinnacle of Baltimore society. By his death in 1721 Aquilla had transformed the moderate legacy his father had left him into an estate approaching 5,000 acres, including forty-two slaves, four servants, and enough personal property to make him one of the wealthiest planters of his day. Paca's conversion to Quakerism forced him to abandon politics, but not before he occupied every significant office Baltimore had to offer—sheriff, justice of the peace, and assemblyman.[13]

Thus the London agents who reached Baltimore expecting to parlay their transatlantic connections into local power discovered that the political arena had been staked out already by a few well-entrenched local families. The two groups differed in significant ways. First, planters were either natives or long-time residents of Maryland; merchants were immigrants whose stay in the colony had been relatively brief. Second, planters included self-made men who had lifted themselves from humble origins; merchants arrived in Baltimore with valuable connections that facilitated their economic ascent. Third, planters tended to cluster at the northern half of the county in the vicinity of the Bush and Gunpowder rivers; merchants settled ten to twenty miles away along the Patapsco River.

Was a clash inevitable? Nothing in the relationship between planters and merchants was inherently antagonistic, for both groups shared an economic commitment to slave labor, the plantation system, and a vigorous tobacco market. But for native planters like Aquilla Paca who had amassed their fortunes on the Chesapeake frontier through a combination of hard work, ruthless acquisition, and prudent marriages, the sudden appearance of merchants enjoying connections with the commercial world of the metropolis posed a real threat. Conversely, on the small stage of Baltimore County, London agents like Richard Colegate undoubtedly expected to play leading roles. It was only natural for them to assume that backwoods planters, whose social origins seemed dubious at best, should step aside. If it came to a simple head count, merchants did not stand a chance against the planters: from 1708 to 1724 they were outnumbered eighteen to four on the county bench and twelve to three in the assembly delegations. But with so much at stake, merchants fought against the odds.[14]

The immediate issue over which merchants and planters clashed— where to build a new courthouse—might seem less momentous than the assembly debates that historians have scrutinized so closely, yet it kept Baltimore in an uproar for seven years and split the county's political leadership down the middle. A close examination of the controversy and its denouement reveals the fragility of a local elite grappling to make sense out of the larger Atlantic world into which Baltimore was being pulled.[15]

Settlement patterns provide the essential backdrop to the story. As the population shifted into the central and lower parts of the county, the old courthouse on the Bush River became an increasingly remote and inconvenient site to do public business. Baltimoreans agreed that a new seat was needed, but they could not agree where to put it. Each part of the county staked a claim to this valuable plum, for the courthouse not only enhanced the value of nearby property but stimulated local business by attracting buyers and sellers to quarterly sessions. The controversy must have simmered below the surface for years, but in 1706 the assembly brought it into the open with an Act for Advancement of Trade. Alarmed at the province's dangerous reliance on tobacco, the assembly proposed to rejuvenate and diversify the economy by requiring each county to establish a specified number of towns that would function as ports of entry. In an effort to conciliate the various sectional interests in Baltimore, the lawmakers designated the Patapsco, Gunpowder, and Bush rivers as sites for the new towns. The crucial decision on the courthouse came a year later—it went to Joppa Town on the Gunpowder.[16]

The new county seat seems to have been the brainchild of several prominent justices of the peace. James Maxwell, James Phillips, and Francis Dollahyde had served in the assemblies that framed the original legislation, and they also sat on the county court that was given the task of constructing the new courthouse. Since these planters lived in the Gunpowder region and owned property there, they all stood to gain from the legislation. Spearheading the opposition was justice Richard Colegate, the preeminent merchant on the bench and the leading spokesman for the Patapsco area. At its November 1709 session the justices took the first step toward executing the measure by assessing the county's inhabitants 40,000 pounds of tobacco to begin construction. Five of the six justices, including stalwart supporters Maxwell, Phillips, and Dollahyde, voted in favor of the assessment. Colegate cast the one negative vote, an unprecedented breakdown of consensus—never before had the clerk been forced to enter a dissenting vote in the court records.[17]

When the court met again in March 1710, it had to resolve another potentially explosive issue—who would receive the lucrative building contract? After four days of discussion, the justices gave the job to their colleague James Maxwell. As the senior member of the court, a regular delegate to the assembly, and a proponent of the new courthouse from the beginning, Maxwell represented a logical but by no means unanimous choice. Although Colegate left his seat in apparent protest before the vote was taken, his fellow Patapsco merchant William Talbot seems to have raised his vote against the contract. For the next three years this pair, Colegate and Talbot, championed the cause of the powerful merchant community, which since the 1690s had operated their stores on the Patapsco and which feared that the proposed county seat would divert trade to the rival Gunpowder.[18]

The beginning of construction did not stifle opposition to the plan. Despite their defeat on the bench, Colegate and Talbot continued to fight against the Joppa Town courthouse and soon drew the entire county into the debate. In November 1710 fifteen members of the grand jury placed a "remonstrance" before the justices, protesting all schemes to relocate the courthouse. To abandon the building then under construction, the jurymen declared, constituted a "palpable Notorious Greevance" because a new round of taxes for yet another courthouse would "reduce us to the Lowest Ebb of Poverty." Nowhere in the remonstrance were Colegate and Talbot mentioned by name, but everyone knew who was leading the opposition. Ten jurymen did not sign the document, perhaps because they were aligned with the merchants. In drawing up the remonstrance, small and middling planters who made up the grand jury demonstrated they were not overawed by their magistrates. Yeomen could speak out when their interests were at stake. It is impossible to know whether the pro-Gunpowder magistrates encouraged this plebeian protest, but immediately upon receiving the remonstrance the court levied another assessment of 45,000 pounds to continue construction. The battlelines remained the same, with Colegate and Talbot voting no. [19]

Outmaneuvered in the court, Colegate shifted his attack to the assembly. When the legislative session opened in October 1711, the delegation was split between Colegate and three other justices who favored the Joppa Town courthouse. The odds were not in his favor, but Colegate nonetheless proposed that the courthouse be relocated to the Middle River, closer to his Patapsco home. In April 1712 the assembly ordered that a countywide referendum be held to settle the troublesome issue once and for all, designating polling sites on the Middle River and at Joppa Town and appointing representatives from both sides to supervise the voting. As the referendum approached, the grand jury once again entered the battle and declared it "a Grievance to remove ye Court house being so near the Center of the County where it now Stands or to build another in Any other part of the County whatsoever." The statement carried the signatures of thirteen of the nineteen members of the jury, probably a fair indication of overall sentiment on the issue, for when the final votes were counted Colegate and his merchant allies had lost the referendum. [20]

But the Patapsco faction was still not finished. The county court convened in June with Colegate and Talbot conspicuously absent. This must have been more than mere coincidence, and it is possible that the opposition was attempting to disrupt local governance by orchestrating a general boycott of the court. On the first day of the session, the justices handed down an exceptionally large number of fines to grand jurymen who had ignored the sheriff's summons and refused to appear at the court. Colegate and his allies might have had their eye on the approaching assembly elections scheduled for October, the first in four years. Colegate formed a ticket with three other Patapsco men—his old friend Talbot, merchant Edward Stevenson, and planter Thomas Hammond—and after a bitter campaign they swept all four assembly seats.[21]

The Patapsco forces now controlled the assembly delegation, but their victory was contested by a number of county residents who protested to the assembly that sheriff James Presbury had intimidated voters who opposed the Colegate ticket. After examining the charges, the assembly ordered a new election for early November and summoned Presbury to explain his misconduct. The sheriff admitted that he had acted illegally, but attributed his behavior to "Ignorance and some menacing Letters he had from some Gentlemen living about Potapsco [sic]." Presbury discretely avoided naming names, but by this point the Patapsco "Gentlemen" were well-known figures. At the same time the council received word that the old courthouse on the Bush River had mysteriously burned down, raising the specter of arson. From the perspective of the provincial government, the courthouse dispute seemed to be getting completely out of hand.[22]

The Colegate ticket triumphed in the new elections and immediately renewed its assault on the Joppa courthouse. Colegate was given one final opportunity to present his case before an understandably exasperated lower house. The assembly rejected his proposal in hopes of killing the issue once and for all, but it also prohibited the county's justices from levying further taxes until the building contract had been studied. In a last desperate attempt to stave off defeat, Colegate and the others petitioned the council, which sent the document back to the lower house without a reading. On November 15 the assembly passed an "Act for settling Baltimore county court at the new court-house at Joppa" and ordered the county to "forbear and desist from raising promoting or prosecuting any Heats, Debates, Reflections or Disturbances." In October 1713, after a review of Maxwell's contract, the assembly permitted the justices to make a final assessment for completing the building.[23]

The courthouse battle symbolized more than a personal defeat for Richard Colegate and the Patapso merchants, for at moments during the controversy the very machinery of local government seemed to be breaking down. It was essential for Baltimoreans to put the issue to rest. The chief obstacles to reconciliation remained the recalcitrant Colegate and Talbot, who in November 1712 refused to take their seats on the court bench, threatening to prolong the battle and impede the administration of justice. This was something neither their friends nor enemies could condone. On this question the grand jury, which had hitherto been polarized over the courthouse issue, spoke with one voice, ordering the two justices to show cause for their failure to appear. No more prodding was necessary, and the next day Colegate and Talbot resumed their customary places alongside their antagonists.[24]

Like any fundamental economic change, the incorporation of Baltimore into the Atlantic economy, signaled by the arrival of the London agents, unsettled established ways of doing things. Ambitious men struggled to understand the new rules of the game and make the most of them, and the courthouse controversy should be seen as part of this adjustment. With hindsight, it seems all but inevitable. But to old-timers who had lived through the tumultuous days of the Glorious Revolution, when Quaker renegade Thomas Thurston successfully challenged the old guard, it must have brought back memories of a local gentry that could not make peace with itself.

But in time peace did come. By 1730 the protagonists of the courthouse war were dead, and the next thirty years saw merchants and planters put aside their differences and pool their resources. One factor underlying the reconciliation was quantitative. Merchants now comprised one of the fastest-growing occupations in Baltimore, their numbers rising steadily from an estimated fifteen in 1730 to forty three decades later (see appendix 2, figure 5). At the same time merchants continued their climb up the wealth hierarchy. Of the 117 merchants active in Baltimore County between 1730 and 1769, forty died before 1769 and left inventories. Eighteen of the forty probated merchants belonged to the economic elite. The average assessment amounted to £1,426, almost double the figure for the second generation.[25]

Merchants also continued down the path of commercial specialization that had been pioneered by the London agents. Between 1740 and 1759 the index of commercialization climbed for both elite merchants and first-tier planters, while dropping slightly for second-tier planters, who remained on the periphery of commercial life (see figure 1). We can only speculate about the factors accounting for this pattern, but two guesses seem plausible. First, it was widely complained that the Tobacco Inspection Act of 1747, which called for the destruction of low-grade tobacco, discriminated against small planters who needed to sell every last leaf to make ends meet. Supporters of the legislation argued that the resulting improvement in the quality of the crop would benefit all classes of producers by raising the general price level in Europe. Whatever its long-term effects, the law may have placed ordinary planters under particularly severe pressure to borrow from their very wealthy neighbors. If this guess is correct, the value of debts receivable in the estates of elite merchants and first-tier planters would have increased, thus driving up the index of commercialization. Second, after 1739 King George's War disrupted shipping lanes, raised freight rates, and threw a pall over the economy. The wartime dislocations, coupled with the new legislation, may have combined to generate a growing demand for local credit that only the wealthiest merchants and planters could supply.[26]

What most clearly set these merchants apart from their predecessors of both the first- and second-generation was their ability to conserve wealth. They succeeded in establishing their children on a sounder economic basis than ever before, in part a reflection of the continued drop in mortality rates during the eighteenth century. Baltimore remained a dangerous place to live, but the epidemiological outlook had brightened. Of the twenty merchants who began their careers in the 1720s and 1730s, the ages of ten are known. They lived to an average age of fifty-nine, ranging from the forty-five-year-old John Moale to the octogenerian Jacob Giles. For these merchants longer lives meant more children. Of fourteen who left wills, thirteen mentioned children. The average number of children was five, but Isaac and Margaret Webster boasted of twelve sons and daughters. For the first time genuine merchant lineages began to emerge, founded by such men as Charles Ridgely, Sr., Darby Lux, Sr., and John Moale, Sr., each of whom had two merchant sons. The economic and political accomplishments of the junior Ridgely, Lux, and Moale eventually surpassed those of their fathers.[27]

The 1730s brought another radical change to commercial life—the emergence of the native-born merchant. The London agent did not disappear, but never again would he dominate the merchant community as in the days of Richard Colegate. This change can be charted through an examination of twenty merchants who launched their careers between 1720 and 1740 and who typified the group as a whole; their average assessed wealth of £1,648 was close to the figure for all probated merchants active from 1730 to 1769. For the first time in Baltimore's history native merchants outnumbered immigrants. Ten of the seventeen whose origins have been determined were born in Maryland, in stark contrast to the pre-1720 years when not a single known merchant was "country-born." Like many younger sons throughout colonial America, native merchants may have adopted trade in part because their fathers could not establish them on land. The six fathers who appear in the records were moderately successful planters, but by no means aristocrats, owning an average of 700 acres of land and £378 in personal property, which would have put them in the top quarter of the county's probated decedents. In their wills, men of this economic standing frequently set aside undeveloped tracts for their younger sons, who had the choice of either developing their unbroken land or starting a career outside of planting. No fewer than three of the six known native merchants were younger sons, and at least two of them watched the home plantation go to their older brothers. While merchant William Hammond was a firstborn son, his failure to inherit exclusive rights to the home plantation put him in the same squeeze as younger sons. In 1725 his father willed that William and his younger brother should possess the home plantation jointly upon their mother's death.[28]

With planting a distant prospect, native merchants made an early decision to enter the world of trade. Six of the ten called themselves merchants from the very beginning of their careers to the end, and another three switched to trade in their late twenties or early thirties. As mortality rates declined throughout the Chesapeake, the abrupt generational breaks that wreaked havoc among earlier merchant families subsided, with the result that many young men could now count on parental assistance when they launched their careers because their fathers were still living. Although Charles Ridgely, Sr., and Richard Gist lost their fathers at the ages of three and eight respectively, other merchants were adult men at their fathers' deaths: Jacob Giles was twenty-one, William Hammond twenty-three, and Isaac Webster probably in his fifties. When Webster's father died at the age of ninety-one, even the provincial newspaper marveled that he "lived to see One Hundred and Eight of his Posterity, Twenty-two of which died before him."[29]

After 1730 immigrants were outnumbered by natives, but they nonetheless continued to make up a vital component of the merchant community by representing the commercial interests of the metropolis. Three of seven whose birthplaces are known came from the western counties of Lancashire and Devonshire. Like John Moale who reached the province in 1719 at the age of twenty-two and Josias Middlemore a year later at thirty-eight, immigrant merchants were mature men upon their arrival. No fewer than six of the seven served as partners, attorneys, or factors of London merchants. In 1724 Edward Fell registered a power of attorney for the London merchant Thomas Bond,

giving him jurisdiction over both Virginia and Maryland. His brother
William came as the partner of the London merchant John Philpot. At
various points during his long career Middlemore acted as the attorney
for the London merchants Richard Partridge, Samuel Lawrence, and
Edward Hankin. He also appeared as the factor of the London merchant Daniel Herbert. Brian Taylor established a store in partnership
with London's Philip Smith, who supplied most of the capital. Both
John Moale and Darby Lux served as attorneys for the London merchant Jonathan Forward.[30]

The consolidation of the merchant community was advanced
through the intermarriage of native and immigrant merchants, an arrangement that enabled both groups to pool their local and overseas
contacts. By the mid-eighteenth century the twenty merchants who
began in the 1720s and 1730s were entangled in a variety of kinship
networks, usually because their children intermarried. The major
constraint on these marital alliances was church affiliation, for the
majority Anglicans and minority Quakers chose their spouses from
among coreligionists. With so much hinging on the proper match,
courtship could elicit intense rivalry. When Robert North died in 1749,
his daughter Ellen received a handsome inheritance of 500 acres of
land, two lots in Baltimore Town, and £125 sterling for her "Education." Nine years later she married the son and namesake of John
Moale, Sr. Charles Ridgely, Jr., who had also courted Ellen, received
the bad news from his older brother John: "This Day Mr. J. Moale
is to be Married to Miss North happy for You that you did not engage with her but Suppose you'd be Angry with yourself for not
Plucking the Bud as without Doubt it was in your Power. I wish you
had, as it might have saved Poore Johnny Some Trouble in Entering."
The incident is remarkable because every man involved was a
merchant—Robert North, John Moale, Jr., Charles Ridgely, Jr., and
John Ridgely.[31]

The native and immigrant merchants who intermarried after the
1730s consolidated their economic position by creating credit networks
entangling virtually every planter in the county. At their deaths they
had extended an average of £729 in good credit to ninety-eight persons, compared to only £95 for the second generation and £45 for the
first. These credit networks went deep into the county. It is possible to
locate the debtors of four merchants who died within a few years of the
1737 assessment list. These merchants extended most credit to customers who lived within five to ten miles of their stores. John Moale and
Richard Gist lived in Upper Patapsco Hundred, which accounted for

Mrs. Ellen Moale was the daughter of Capt. Robert North, one of the leading traders of his day. Not surprisingly, she attracted the attention of several of Baltimore's aspiring young merchants, including John Moale and Charles Ridgely, Jr. She was in her late twenties when John Hesselius painted this portrait. Courtesy of the Maryland Historical Society, Baltimore.

38 percent and 41 percent of their respective debtors, while Brian Taylor operated a store in one of the Gunpowder hundreds where 57 percent of his debtors lived. Only William Smith of Upper Spesutia Hundred diverged from the pattern and drew his debtors evenly from across the county. These merchants knew that many debtors would never make good. In eight merchant inventories appraisors included both good and bad debts. For every £7 of credit advanced, merchants lost £2. Although desperate debtors were not necessarily limited to the indigent, poor planters definitely posed the greatest risk. Of thirty-three desperate debtors identified in the 1737 list, thirty-one did not own slaves.[32]

A clear indication of the merchants' growing influence as creditors comes from the 9,464 cases recorded in county court records between 1710 and 1769, the overwhelming majority of which were suits for recovery of debt. From 1710 through 1729 merchants accounted for only 10 percent of the cases that the court handled, but the emergence of men like Col. Charles Ridgely in the 1730s coincided with a dramatic increase in merchant litigation, for during that decade traders doubled their share of court cases to 20 percent. Merchants accounted for 35 percent of the total cases in the 1740s, 30 percent in the 1750s, and 35 percent in the 1760s.[33]

Col. Charles Ridgely was a slaveholder, landlord, employer, and merchant. In his evolution from dry goods merchant, to money lender, to backwoods grocer, to gentleman planter, he exemplified the career patterns of many elite merchants who saw trade not as an end in itself but as a means to securing a privileged place in landed society. The accounts the colonel kept allow us not only to reconstruct in detail how he ran his business, but also to identify the people who shopped at his store. They leave little doubt that elite merchants like Colonel Ridgely exercised enormous economic power over their neighbors.

Around 1732 the colonel, then thirty years old, opened a store on the Patapsco River, where he traded for over a decade. Two surviving ledgers for 1734 and 1735 and a series of day books covering the 1740s and 1750s offer a glimpse into the business dealings of a successful merchant. They provide answers to these questions: What did people buy at the store? How did they pay? What sorts of people did Ridgely do business with? How often and how far did they fall in debt?[34]

On the left side of the ledgers Ridgely itemized his customers' debits. The largest category of accounts receivable consisted of purchases of merchandise. Each spring the colonel laid in his stock of supplies, the same assortment of "new goods" merchants received up and down the Atlantic seaboard. In 1734-35 he sold £806 of such merchandise, which represented about three-fifths of his accounts receivable.

It is convenient to divide merchandise into four groups (see table 12). The first in importance was cloth. The colonel carried a wide variety of fabrics, including the finer types of hollands, shaloons, linens, kerseys, cottons, druggets, friezes, and calicos that might sell as high 6s. per yard. But these fabrics were sidelines brought out only on special occasions. It was the coarse and durable osnaburg, priced at 1s.6d. per ell, that represented the staple of Ridgely's dry goods trade. This one item made up 35 percent of cloth sales, 18 percent of total sales, and 10 percent of accounts receivable. The second leading class of merchandise encompassed various types of clothing. For about £1 a person could attire himself in a new pair of falls, hose, and a felt hat; these three articles accounted for three-fourths of clothing sales. The third category included a miscellany of manufactured goods, chiefly hardware: nails were in the lead, followed by gunpowder, shot, lead, knives, and forks. The last type of merchandise available at the store was food, most of it in liquid form. In the two years covered by the

Table 12. Accounts Receivable and Payable in the Ledgers of Col. Charles Ridgely: 1733-35

Accounts Receivable		Accounts Payable	
Cloth	29%	Tobacco	43%
Loans	20	Notes	23
Brought Forward	20	Cash	11
Clothing	15	Work	7
Manufactures	10	Goods	7
Food	4	Cash Transfer	5
Unknown	2	Miscellaneous	4
TOTAL	100%	TOTAL	100%

SOURCES: Ledger 1734; Ledger 1735, MS 691, Ridgely Account Books, Maryland Historical Society.

NOTES: Brought Forward includes debts that Ridgely's customers had accumulated in previous daybooks that have disappeared. For a discussion of eighteenth-century bookkeeping, see W.T. Baxter, *The House of Hancock: Business in Boston, 1734-1735* (Cambridge, Mass., 1945), 11-38.

ledgers, the colonel poured out about 150 gallons of rum for his thirsty customers, making up three-fourths of all food sales. He also sold a few dozen bushels of salt and corn.

It should not be concluded from this detailed breakdown of merchandise sales that Ridgely was operating an eighteenth-century department store with a complete line of consumer products. Planters of the Patapsco River came to the colonel's store looking for essential dry goods, not luxuries or trifles. Although he stocked his shelves with eighty individual items, osnaburg, cotton, hats, and hose accounted for two-fifths of sales.

The second category of acccounts receivable, comprising one-fifth of the total, was made up of loans. The colonel often issued cash directly to a customer (call him Mr. X) and charged it against his account. Since the lord proprietor demanded his quitrents, alienation fines, and escheats in sterling money, it is no surprise that Ridgely's most frequent entry read: "Cash paid for land rents." On some occasions, Mr. X needed tobacco rather than cash. All local taxes, court fines, and officials' fees were payable in tobacco; nearly half of the tobacco payments Ridgely made were earmarked for the county sheriff in charge of collection. At Mr. X's request, the colonel could extend cash or credit to another person (Mr. Y) and deduct it from Mr. X's account. A variant on the transaction occurred when Mr. Y preferred something on the shelf; Ridgely then charged the merchandise to Mr. X's account. In several instances, Mr. X had given Ridgely a promissory note for goods received but failed to make payment. If Mr. X was a neighbor, friend, or faithful customer, Ridgely might transform the bad note into a debt and charge it against Mr. X's account, although he always collected interest. The Xs and Ys were real people, of course, for whom Ridgely represented an indispensable source of credit. In 1734-35 the widow Sarah Parrish, her son John, Sr., and her grandson John, Jr., borrowed a total of £17 from Ridgely, a substantial sum for a family of ordinary planters.[35]

Now consider the right side of the ledger, where Ridgely recorded how customers paid for their goods and services. There were three types of credits (see table 12). The most important was tobacco payments. In 1734-35 Ridgely received over 65,000 pounds of tobacco packed into 147 hogsheads and valued at £349. A successful merchant had to have a good eye, nose, and touch for tobacco, and Ridgely must have spent hundreds of hours scrutinizing each delivery for its texture, aroma, color, and condition. Ridgely knew his business and calibrated his prices to the twentieth of a penny. The average leaf brought 1.2 pence per pound. Below this came "trash" or "under" tobacco that fetched as little as a farthing and made up only 10 percent of his tobacco payments. At the other end of the spectrum was "good," "fine," or "brite" tobacco, which cost Ridgely up to 2d. per pound and comprised 31 percent of his payments. He apparently bought as much bright tobacco as he could, confident that it would find a ready market in Europe and England.

The second leading item under accounts payable was composed of promissory notes. In 1734-35 he received thirty-three notes, of which twenty-nine specified payment in tobacco. Given the fact that virtually all his customers were in debt, why did Ridgely demand a promissory note from one debtor and not another? First, he may have required extra security from small planters who were always at risk of going under with one bad harvest. This is a partial answer at best, since note-givers included customers who belonged to the vestry, served on grand juries, and occupied local offices—in short, reliable and trustworthy men. Second, Ridgely may have wanted a ready stock of promissory notes from reputable individuals whose credit was secure, for these circulated as local currency and could help the colonel settle his own debts. October was the busiest month for promissory notes, presumably because many planters had harvested their tobacco but not yet delivered it to the landings for credit.

The third category of payments took the form of cash, work, and barter. Here emerges most clearly the highly personalized relations between the colonel and his customers, the thick web of dependency centered on his store, and the primitive nature of the market mechanism in eighteenth-century Baltimore. Of the 159 customers who appear in the ledgers, twenty-three paid off their debts with labor. Most of them did odd jobs like trimming Ridgely's garden, plowing his fields, mowing his oats, running errands to Annapolis or Joppa, tanning a side of leather, or burning bricks at his kiln. Nine men found regular employment from Ridgely. In 1735 Richard Clark was credited £7/10 for "One year's service p. agreement," and he earned another £3 packing Ridgely's tobacco into hogsheads. These jobs did not prevent Clark from producing his own tobacco crop of 1,307 pounds, which he turned over to Ridgely. No other customer bound himself for a year, but Isaac Bennett served two months and John Hagon one month and ten days. In addition to paying off their debts in labor, Ridgely's customers resorted to barter. The long list of goods taken in trade included horses, beef, pork, oats, corn, wheat, lumber, rum, cider, and even "squirrel scalps."[36]

In addition to illuminating what was being exchanged at the store, the ledgers allow us to sketch a rough profile of the people who traded there. It is not a wild exaggeration to say that country stores like Ridgely's represented the most socially inclusive institution on the local scene, bringing together impoverished laborers, middling planters, and great slaveholders, while at the same time laying bare the complicated ties of economic dependency among them.

Colonel Ridgely seems to have traded with everyone who walked into his store, even the most obvious credit risks. In 1737, a few years after the colonel compiled his ledgers, local officials drew up a tax list of county residents. Of the 159 customers, sixty appear in this document. The striking thing about them is how many came from the bottom of white society. About half of the taxable customers (thirty-one) were inmates, that is subordinate members of a household. Since none of them had the same last name as the head of the household, it is safe to say they consisted mainly of overseers, laborers, and servants. The colonel also did a surprisingly brisk trade with teenagers. In 1737 the county court granted bounties for wolf and squirrel heads to nineteen of the ninety-nine customers who did not appear in the tax list for that year. It is likely that these marksmen were under sixteen years old, the age of assessment. Another indication of the plebeian cast of Ridgely's business is the large number of landless customers. Of the 125 customers who can be traced through the proprietary rent rolls and county land records, fifty (40 percent) did not own land.[37]

Artisans composed a sizable segment of the population in every Chesapeake county and a not insignificant part of Ridgely's clientele. Of the 159 customers, it was possible to identify the occupations of forty-eight in the land records of the 1730s: almost one-fifth (eight) were craftsmen. They included three carpenters, a tanner, a cordwainer, a shipwright, a painter, and a bricklayer. It is no surprise that artisans worked off much of their debt, either by plying their specific trade or by doing simple day labor. In most cases, the colonel merely noted "Work done," but he occasionally itemized the accounts: tanner William Raymon curried eighteen sides of leather, cordwainer John Peter Sarter made forty-five pairs of boots and shoes, bricklayer William Wells earned a few pounds for "fetching tobacco" and delivering it to Ridgely's tobacco houses, and bookish shipwright Peter Johnson received credit for "Schooling" his daughter.[38]

It should not be assumed that Ridgely dealt exclusively with servants, tenants, overseers, teenagers, and artisans. Quite the contrary: he welcomed all his neighbors. The colonel lived in Upper Patapsco Hundred, which in 1737 had a population of 261 adult white men and 171 adult slaves. Of the sixty customers who appear in the tax list, thirty-three resided in Upper Patapsco and another eight a few miles away in Lower Patapsco Hundred. Most of the rest were scattered along the Back and Gunpowder rivers, while only four customers lived in the northern reaches of the county. There is no more striking proof of how thoroughly the operations of a simple country store could penetrate the surrounding neighborhood than this: Ridgely's customers comprised 13 percent of the white taxables of Upper Patapsco, 15 percent of its household heads, and 25 percent of its slaveholders.[39]

Dissecting the ledgers item by item and tracing the customers through tax and land records should not obscure the central fact of Ridgely's operations: virtually all of his customers were in debt. Of 161 accounts in the ledgers, 137 were in the red. And the debts were considerable. In 1734 and 1735 Ridgely collected only 59 percent of the £1,226 owed him. The individual debts ranged from a few pennies to nearly £40, with the average at £3/11/8. Given the relatively large number of customers who were at or near the bottom of white society, this was a very large sum of money. It has been estimated that in the

mid-eighteenth century the average tenant farmer cleared only about
£3 a year from tobacco after expenses, a nonslaveholding landowner
£3-£6, and a slaveholder £15-£20. For even a prosperous planter a debt
of £3/11/8 meant that Ridgely might take a big share of the tobacco
crop, for landless tenants and sharecroppers he might take the whole
thing, and for the small operator cursed by a bad harvest or bad health,
he might get next year's crop too. In the eyes of his neighbors, Colonel
Ridgely was a powerful man.[40]

This power was in full view when Ridgely took his customers to
court. From the moment he opened his store until 1757, Ridgely
brought a total of twenty-seven suits before the Baltimore County
Court and another thirty before the Anne Arundel County Court. Only
one came during the 1730s when he was just establishing his business
and hoping to attract customers, but it was typical of the rest. On November 13, 1736, the Baltimore sheriff was ordered to attach the property of planter James Hopkins for a debt of 2,103 pounds of tobacco in
addition to court costs of 701 pounds. At the March 1737 session the
sheriff reported having attached 1,102 pounds of tobacco and eight barrels of corn worth 600 pounds. Meantime, Hopkins seems to have
skipped the county. He does not appear in the 1737 tax list, compiled
only a few months after his property was condemned. It is impossible
to know why Ridgely singled out Hopkins among the many people
who owed him money, but the size of the debt probably was an important consideration. At the going rate of 1.2 pence per pound Hopkins was over £10 in debt, a substantial figure judging from the fact
that only seven of the 161 accounts in Ridgely's 1734-35 ledgers were
so far in arrears.[41]

But within a decade Ridgely was squeezing his debors harder
than he had dared in the past. From 1741 through 1746 he brought
twenty-six suits before the Baltimore and Anne Arundel courts. One
possible explanation is that by the 1740s Ridgely was extending larger
amounts of credit to individuals, the collection of which justified the
time and trouble of a lawsuit. In forty of the fifty-seven suits, the debt
was recorded in tobacco and averaged 4,486 pounds. Only three debts
dipped below 1,000 pounds and one reached 23,830 pounds. During
the 1730s Ridgely had done little business on this scale: of the promissory notes he recorded in his 1734-35 ledgers, the average was for
844 pounds. If Ridgely was taking larger notes during the 1740s than
he had before, it is easy to understand why he became increasingly
willing to incur the various costs and headaches of a lawsuit to recover
his money.[42]

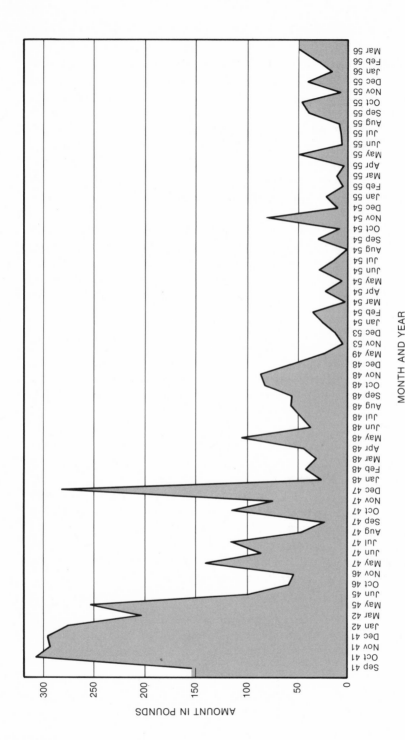

MONTH AND YEAR

Figure 2: Monthly Receipts at Ridgely Store: 1741-55

SOURCES: Day Books, 1741-56, MS. 691, Ridgely Account Books, Maryland Historical Society

There is another possible reason why Ridgely was in court so often during the 1740s—he was sitting on the bench. His rise to local office began in 1731 when, at the age of twenty-nine, he received an appointment as press master. Three years later Ridgely advanced to overseer of the roads in his neighborhood. Like so many aspiring gentlemen, Ridgely was traveling a familiar path that in 1741 led to the county court. Except for a brief interruption in 1754, Ridgely served as a justice of the peace for fourteen years. As a judge attending the quarterly sessions at the county seat in Joppa, Ridgely found himself at the political and economic center of Baltimore. It is probably not too cynical to assume he could except his colleagues on the court to look favorably on his own suits.[43]

The last explanation for the increase in litigation during the 1740s is that the colonel was beginning to withdraw from trade, as evidenced by the dramatic drop in monthly receipts at the store after 1741 (see figure 2). These were the years when Ridgely gave his Patapsco plantation to his son and established a new estate, Northampton, along the Gunpowder River. In closing down his business, the court was the most direct way to settle old accounts. After 1747 Ridgely did very little trade, in some months none at all. As business dwindled, he made fewer appearances before the court. From 1747 through 1755 he brought suit seventeen times in Baltimore and Anne Arundel, an average of 1.9 per year as compared to 4.3 per year in 1741-46.[44]

Throughout the Chesapeake merchants constituted a vital component of the elite, but this was especially so in the remarkably fluid social milieu of Baltimore. The top traders who had emerged by the 1730s never considered themselves a group apart but were drawn into the elite by a network of commercial and familial ties. So it is not surprising that the resolution of the courthouse controversy brought an end to the merchant-planter rift and inaugurated a half century of harmony among the leading families of the county. That merchants succeeded in gaining for themselves such a prominent economic and political station alongside planters testified to the wide-ranging possibilities for advancement at the top rung of Baltimore society.

6
The Established Church

Most Chesapeake gentlemen were born, married, and buried in the Church of England. With its establishment in Maryland in the aftermath of the Glorious Revolution, the Anglican church became an indispensable feature of local life, not only setting moral standards for the community but enforcing them with the resources of the state at its command. Whoever controlled the church, which was the only place (aside from the court) where large numbers of people from all ranks of society regularly gathered, exercised authority that went far beyond the spiritual concerns and everyday activities of the congregation. Hence an examination of the tone and texture of social relationships in the principal arena in which the gentry endeavored to assert the moral legitimacy of its rule illuminates the dynamics of power in the colonial Chesapeake.

If the institutional structure of the established church varied little between Baltimore and tidewater counties, the formal similarities concealed vastly different patterns of class relationships. In tidewater Virginia, the church came under the sway of the provincial gentry, who monopolized lay leadership, dominated the ministry, and molded the message conveyed from the pulpits to suit its own interests. The Anglican parish was, in effect, an extension of the great plantation. By contrast, in Baltimore the church did not cater exclusively to the interests of the county gentry, but reached out to ordinary parishoners as well. Middling and upper-middling planters, who rose to positions of leadership in the vestry and who were extolled from the pulpit as paragons of true Christianity, found a respected place in the church. Likewise, the Baltimore clergy enjoyed much more freedom of action than the conservative watchdogs of gentry rule who occupied the rectorships of tidewater parishes. In their struggle to preserve learning and letters amid the rough-and-tumble of provincial society, these defenders of rational Christianity offered their parishoners, great and humble, a bridge to the enlightened culture of the mother country. It seems only logical that in a county whose economic elite was characterized by openness and accessibility, the established church would throw open its doors to the wider community.

By the second quarter of the eighteenth century the Baltimore church had succeeded in overcoming many, but not all, of the problems that had bedeviled rectors and parishoners alike in the generation since its establishment. Parish boundaries had been laid out, ministers had taken up their posts, tax revenues had been earmarked for support of the church. Yet the very structure of ecclesiastical power in Maryland tended to set ministers and vestries at each other's throats. Unlike their counterparts in neighboring Virginia who had considerable influence over the hiring and firing of ministers, Maryland's vestrymen failed to secure the power to present clerics to their livings. These positions were valuable sources of power and profit, and the Lords Baltimore, ever vigilant on questions of patronage, refused to give them up. Stripped of any formal means of disciplining their parsons, vestrymen regularly vented their frustrations in vicious verbal assaults—sometimes deserved, more often not—on the character of their ministers. It was this institutional arrangement, more than the dissolute behavior of the specific individuals involved, that accounted for the Maryland clergy's unsavory reputation as gamblers, drunkards, and fornicators.[1]

Given the inherently prickly relationship with the vestry, the rector walked a difficult line. If he asserted his independence too aggressively, he alienated the lay leadership, whose support he needed, risked having his name dragged through the mud, and poisoned relations within the congregation. But if he acquiesced in a subservient role and submitted meekly to the vestry, he forfeited the persuasive power of the pulpit. The bitter experiences of Rev. William Tibbs and Rev. Stephen Wilkinson suggest that before 1750 the clergy failed to resolve this dilemma and paid the price in a festering anticlericalism that could erupt at any time.

Among Baltimore's clerics none had a stormier career than William Tibbs. A graduate of Merton College, Oxford, Tibbs assumed the rectorship of St. Paul's Parish in 1702 and held it tenaciously for thirty years. Everyone seemed to agree that he was a stubborn and cantankerous man, and within thirteen years of his appointment the parishoners of St. Paul's were petitioning the governor for Tibbs's removal. Most of the charges leveled against him spoke in general terms of the parson's sottishness: "he is a common Drunkard," "he is guilty of Sins & Actions in his Drink that will make a modest man blush to mention them," "he will be drunk on his taking the Sacrament before it can be supposed that the bread and wine is dijested in his Stomach." In addition, the petitioners accused Tibbs of being a crass moneygrubber who demanded a fee before consenting to baptize desperately sick children or to administer communion to the dying in private homes.[2]

These allegations could not be ignored because some very powerful men were making them. Vestryman Thomas Todd, Jr., a prominent member of the elite who spearheaded the movement to break the minister, blasted Tibbs for ignoring his priestly duties, cheating the parish of five thousand pounds of tobacco, and preaching what Todd could only describe as "Nonsense." What most infuriated Todd was the powerlessness of the vestry in the face of a minister so patently beyond redemption, and this frustration led him to the radical stance of questioning the legitimacy of the proprietor's prerogatives in church affairs. By what "power and authority," he asked, did the governor and council saddle the parish with a minister whom the vestry judged unacceptable? Todd found a powerful ally in the leading merchant of the period, Richard Colegate, who had also crossed swords with Tibbs. In 1714, a year before the petition for dismissal, Colegate asked Tibbs to deliver communion to his mother-in-law, who seemed close to death. The family went into a rage when the minister demanded a fee of twenty shillings for his services. In testimony before church authorities, Rebecca Colegate, Richard's wife, claimed that Tibbs had no sooner finished his business and collected his fee than he began to imbibe. When he finally staggered out of the Colegates' house, twenty shillings stuffed in his pocket, a family servant had to lead the inebriated parson home.[3]

The movement to oust Tibbs culminated in the most serious challenge to the Baltimore's Anglican establishment before 1760. The governor referred the petition to four clergymen whose objectivity might be open to question, since Tibbs received a seat on the panel. After deliberating on the matter, the judges concluded that while the charges were too general to warrant formal disciplinary action, Tibbs should be admonished to make peace with his flock. The wounds refused to heal, however, and soon after Todd resigned his position on the vestry and petitioned the county court to permit Presbyterian meetings at his home. A year later Rev. Hugh Conn, a twenty-nine-year-old Scotch-Irishman with impressive academic credentials from the University of Glasgow, arrived in Baltimore to head the fledgling congregation. Todd died shortly after the establishment of the new church, and young Conn immediately married his widow. The congregation built a meeting house on the Patapsco River and began to hold regular services there, but within a few years Conn had grown discouraged by the "paucity of his flock" and packed off for Virginia. Another forty years passed before a new generation of Presbyterians renewed the challenge to Anglican dominance.[4]

Despite his victory over the vestry and the collapse of the Presbyterian experiment, Tibbs could not avoid further confrontations with his parishoners. In 1731 the St. Paul's vestry issued another protest against the behavior of their aged parson, this time placing it before the commissary who was acting in the colonies as the personal representative of the bishop of London. Once more the vestry included some weighty names: Thomas Sheredine, John Moale, and George Buchanan, all members of the elite. The spiritual needs of St. Paul's were going unattended, explained the parishoners, because Tibbs had taken over the incumbency of neighboring St. John's Parish and had apparently moved there. To keep an eye on his old congregation Tibbs appointed his clerk, whose dubious qualifications included a conviction of felony. Tibbs was not prepared to forget the bad blood from previous years, for he refused to administer a deathbed communion to John Hillen, an old enemy from the earlier removal drive. Only Tibbs's death in 1732 brought an end to the controversy. For three decades he had defied his vestry, defeated all attempts to fire him, and exhibited a pattern of behavior that the commissary himself judged to be "incorrigible."[5]

Stephen Wilkinson of St. George's Parish enjoyed no more success cultivating peace and harmony among his congregation. In 1728, two years after taking over the incumbency, Wilkinson petitioned the county court against an alteration in parish boundaries that would have deprived him of tax-paying congregants. The minister took the high ground of principle in demanding the "recovery of my Just rights," but he seemed most worried—or so many county residents suspected—about his salary. Hoping to appease Wilkinson and to "put a Stop to all Debates and Controversies," the local magistrates ordered new parish boundaries to be laid out. Whether the controversy caused agitation among his own congregation is unknown, but a year later the St. George's vestry requested that their parson present an inventory of the parish library, thereby preciptating a battle that would continue until Wilkinson's death. By 1736 relations had deteriorated so badly—Wilkinson and his vestry were no longer speaking to each other—that the lay leaders placed a long list of accumulated grievances before the commissary, in which they claimed that the minister's refusal to attend vestry meetings disrupted business vital to the interests of the parish.[6]

As if these problems were not bad enough, Wilkinson was sinking in a financial morass. In 1741 and again a year later, he signed over his salary to Aquilla Paca, a local merchant and church leader, who agreed to pay off the minister's numerous debts. But even this drastic recourse could not steady Wilkinson's tottering financial affairs, for at the same time he mortgaged his plantation, livestock, and tobacco to the merchant Thomas Harrison of St. Paul's Parish. Then in 1743 the vestry tried to deliver to Wilkinson another list of grievances, which included his continued failure to account for the parish library and to maintain the parish glebe in good condition. The elusive minister never received the document because he "heard of their coming and Went out of the Way." In 1744, after eight years of remonstrances and petitions, the lay officers finally secured the much-disputed books and carefully lodged them in the vestry house under lock and key. The death of Wilkinson in the same year left such bitter memories that the parishoners of St. George's urged the governor to end almost two decades of turmoil and rancor by appointing a new rector agreeable to them.[7]

From this distance it is impossible to unravel the tangle of personalities and principles that set minister against vestry. If the admittedly partisan petitions are any indication, both Tibbs and Wilkinson were difficult men with flinty egos. But they were not wholly to blame for the breakdown of Christian brotherhood in their parishes. Thomas Todd, Jr., and Richard Colegate also displayed an an explosive mix of pridefulness and inflexibility, perhaps because they saw the church as their private domain and the minister as their social subordinate. At stake in the disputes swirling around these two rectors was much more than a twenty-shilling fee or the parish library; at stake was whether the proudest families of Baltimore could put headstrong priests in their place.

A generation later Tibbs and Wilkinson would have been astounded at the spirit of quiet harmony and mutual respect that reigned in their parishes. Even Rev. Thomas Chase of St. Paul's Parish, whose acid tongue kept him at the center of controversy throughout his entire life, managed to avoid an open clash with his vestry during his exceptionally long incumbency between 1745 and 1779. To uncover the sources of this happy equilibrium we must examine the expanded role clergymen played in their parishes during the third quarter of the eighteenth century. The rectors who succeeded Tibbs and Wilkinson gained the respect of their parishoners because they were men of

learning who brought to the remote reaches of the upper Chesapeake
a cosmopolitan culture that one historian has termed the "moderate
Enlightenment." As spokesmen for a "rational Christianity" that appealed to the head no less than to the heart, the clergy became channels to the literate culture of the mother country.[8]

Thomas Cradock personified a generation of uprooted English
ministers who struggled to preserve the high culture of the metropolis
in the backwoods of the North American colonies. Born in Stafford-
shire in 1718, Cradock came from a family of prosperous tenant farmers who managed to provide their nineteen-year old son with enough
education to enter Oxford. After four years of study he returned home
to become master of the school he had attended as a youth. In 1743
Cradock received his ordination and under somewhat cloudy circumstances set out for Maryland. Some who knew him speculated that the
ambitious young clergyman had secret hopes of becoming the first
bishop of Lord Baltimore's colony, while others whispered about a
broken romance. Whatever the case, by 1745 Cradock had been in-
stalled as the rector of St. Thomas's Parish in northern Baltimore. A
few years later he married Catherine Risteau, the daughter of a rich
Huguenot refugee and prominent local merchant, thus gaining a foot-
hold in the uppermost social circle of the county.[9]

By temperament Cradock was a teacher and scholar. Upon reaching Baltimore he opened a school for the sons of well-to-do families
who desired a classical education. Amid his parochial and pedagogi-
cal duties Cradock found ample time for writing. In addition to his
voluminous sermons, he composed poetry, both religious and secular,
as well as a set of picaresque satires on Maryland life patterned on the
eclogues of Virgil. Perhaps his most ambitious and erudite work was
a play on the death of Socrates, whom the open-minded minister regarded as a paragon of classical virtue and an embodiment of true
Christianity. He published translations of psalms in both Annapolis
and London, which caught the attention of metropolitan readers, since
his death in 1770 elicited an obituary in the cosmopolitan *Gentlemen's
Magazine*. As comfortable as Cradock was in his study, he made several noteworthy sallies into the public arena, including a much-
discussed sermon before the provincial assembly calling for the
establishment of a colonial bishop and another in Philadelphia on a
proposed curriculum that would combine the best of classical wisdom
and Christian virtue. In the 1740s Cradock belonged to a local social
and literary club that Dr. Alexander Hamilton good-naturedly dubbed
the "Baltimore Bards," and he also held an honorary membership in

Hamilton's irreverent Tuesday Club. For a parson stuck in the back-woods of the British empire, Cradock managed to cut an impressive figure in the literary world of his day.[10]

Cradock and Chase, together with several dozen of their Maryland colleagues, have left behind an impressive body of manuscript sermons and other writings at the Maryland Diocesan Archives that throw light on the intellectual qualities of the Anglican ministry. They espoused an enlightened brand of religion premised on the compatibility of reason and revelation. "Thus are Reason & Faith distinguished," Rev. Cradock wrote, "both excellent in their Kinds; nor need we set them at Variance, nor disparage the One by over praising the other. They are distinct but not contrary. Reason, no doubt of it, is the Gift of God, as well as Faith & a most distinguishing Excellency it is." For Anglican ministers like Cradock the Protestant Reformation had represented a giant step forward in the march of progress, because by challenging the hoary superstitions of the Roman Catholic church it ushered in a new era of rational Christianity. In tracing the living legacy of the Reformation to their own type of cool rationalism, they rejected as irrational the predestinarianism and enthusiasm they ascribed their opponents. Cradock carefully distanced himself from the teachings of John Calvin. He directly attacked the doctrine of predestination because of what he saw as its inevitable corollary, that man was not a free and rational moral agent who controlled his own fate. This same commitment to rational Christianity led him to condemn the Quaker notion of the "inner light," since the idea that a sudden infusion of divine presence could fill a man or woman with moral certainty transcending the laws and conventions of society not only posed a threat to all existing authority but, most important, undermined the efficacy of reason. For Chase the only inner light that Christians received was emitted by reason itself. "The Light, which God originally implanted in Man is Reason," he asserted, "or their natural Sense of the Difference of Good & Evil: the Light of Revelation is a Confirmation, & Improvement of the natural Light of Reason."[11]

The Anglican clergy saved some of its harshest words for the growing army of "enthusiasts" who seemed to pose the greatest danger to rational Christianity. Because they encouraged unrestrained and excessive displays of religious fervor, enthusiasts disparaged the believer's rational faculties. A true Christian should be free of all religious "passion" that clouded reason. As a student of Lockean psychology, the Rev. John Eversfield attempted to press the insights of science into the campaign against enthusiasm. He saw religious passions in strictly biological terms, arguing that they resulted from "different Motions the animal fluids are put into by the various impressions made upon the Nerves by objects more or less Agreeable or disagreeable from without." Only when passions rooted in physical sensations are mediated through reason, according to Rev. Henry Addison, do we become "Masters of ourselves, which is in Truth a greater Conquest than Man subduing a City."[12]

The clergy's vision of rational Christianity produced a distinctive type of preaching, one that was a negative image of the evangelical style. Cradock's congregation could expect a sermon lasting no more than twenty to thirty minutes. On special occasions the parson might speak for an hour, but he generally preferred not to test the patience of his listeners. This subdued style put Anglicans at odds with "enthusiastical" divines who attempted to "transport some whimsical Men by fitts and Starts, as they think, into the third Heaven." Rev. George Goundrill summarized the Anglican contempt for enthusiasts who "relish nothing from the Pulpit, but what is addressed to their Passions." Whatever their immediate impact, these harangues invariably left the congregation with a sense of emptiness and despair.[13]

Because rational Christians had mastered their own passions, they enjoyed an emotional equilibrium between the dangerous extremes of exuberance and despondency. They could enjoy the earthly pleasures that God had provided for mankind without succumbing to their seductive powers. In short, the rational Christian was an agreeable fellow and a fine companion. In one of his most popular sermons aimed directly at the enthusiasts, *Innocent Mirth Not Inconsistent with Religion,* Cradock argued that a "gay social Temper" became a Christian since every man was born "to promote the Happiness and Benefit of his Neighbor," an essential truth that Calvinists and enthusiasts could never understand because they "dress'd up Religion in such a gloomy, frightening Manner." The telltale signs of enthusiasm could be seen in the "sullen" and "sour" faces of the deluded believers. Chase acknowledged that rational Christianity frequently lacked the fire that enthusiasts kindled in their followers, but he explained the fact in sociological terms. The Anglican church service had no choice but to aim at a lowest common denominator of religious sentiment, because congregations generally included "Men of all Ranks, Distinctions & Attainments." In such mixed company, decent restraint was necessary to maintain order. Chase understood that many men and women in his own congregation craved a more intense religious experience, and for them he recommended the private "retreat" as a sort of emotional safety valve. In solitude, a rational Christian might experience the ecstatic and sublime. Even so, the minister warned his parishoners to respect social proprieties and keep their private piety "in the Closet."[14]

The Anglicans' belief in the religious power of disciplined reason and book learning emerges in their approach to education. Eversfield, the loyal disciple of Locke, implied that all morality was learned behavior. He dismissed the argument that moral sense was engraved on us at birth as the rantings of "Some Enthusiastical Divines." Nor did Eversfield hesitate to draw the elitist conclusion that learned men who had cultivated their reasoning powers were subject to a higher standard of morality than the "Ignorant people." For this conservative divine, individuals "without Educations" lacked the intellectual tools to understand many of the "Duties of Natural Religion."[15]

Other clergymen, such as Cradock, balked at condemning the masses to second-class status in the church. "The Love of God is qualified to warm the heart of the most vulgar Breast," he insisted. Yet even he had to concede that while God had endowed all men and women with sufficient knowledge to comprehend the basics of morality, a liberal education deepened Christian understanding. This dilemma emerged in a highly political sermon Cradock delivered during the French and Indian War, in which he argued that religion was the underlying cause of the conflict. For the people of St. Thomas's Parish, the issue was frighteningly real. In 1755, after hearing reports that Indians had attacked settlements only sixty or seventy miles from St. Thomas's, Cradock's parishoners began stacking their firearms in the corners of the pews during service. Their rector explained that, unlike Protestants, Catholics held that common people were incapable of understanding the Bible without a vast array of professional specialists explaining it to them, and for this reason the Catholic hierarchy refused to translate the Scriptures into the vernacular. The Anglo-American armies arrayed against France were fighting for the principle declared by Luther more than two centuries before—every man his own priest.[16]

Yet even as he attacked the elitism of the Roman church, Cradock could not prevent his own faith in a liberal education from leading him a similar conclusion. He admitted that certain scriptural passages involving tropes, metaphors, and allegories posed difficulties of interpretation. While a resourceful layperson might decipher an intractable passage with the help of a "good Exposition," Cradock advised his uneducated parishoners to submit to the authority of "their Teachers" rather than seek their own solutions to questions beyond their comprehension. In the end, Cradock reached a conclusion that would have pleased Eversfield: "A very ignorant man can not well be a good man; he may indeed have some virtues but his virtues are such merely as nature herself has been pleased to give him, and he also may have some religion, but tis such a religion as others chuse for him, & he plods dully on the exercise of its duties, without giving himself any concern, nay indeed often without being able to know, whether he is in the way that will lead him into happiness or not."[17]

The tremendous stress placed on book learning made the Anglican clergymen lukewarm missionaries at best. Their apathy became especially clear in their approach to proselytizing among the slaves who lived in their parishes. Not until the evangelical awakening of the late eighteenth and early nineteenth centuries would Baltimore's blacks begin the process of grafting Christianity to their own stock of African-American religious perceptions and practices. Although before 1776 a few Maryland divines attempted to preach in the quarters, they had very little success, in part because slaves seemed little interested in their masters' religion. As early as 1724 Tibbs prepared a report for his superiors in England on the state of the church under his rectorship. While he had every reason to puff up his accomplishments, Tibbs did not try to conceal the fact that slaves under his care seemed unmoved by God's word: "Many of them I have baptized & instructed in the principles of the Christian Religion but most have refused instruction."[18]

A generation later Cradock was also forced to acknowledge that slaves moved in a half-hidden culture outside the institutional framework of the master race. In one of the satires he wrote based on the people he had come to know in Baltimore, Cradock tells the story of an ordinary white woman, Jemima, who is seduced by a certain Dr. Crocus. When the doctor reneges on his promise of marriage after finding a richer bride, Jemima seeks out Granny, "an old Midwife, famous among Planter's Wives & Daughters for her great Skill in Charms & Enchantments." Granny then concocts a love potion for Jemima. For our purposes the crucial detail of the story is that the secret ingredient guaranteed to bring back Dr. Crocus is recommended to Granny by an "old *Negro*" whose ability to cast spells and brew poisons is universal knowledge throughout the community. In telling this story, Cradock was revealing a great deal about himself and the slaves who belonged to his parishoners. If he had been genuinely committed to converting the slaves in his parish, he undoubtedly would have viewed the "old

Negro" as a dangerous competitor for the loyalties of his black congregation. But Cradock assumed that the chasm between the enlightened culture he personified and the shadowy sphere of the "old *Negro"* could not, and should not, be bridged.[19]

In celebrating the virtues of learning in sermons that brimmed with references to Seneca, Plutarch, Addison, and Tillotson, the Anglican clergy gave churchgoers a satisfying taste of English high culture that could be obtained nowhere else in Baltimore County. It is impossible to say how the congregation responded to this display of erudition, but the appeal to learning probably struck a positive chord among the foremost families sitting at the front of the church. For wealthy provincials striving to emulate the life-style of their English counterparts, Sunday service involved not only a declaration of religious faith but an entrée into the literary life of the mother country. This is not to suggest the gentlemen were a bookish people. On the contrary, it was precisely because members of the economic elite had so little personal contact with the high culture of the mother country that they looked to the Anglican church and clergy for intellectual guidance.

An examination of the books in elite inventories illuminates the cultural life of the highest circle of white society. A few words of caution are in order. First, rather than noting the title and value of each book they found, estate appraisers usually jotted down the catchphrase "parcel of books," together with an estimate of overall value. Thus it is impossible in most cases to determine the type or number of books that individual decedents owned. Second, in the handful of cases where appraisers listed each book individually, they frequently omitted the name of the author and the full title of the work. For example, at his death in 1735 William Smith owned a book that appraisors listed as *On Christ's Incarnation.* There must have been hundreds of pamphlets, sermons, and books published in England during the seventeenth and early eighteenth centuries on this topic. In many cases we can do no more than guess from the book's abbreviated title the general category into which it fell—religion, history, law, medicine, and so on. Third, books owned were not necessarily books read, and vice versa. We should be exceedingly cautious in assuming that the reading tastes of the elite corresponded exactly to what we find on the shelves of their libraries.[20]

A case in point is that of John Moale, who died in 1740 and left behind a collection of books that appraisors carefully itemized. In his will, Moale divided his landed estate between his two sons and his

Table 13. Value of Bookholdings of Baltimore Elite:
1660-1776

Value of Books	% of Elite (N = 181)
No Books	17
1d-8s. 3d.	13
8s. 4d.-16s. 7d.	19
16s. 7d.-£1.13.3	19
£1.13.4-£4.19.11	21
£5.0.0-£20.3.2	11
TOTAL	100

SOURCES: Inventories & Accounts, Inventories; Baltimore
County Inventories, Maryland State Archives.

NOTES: The values have been adjusted with the price deflator
of St. Mary's City Historical Commission.

personal estate between his sons and two daughters, stipulating that if
the division did not provide each of the girls with at least £50 sterling,
then the sons were to make up the difference from their own inheritances. In settling the estate, the male heirs were probably forced to sell
some of their father's personal property to fulfill the conditions of the
will, for three years later, when appraisors inventoried the estate of
George Bailey, Jr., they listed the same books Moale had owned. If
Bailey purchased Moale's entire collection in 1741 or 1742—which
seems likely—he could not have read them all in the year that remained of his life. If Moale's sons insisted that the collection be sold
intact—which also seems likely—then Bailey probably never intended to read everything he bought.[21]

The elite's libraries were modest in every way. Indeed, almost a
fifth of the elite did not own a single book (see table 13). Since almost
all itemized libraries included a Bible, it is probably safe to assume
that virtually every book owner had a copy of the Scriptures on hand.
The average value of the forty-nine Bibles that appeared in elite
inventories was 9s.4d., and ranged from over a pound to under a
shilling. Thus one-third of the elite had no books or nothing more
than a family Bible. Another way of estimating the size of the elite's
libraries is by considering the number of books a person could buy
with £1.14.3, the median value of the libraries. In thirteen inventories

appraisors either gave the value of each book or listed the total number and value of the books. These inventories included 619 books worth £79.11.4, or 2s.7d. a piece. Based on these figures and assuming that everyone had a copy of the Testament, the typical elite library consisted of one Bible and ten books. It would have fit easily in a small box.

During the eighteenth century, the value of libraries increased, but the Baltimore elite remained a nonbookish people on the eve of independence. This trend should be seen as part of the overall improvement in material living conditions, and the pervasive ramifications of the consumer revolution that also brought fancy linen, silver tea sets, and mahogany furniture into elite homes. The average value of elite book holdings before 1720 fluctuated between thirteen and seventeen shillings, then rose steeply to £5.9 in the 1730s. In this decade of relative peace and tranquility, which fell between Queen Anne's War and King George's War, the elite perhaps found time to cultivate such leisure pursuits as the reading and collecting of books. The subsequent decline in the value of book holdings to £1.9 in the 1760s may have mirrored the disruptions of the French and Indian War and the ensuing imperial crisis, although one would think that the politically charged atmosphere after 1763 would generate an even greater demand for books and pamphlets. The colonial years witnessed an overall upward trend in the value of the elite's book holdings, but it would be a mistake to exaggerate the quantitative dimensions of this change. Between 1770 and 1776 the mean book holding of the elite amounted to only £2.3.5, a sum that at going rates would have bought a modest collection of one Bible and thirteen other books.

Yet a handful of men did assemble impressive book collections, at least by the standards of the county. Who were they? Among Baltimore's bibliophiles none could rival William Young, who owned the most valuable library, appraised in the 1770s at over £20. The largest collection of itemized books belonged to William Smith, who died four decades earlier with ninety-seven volumes and an unspecified "parcel of old books." In addition to their love of books, Young and Smith had something else in common—they were merchants. The thirty-three merchants who belonged to the elite had book holdings appraised at an average of £3.14.8, while the average library of the remaining 148 gentlemen was worth only £1.12.7. Additional evidence for the bookish tendencies of the merchants is the fact that they made up nine of the twenty elite decedents whose book holdings were appraised at £5 or more. Another group that invested heavily in books

Table 14. Types of Books in Libraries of Baltimore Elite: 1660-1776

Religion	37%	Technical	7
Literature	22	Travel	3
History	11	Dictionaries	3
Law	8	Other	2
Philosophy	7	TOTAL	100%

SOURCES: Baltimore County Inventories, II, 183-94; V, 149-56, 247-68; XI, 75-82; VI, 217-25; IV, 421-22, 435-46, 521-34; Inventories, XVII, 558-69; XXVIII, 422-27, Maryland State Archives.

NOTES: Based on book holdings of James Heath, John Moale, George Bailey, Jr., James Maxwell, John Crockett, John Stokes, William Smith, and Christopher Carnan. There were a total of 435 volumes in these eight collections, of which 378 could be placed in one of the above categories.

was professionals—clergymen, physicians, and lawyers—who accounted for four of the twenty leading collectors. To sum up, merchants and professionals comprised two-thirds of the largest book holders of the elite.[22]

That merchants exhibited a lively interest in books should come as no surprise, for they maintained the strongest links to the mother country and strove to keep abreast of developments on both sides of the Atlantic. Merchants had to know what was happening in London—their businesses depended on it. Yet the interest that local merchants showed in English affairs went beyond narrow matters of pounds and pence. Collecting books enabled merchants to cultivate a cosmopolitan life-style that gave special meaning to their transatlantic business connections; it enabled them to identify with the literary and business world of the mother country.

What kinds of books did the elite buy? It is possible to answer this question for eight of the elite who had major collections and whose inventories included an itemized account of all their books. Not surprisingly, religious works ranked at the top of the list (see table 14). Gentlemen carefully selected writings that carried the imprimatur of Anglican orthodoxy while avoiding anything that smacked of deism. One exception was the merchant John Crockett, something of a free thinker, who shortly before his death in 1736 purchased a copy of *Religion of Nature Delineated,* in which Anglican clergyman William Wollaston presented an argument for natural religion that stopped short of denying revelation. Crockett notwithstanding, the elite felt most comfortable with religious works that eschewed both boiling polemics and theological perplexities.[23]

To satisfy their appetite for this moderate brand of Christianity the elite turned to the great Anglican divines of the late seventeenth and early eighteenth centuries. The names that stand out were those of John Tillotson, Jeremy Taylor, Robert Sanderson, Thomas Sherlock, Henry Hammond, George Stanhope, Isaac Barrow, Edward Fowler, Edward Synge, John Scott, and John Kettlewell. The elite filled their libraries with manuals on everyday devotion and piety like Scott's *Christian Life* (1691), Taylor's *Rule and Exercises of Holy Dying* (1650), and Kettlewell's *Practical Believer* (1688). Precisely because these authors appealed to the widest possible audience and attempted to sooth the still raw religious sensibilities of the English Civil War and Restoration periods, their works became enormously popular in both England and the colonies. By 1712 *The Christian Life* was in its ninth edition, while Taylor's tracts on living and dying had reached their nineteenth printing as early as 1695.

Literature followed religion as the second most popular category (see table 14), and with respect to both genres, the tastes of the gentry can be summed up in one word: conventional. It was taken for granted that a gentleman's library should contain a classical section reserved for Seneca and Plutarch, whose diagnosis of the evils besetting the Roman Republic seemed to reinforce what Anglican divines stressed in their writings—that restraint, moderation, and temperance provided the keys to private serenity and public prosperity. Indeed, these two figures enjoyed greater popularity among the elite than any other classical or contemporary authors, including the giants Shakespeare and Milton. William Smith had the most complete classical collection with three volumes of Plutarch's *Lives,* three volumes of his *Morals,* and both the *Morals* and *Tragedies* of Seneca. Through *Spectator,* edited by Joseph Addison and Richard Steele, the elite followed contemporary literary fashions in England. Published at the start of the eighteenth century, *Spectator* provided its readers with a potpourri of literary essays, satire, and commentary on the issues of the day, written within a tradition of enlightened moderation that easily accommodated the nostalgic republicanism of Seneca and Plutarch and the latitudinarian leanings of Scott, Taylor, and Kettlewell. Taken together, Seneca, Plutarch and *Spectator* accounted for over half of the volumes in the literature catgegory.

With the exception of maverick James Heath who by his death in 1768 had brought together a sophisticated assortment of contemporary

writings, none of the elite demonstrated an interest in the literary revolution that was giving birth to the modern novel. In addition to Le
Sage's picaresque *Gil Blas,* Heath owned Tobias Smollett's *Peregrine
Pickle* and Lawrence Stern's *Tristram Shandy.* Unlike Heath, the vast
majority of the elite preferred the rock-ribbed republicanism of Seneca
and the dignified moderation of Addison to the dubious moral themes
of contemporary novelists.[24]

History and philosophy made up the third category of books (see
table 14). Elite decedents were not greatly interested in the past, and
what history they did absorb came through Plutarch, *Spectator,* and
the perennial favorite, *History of the World,* by Sir Walter Raleigh.
Philosophy did not captivate many readers. This is not surprising
given the elite's distaste for weighty argumentation. Towering above
all other philosophers was John Locke, whose *Essay on Human Understanding* appeared in three of the eight libraries. By contrast, the
political writings of this revolutionary theoretician were conspicuously absent from the elite's collections, although Crockett's three-
volume collection of Locke may have contained the *First and Second
Treatise of Government.* The fact that Crockett also owned several
volumes of Pufendorff and Shaftesbury's *Chracteristics* suggests
that he had Whiggish leanings, but not so pronounced as to exclude
from his library *The Fable of the Bees,* by the Tory skeptic Bernard
Mandeville.

Only one other member of the elite indulged an interest in history and philosophy. Alongside his collection of contemporary
novels, Heath had two volumes on Roman history, a volume on King
Charles XII of Sweden, eight volumes on English history, eight
volumes of debates of the House of Lords, and three volumes of
Voltaire's *General History of Europe.* It is likely that Heath put a
Whiggish interpretation on his historical readings, for only a man with
left-of-center politics and a skeptical view of the church would purchase Algernon Sidney's *Discourse Concerning Government* and
David Hume's philosophical essays. Yet in politics as in literature,
Heath stands out as an exception to the overwhelmingly conventional
reading tastes of the elite.[25]

Baltimore was a long way from London, and the skimpy libraries
of the county gentry showed it. But it was precisely this remoteness
from the cultural life of the metropolis that invested the local rector
with such symbolic importance. In the eyes of wealthy provincials
who realized that the highest standards of gentlemanly behavior to
which they might aspire were established across the ocean, the church

brought the larger transatlantic community of enlightened learning
and polite letters within reach.[26]

The appeal of the Anglican church was not limited to the county
gentry. Ordinary planters, who prided themselves on the economic independence that came with owning land, took their seats alongside
gentlemen at church services and listened no less attentively to the
pastor's sermons. It is does a grave injustice to these yeomen families
to suggest that they attended merely to show their respect for the local
big men or to curry favor among the powerful. The church offered
them tangible and intangible benefits.[27]

One of those benefits was a place on the vestry. By the third
quarter of the century, if not earlier, the governing board of the local
parishes had opened its doors to planters who did not necessarily come
from genteel circumstances. While it would be a mistake to call this
"democratization"—landless laborers, tenant farmers, and the poor-
est sectors of white society remained excluded from office—perhaps
in no other sphere of community life could one find a comparable
leveling of social distinctions. It has been possible to identify 167
vestrymen, wardens, clerks, and registers of colonial St. Paul's Parish, of whom sixty-two died before the Revolution and left inventories.
While 34 percent of the sixty-two vestrymen belonged to the richest
decile of probated decedents and therefore fell into the group defined
here as elite, what seems most striking about the composition of the
lay board is the prominence of those in the upper-middle range of the
wealth hierarchy: 55 percent of the officers ranked in the top 11-25
percent of decedents. All but two of the sixty-two officers belonged in
the top 50 percent.[28]

The vestrymen did not constitute a political clique that controlled
the most important positions in the community. Only 18 percent of the
141 lay officers between 1720 and 1763 sat on the county court. The
vestry drew largely on solid planters who faithfully served their church
without expectation of further political advancement. It would be a
mistake to measure the gentry's influence in church affairs solely in
terms of their numbers, for in the everyday operations of the parish
the wealthiest lay leaders may have overawed their colleagues who
came from the middling or upper-middling classes. Nonetheless, the
socioeconomic composition of the vestry at St. Paul's offers little evidence to support a picture of a rigidly hierarchical church dominated
by the local gentry.

While it is doubtful that clergymen deliberately tailored their sermons to appeal to the relatively wide social spectrum represented on

the vestry and present in the congregation, they preached a social philosophy glorifying the nongentry planters who occupied such a prominent place in the church. And this was the second benefit, no less important for being less tangible, that middling planters received from the church. It might be summarized as respect.

The social philosophy of the clergy began with the conventional proposition that in a society constructed as an organic and harmonious whole, man reached his highest development in cooperation with others. Reverend Chase agreed with the ancient philosophers who described man as "a sociable Creature, as if this did belong to the Essence & were one of the Properties of human Nature." In making the same point, Rev. John Claggett of Calvert County used the analogy of love. Without love, "the cement of Society, & the source of social Happiness," Claggett could only envision a nightmare of egoistic individuals detached from all human affections, a Hobbesian world of one against all in which "the great Community of the rational universe would dissolve, & Men and Angels would turn Savages & roam apart in barbarous solitude."[29]

The clergy also remained safely within the realm of conventional wisdom in asserting that individuals who comprised this harmonious whole were intended not to be equal in their temporal stations but to occupy well-defined ranks in the social hierarchy. Cradock conceded that this arrangement might seem unjust and oppressive, since the "Distinctions which arise from Power & Subjection, from Riches & Poverty, from Ease & Affection, appear so unequally & irregularly divided among Men & with so little Regard to Moral Reasons." But he reminded his listeners that hierarchy fit within a larger divine scheme to "unite & endear Mankind to One Another." By laboring at even the most humble station, a person not only made a unique contribution to the good of the whole but benefited from the labor of his fellow men.[30]

In this social framework the gentry had a special obligation as God's stewards to dispense their wealth in a Christ-like manner, since the earthly treasures that providence bestowed on a few individuals constituted a "publick Fund & Respository" that could not be wasted on "Splendor & Ease; or to make our Families great in Riches." Given this emphasis on stewardship, it is not surprising that the Anglican clergy poured some of their harshest criticism on gentlemen who failed to do their duty, with Rev. John Trusler going so far as to assert that the poor might rightfully demand charity as "their strict due, & just debt." Yet neither Trusler nor other Anglican divines envisioned a fundamental redistribution of wealth, and the radical implications of stewardship were blunted by the assumption that only "deserving poor" had a legitimate claim to alms. Notwithstanding his paeans to the harmonious nature of society, Cradock had little compassion for able-bodied men who became economically dependent on community charity. Their misery, he argued, usually resulted from "laziness, negligence, and intemperance," for with a reasonable amount of diligence "most" people could attain the "common accomodations of life." Thus Cradock and his peers placed strict limits on the gentry's social obligations, stressing that the just demands of "Flesh & Blood" always took precedence over those of nonkinsmen.[31]

If gentlemen had a responsibility to care for "widows and fatherless orphans," the lower classes were obliged to reciprocate by honoring their superiors. Society should be bound with the ties of deference. For Cradock, doffing the cap or bending the knee exemplified the outward aspect of deference, admittedly mechanical gestures but nonetheless "necessary, for the peace or at least convenience of Society." But real deference went much deeper. Rev. George Goundrill insisted that the lower and upper orders must be held together through "Habitual Reverence," which he defined as a "Regard, not formal or affected, not superstitious and troublesome, scrupulous and precise; but an habitual and an easy and unperceived Regard, such as Men bear towards a Governor whom they esteem and Love."[32]

Harmony, hierarchy, stewardship, deference—these shibboleths were the stock-in-trade of conservative social theory during the eighteenth century. Yet it would be a mistake to leave the impression that Anglican divines were nothing more than rock-ribbed defenders of the status quo. Below the surface of conventional generalities the clergy not only recognized the fluid nature of colonial society but also endorsed it. They understood that the values of the marketplace had seeped into every corner of eighteenth-century life and threatened to disrupt the traditional order by enticing men to reach beyond their ordained station in life. Rather than attempting to turn back the clock by condemning these new forces, the clerics gave qualified endorsement to the unprecedented social mobility they saw around them.

The dynamic dimension of Anglican thought emerges in discussions of the marketplace. Although clergymen always paid lip service to the idea of a stable social order, they understood that the spread of market relations doomed the social hierarchies of the Old World. The commercialization of society troubled many clerics, but they ultimately came to accept the forces of change as both inevitable and desirable. Cradock reached this conclusion with misgivings. In thoroughly conventional terms, he exhorted his parishoners to pursue their callings diligently but warned them against becoming slaves to ambition. Each man had a right to "desire and seek after so much as is necessary to supply all his real, not imaginary wants, in the Station which Providence has placed him." It would be improper to desire more than one's rank permitted, for "what is truly a competence for men in one station, is not so for those in another to enable them to live comfortably." Assuming that each man accepted his station and competence, the question then arose whether an individual could aspire to a higher place if, for reasons beyond human understanding, God should "open a fair way to us, to better our present station?" In this case, Cradock would allow us to unleash our ambition and "to enlarge our desires and endeavour after a Provision proportionable," thus giving his tacit sanction to a society in which each individual was permitted to scramble up the ladder as far as he could.[33]

Another example of this quandry arose over the issue of prices. The medieval notion of a just price was very much alive in the eighteenth century, presenting clergymen with a difficult dilemma as they tried to steer a safe path between wholesale rejection of the profit motive and complete acceptance of the marketplace. Cradock saw nothing inherently wrong in a simple market transaction where buyer and seller "are well employed, each of them proposing a reasonable gain and advantage to himself." Since such activities benefited the "whole Society," Cradock acknowledged the need to charge high prices "as a due recompense for extraordinary diligence or uncommon skill in some art, profession, or employment." But at all times men must consider "the publick Good," for when they charged extortionate prices, magistrates had the duty to intervene and regulate their "inordinate desire" for gain. Yet Cradock could propose only the most elusive yardstick for determining what consituted a legitimate return—"plain Reason grounded upon Self-Interest." By making individual self-interest the arbiter of the public good, this Anglican pastor once again found himself on the side of the market economy.[34]

In an effort to resolve this dilemma, Cradock put his faith in the redemptive qualities of middling planters. Men of this class aspired to better themselves through hard work and shrewd management of their resources, but they kept their ambition within the bounds of moderation, seeking "neither riches nor poverty." For Cradock "the middle State . . . is the mark at which we ought to aim in our pursuits in this life." The rector of St. Thomas's Parish always considered himself a loyal son of the mother country, but in extolling the virtues of the "middle State," he came close to suggesting that the New World was capable of producing a morally regenerate society of the middling classes. "You then enjoy yourselves in the bosom of your Farms & plantations, clear from the noise & bustle of a vain & ambitious world, free from the fears & apprehensions of poverty & distress, happy if you choose to be so, in your families, in your children, in yourselves." These were words to please the middling planters of St. Thomas's Parish.[35]

The established church reflected the structure of Baltimore society. At the top of that society was a county gentry that, by comparison with the provincial gentry of tidewater Virginia and lower Maryland, lacked the economic, political, and cultural resources to become a cohesive and confident ruling class. In contrast with tidewater counties where Anglican parishes buttressed the cultural hegemony of the foremost local families, Baltimore developed a more open church in which the county gentry shared the stage with enlightened clergymen and middling planters.

7

Baltimore Town

In the two decades before the Revolution, Baltimore County embarked on a radically new course of social and economic development. Since the establishment of Virginia and Maryland, both provincial and imperial authorities had agonized over the long train of deleterious consequences that, they assumed, would inevitably follow from the absence of towns. For men steeped in a classical tradition according to which commerce and culture could flourish only in an urban setting, it was difficult to envision civilization without cities. Over the years numerous schemes were proposed to remedy this perceived defect in the Chesapeake social order, but none of them were successful. Even if the king had not consistently opposed every initiative that threatened to reduce his lucrative tobacco revenues, the natural transportation network of the Chesapeake Bay would have imposed severe limits on urban development. So the society that eventually took shape in the region was marked, when compared to the Middle Atlantic and New England colonies, by the absence of towns.

With the spectacular rise of Baltimore Town during the third quarter of the eighteenth century, the dream of urban development in the Chesapeake finally became a reality, but at a high cost—the fragmentation of regional unity. The increase in wheat production, the decline of plantation slavery, and the acceleration of urban development propelled northern Maryland along the same economic and social trajectory as neighboring Pennsylvania. At the same time the deepening crisis in imperial affairs after 1763 opened the way for a coterie of Scotch-Irish merchants, most with Pennsylvania connections, to emerge as leading political figures in booming Baltimore Town. One might have expected an old guard of established gentry families to mobilize against the newcomers, who swiftly consolidated their urban base of power. But nothing of the sort happened. While the sudden eclipse of prominent local families elicited protest among a few traditionalists, the new merchants flooding into Baltimore Town were assimilated rapidly and with remarkably little discord. Indeed, the

Baltimore Town, an engraving printed in 1817, based on a sketch done by John Moale in 1752. The two ships in the harbor portend a dynamic future for the young settlement. Courtesy of the Maryland Historical Society, Baltimore.

striking feature of Baltimore politics between 1763 and 1776 was the general willingness of gentlemen to accommodate themselves to the new economic and political order. Hence the tumultuous closing years of the colonial era are best seen not as an abrupt break in the mainlines of Baltimore's historical development but as the logical outcome of the openness, fluidity, and impermanence that had characterized the county elite throughout the eighteenth century.

Not even the most sanguine booster could have forseen before 1750 that Baltimore Town would rise to become one of the most dramatic examples of colonial urban development during the third quarter of the eighteenth century. Created by an act of the assembly in 1729, the small settlement on the northwest branch of the Patapsco River seemed destined for no greater future than that of an ordinary hamlet whose quiet streets and empty taverns stirred briefly to life during the trading season, then slipped back into sleepy normalcy. In 1750, a full generation after its founding, Baltimore Town could boast of a population of no more than a few hundred.[1]

During those early years even the commissioners who had been appointed to oversee the sale of town lots must have wondered whether they were wasting their time pursuing the chimera of urban development. They divided the site into sixty lots of roughly one acre each (see map 3). Buyers were required on pain of forfeiture to build a house on each of their lots within eighteen months of taking possession. The anemic market for land and the frequent incidence of forfeiture suggest that few people were foolhardy enough to sink a substantial sum of money in a town whose future seemed doubtful at best (see figure 3). A year after opening their books, the commissioners could congratulate themselves on finding twelve buyers for fourteen lots. But the burst of excitement that greeted the opening round of auctions could not be sustained. The commissioners had little business to do until 1736, when Charles Carroll of Annapolis, a lawyer from one of Maryland's richest families, purchased twenty-six lots to add to the one he had acquired earlier. This deal made Carroll the largest single landowner in Baltimore Town (he held 44 percent of the square footage on the town plat), but it did not make him a quick profit. Eight years passed before he sold a single lot or earned the first penny on his investment.[2]

Whether Carroll knew it or not, dramatic developments unfolding thousands of miles away were protecting his investment. After 1750 the relentless Anglo-French struggle for global supremacy, a disastrous

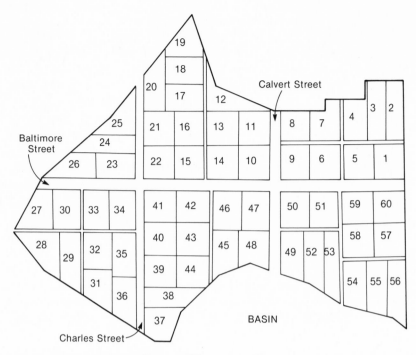

Map 3. Plat of Baltimore Town: 1729

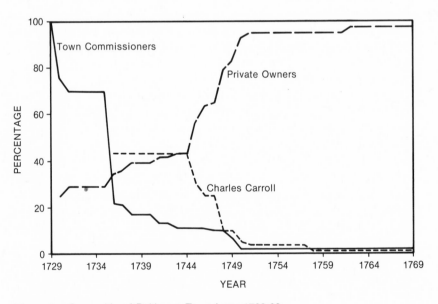

Figure 3: Ownership of Baltimore Town Lots: 1729-69

SOURCES: Baltimore County Land Records, Maryland State Archives; First Records of Baltimore Town and Jones' Town, 1729-1797 (Baltimore, 1905)

run of harvest failures in Europe, the development of improved methods for marketing and financing colonial exports, and the expansion of sugar production in the West Indies combined to transform the Atlantic trading basin. The cumulative impact of these economic and political forces echoed in places as far away as Baltimore Town. The stepped-up demand for foodstuffs in the West Indies and southern Europe fueled the expansion of grain production throughout southeastern Pennsylvania, the Delmarva Peninsula, and newly opened regions of western Maryland, where the growing population of German immigrants continued to cultivate wheat as they had for generations. The result was that the Middle Atlantic region of British North America, the sugar-producing islands of the Caribbean, and large zones of Mediterranean Europe became interlocking parts of a sprawling commercial network.[3]

This shift from tobacco to grain production redefined the regional identity of the upper Chesapeake. One by one, the ties that fastened Baltimore County to the Greater Tidewater stretched and then snapped as northern Maryland was pulled into the economic orbit of the Middle Atlantic region. Urbanization brought this underlying transformation into full view, because the backcountry wheat trade generated an unprecedented demand for mills, roads, bridges, ferries, and—above all—towns. By the eve of the Revolution, Baltimore Town, a bustling port of some seven thousand inhabitants, had emerged as the principal depot for the backcountry wheat trade and the outstanding symbol for the new course of diversified economic development in northern Maryland.

So the faith in urban growth that had moved Carroll to purchase nearly half of Baltimore Town was eventually borne out. In 1744 he began marketing his lots at so brisk a pace that seven years later only three of the original twenty-seven remained in his possession (see figure 3). Meanwhile, the commissioners succeeded in locating buyers for the handful of lots they continued to hold. The twelve parties who in 1730 had secured legal title to town property mushroomed to thirty in 1749, forty in 1759, and sixty-three in 1769. As an economic interest group of growing cohesiveness and confidence, these propertied townspeople were firmly committed to the prosperity of the community they were literally building from the ground up.[4]

The price of land provides a useful barometer of urban expansion. The data are far from perfect, partly because it is impossible to know whether the parties to the transaction reported the full selling price in the deed. Further, average prices tended to swing wildly from year to

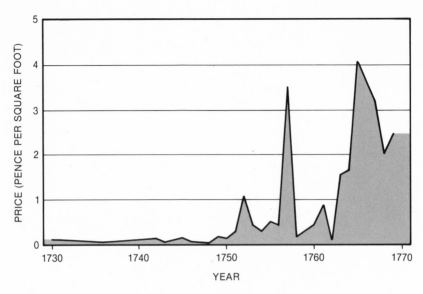

Figure 4.   Price of Baltimore Town Lots: 1729-69
SOURCES: Baltimore Land Records, Maryland State Archives

year, since land value hinged on a multitude of variables that cannot be
unraveled at this distance. Even so, the overall price trend clearly
shows that by 1750, after twenty years of bare survival, Baltimore
Town had finally crossed the threshold to self-sustained growth (see
figure 4). From 1730 to 1750 the average selling price of town land
remained stable at less than .2d per square foot. During the next decade, as the Anglo-French conflict buffeted old trading patterns and
created new ones, the burgeoning port of Baltimore Town confronted
a dizzying mix of opportunities and risks. It is no surprise that against
this backdrop of commerical uncertainity prices underwent dramatic
fluctuations, with the average reaching all-time highs of 1.1d in 1752
and 3.5d in 1757, before plunging back down to .2d a year later. The
official end of the Seven Years' War coincided with another steep
climb in prices to a peak of 4.1d in 1765.

One of the reasons why land prices increased was that townspeople steadily added value to their property by constructing homes,
stores, wells, warehouses, wharves, fences, and stables. Although
deeds rarely mention specific improvements, occasional references
hint at a small-time construction boom in the generation prior to the
Revolution. For townspeople accustomed to ordinary clapboard construction, the brick structures that began to appear on Baltimore Street
(originally Long Street), where many of the principal merchants kept
their homes, stores, and counting houses, signaled prosperity and per-

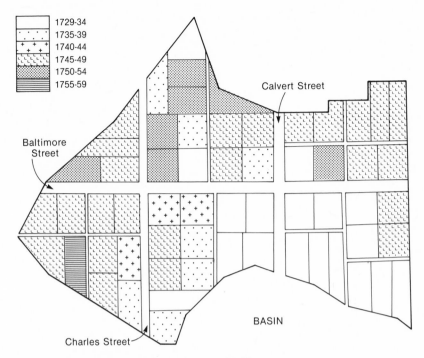

Map 4.   Sale of Baltimore Town Lots: 1729-59

SOURCES: Baltimore County Land Records, Maryland State Archives: <u>First Records of Baltimore Town and Jones' Town, 1729-1797</u> (Baltimore, 1905)

manence. As early as 1751 merchant William Hammond lived in a brick house at the east end of Baltimore Street. Within a decade other brick dwellings were strung along the main residential avenue as far west as Charles Street and beyond. When merchant Richard Croxall built brick stables for his horses at the northwest corner of Baltimore and Charles Streets, he gave concrete expression to the spirit of bouyant confidence pervading the town.[5]

Location was another factor that determined the value of urban real estate. Everyone wanted to own land as close as possible to the water's edge. Of the nine lots that had footage on the basin, seven were snapped up in the first year of sales and the remaining two soon after (see map 4). From the outset townspeople clearly expected the area between Baltimore Street and the basin to fill up most rapidly, and Calvert Street to emerge as the commercial hub of the town. Most of the lots in the section bordered by Baltimore Street, Charles Street (originally Forest Street), and the eastern perimeter of the town plat were already in private hands by 1739. As one crossed over Baltimore Street and moved away from the waterfront, the demand for town lots flagged noticeably. The majority of lots north of Baltimore Street did not find buyers until after 1745.

As prices shot upward with the growing demand for land, a few property holders could not resist the temptation of a safe and steady income offered by long-term leases. The first recorded lease involved Lot No. 49, one of the choicest pieces of real estate bordered on two sides by Calvert Street and the basin. In 1752 Charles Carroll leased 3,267 of the lot's 34,850 square feet to merchant Charles Croxall, at ninety-nine years, for 15 shillings sterling per year. While the leased property did not front the basin, it did include ninety-nine feet on Calvert Street. But the conditions were not yet ripe for the emergence of a class of urban rentiers, and for almost a decade few other townsmen followed Carroll's lead. The turning point came in 1763, when Baltimore Town witnessed a steep increase in both the price of land and the number of leases. Between 1760 and 1769, as Baltimore Town converted to a peacetime economy, the total square footage under lease and assignment skyrocketed from 6,534 to 87,855, the equivalent of nearly three town lots.[6]

Virtually all of the leased land was located in the commercial center of town. In 1769 all or parts of six lots were under lease, four of which were on the basin (Nos. 48, 49, 54, 55) and two on Baltimore Street (Nos. 6, 47). While leased land accounted for only 4 percent of the town as a whole, it constituted 13 percent of the square footage of the nine waterfront lots. The history of Lot No. 47 on the southwest corner of Calvert and Baltimore Streets furnishes a clear, if extreme, illustration of the leasing arrangements devised by the pioneering generation of the landlords. In 1730 town commissioners sold the lot to blacksmith David Robinson, who promptly resold it to merchant Richard Gist for 510 pounds of tobacco. The lot remained in the Gist family for nearly three decades until 1759, when John Mercer "Gent." bought Lots Nos. 47 and 48, together with additional rural lands, for £25 current from Ziporah Gist, who had come into possession of the property at her husband's death. Four years later Mercer divided the lot into ten parts, kept the largest for himself and put out the other nine at ninety-nine-year leases. The leaseholds averaged a mere 2,730 square feet, but all had precious frontage on either Baltimore or Calvert streets. While merchant Jonathan Plowman leased a veritable microlot, thirty feet by twenty feet—barely enough to hold a house or shop—he lost no time in acquiring additional adjoining land through assignments from his neighbors. A bolder investor might have developed the property himself, but Mercer preferred to play it safe with an annual rental income of £31.17.6 sterling.[7]

The growing demand for urban land reflected in rising prices not only spurred a trend toward long-term leases but contributed to growing disparities in the concentration of landed wealth. The top 10 percent of landowners (excluding Charles Carroll) accounted for 22 percent of the total number of square feet under deed or lease in 1739, 23 percent in 1749, 25 percent in 1759, and 32 percent in 1769. The growth of inequality can also be measured with the Gini coefficient, which ranges from 0 (perfect equality) to 1 (perfect inequality). In every decade the coefficient moved in the direction of inequality: .128 in 1730, .197 in 1739, .319 in 1749, .377 in 1759, and .493 in 1769. While these figures fail to take into account the large numbers of townspeople who did not own or lease land, they leave little doubt that youthful Baltimore Town was already exhibiting the same process of economic stratification to be found in the mature cities of Boston, New York, and Philadelphia.[8]

Those squeezed to the margins of the real estate market by rapidly escalating prices were not the only casualties of urbanization. As Baltimore Town steadily tightened its grip on the backcountry wheat trade in western Maryland and made substantial inroads into the Eastern Shore and south-central Pennsylvania, the traditional marketing arrangement of independent merchants operating stores on the principal rivers of the county entered an irreversible process of decline. Planters and farmers who had once sought out the neighborhood trader for imported goods or a line of credit now looked increasingly to the merchants of Baltimore Town. The spreading commercial hegemony of Baltimore Town over the entire county can be seen in the quiet strangulation of Joppa Town on the Gunpowder River, the county seat since 1712. For a time Joppa Town managed to hold its own in competition with its Patapsco rival. But when the wheat trade bypassed the Gunpowder River, it left behind a half-abandoned, crossroads village that awoke only during sessions of the court. According to county debt books, this decline was well under way by 1754, when officials reported that twenty-eight men were paying quitrents on fifty-two lots in Baltimore Town, compared to only eight men and eighteen lots in Joppa Town. Seventeen years later the robust expansion of Baltimore Town (fifty owners, eighty-nine lots) stood in sharp contrast with Joppa Town's downward spiral (four owners, twelve lots). When in 1768 the assembly declared Baltimore Town the new county

seat, it simultaneously acknowledged the economic might of the
Patapsco merchants and stripped Joppa Town of its last remaining
hope for survival.[9]

The expansion of wheat production and the rise of Baltimore
Town also coincided with a major shift in labor arrangements, as slavery entered a slow but steady process of decline. The period framed by
local tax lists of 1737 and 1773 witnessed a drop in the proportion of
working-age slaves from 36 percent to 32 percent of the total population, in striking contrast with the regional trend toward higher black
ratios. By 1782 blacks made up only 20-29 percent of the populations
of the northern Maryland counties of Baltimore, Harford, and Cecil,
while the figure reached 40-49 percent for the southern counties of St.
Mary's, Charles, Calvert, Prince George's, and Anne Arundel. Further, Baltimore County diverged from the regional pattern in that the
relative number of households with slaves did not continue to increase
during the final decades of the colonial period, but instead dropped
sharply from 32 percent to 23 percent. By contrast, most counties in
the Chesapeake colonies resembled Prince George's, where slaveholding households rose from 39 percent to 52 percent in the forty-three
years before independence. Finally, a new pattern of racial segregation
emerged in the county during the third quarter of the eighteenth century (see map 5). As yeomen planters and small farmers moved into
the interior, the slave population became increasingly concentrated
at the mouths of the Patapsco, Back, Middle, and Gunpowder rivers.
Although separated by only twenty or thirty miles, this coastal black
belt was a world apart from inland hundreds like Pipe Creek along the
Pennsylvania frontier, where taxable slaves constituted only 8 percent
of the population.[10]

What distinguished Baltimore Town from first-rank urban centers
such as Boston, Philadelphia, New York, and Charleston or second-
tier towns such as Newport, Providence, Norfolk, and Savannah was
the sheer rapidity of its growth. Within a single generation a thriving
port had replaced the tiny hamlet. Rapid growth placed strains on the
existing social order as newcomers poured into Baltimore Town. And
no group of newcomers was more important in both quantitative and
qualitative terms than the merchants.

The growth of the Patapsco port and the expansion of the merchant
community were integral parts of the same process. After 1760 new
traders swarmed into Baltimore Town and nearly overwhelmed the established merchants who for decades had not only dominated commercial life but supplied indispensable links to the social and cultural

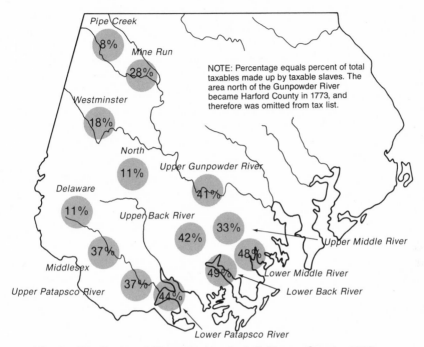

Map 5. Distribution of Slaves by Hundred, Baltimore County: 1773

SOURCES: Wilkins, comp., "Baltimore County Tax List, 1773," Maryland State Archives

world of the metropolis. From the 1750s to the 1770s the average number of merchants per decade shot up almost 150 percent, which represented the largest jump for any twenty-year period in the eighteenth-century. On the eve of the Revolution about one hundred men were trading in the county, the vast majority of whom had settled in Baltimore Town and arrived after 1760 (see appendix 2, figure 5). From 1777 to 1783 another hundred merchants who had never before appeared in the local records registered deeds at the county court, testifying to the commercial prosperity Baltimore Town enjoyed during the war years.[11]

Merchants took the lead in the physical development of Baltimore Town. One way of measuring their contribution is to examine the distinctive investment strategies of the thirty-three merchants and 148 planters and professionals who together made up the economic elite. Representing 18 percent of the elite but 46 percent of the total transactions recorded in the deeds, merchants were clearly enmeshed in the

Table 15. Land Transactions of Elite Merchants and Elite Non-Merchants in Baltimore County: 1660-1776

	A Elite Merchants (N = 406)	B Elite Planters (N = 463)	C Total Elite (N = 869)
Rural Transactions			
Conveyances	66%	85%	76%
Leases	1	4	3
Assignments	1	3	2
Mortgages	7	4	5
Urban Transactions			
Conveyances	15	3	8
Leases	7	-	3
Assignments	1	-	1
Mortgages	2	1	2
TOTAL	100%	100%	100%

SOURCES: Baltimore County Land Records.

NOTES: Column A refers to the 33 members of the elite who identified themselves as merchants in the land records, Column B to the remaining 148 who did not appear as merchants, and Column C to the two groups combined.

land market to a far greater degree than planters were. Put differently, elite merchants registered an average of 10.7 transactions, compared to only 3.2 for elite planters. Seven of the eleven members of the elite who had twenty or more transactions were merchants. In contrast to elite planters, who dealt almost exclusively in rural land close to their dwelling plantations, elite merchants diversified their investments after 1730 by plowing considerable capital into Joppa Town and, increasingly, into Baltimore Town. Urban transactions in these two locations accounted for 27 percent of the elite merchants' transactions, compared to only 8 percent for elite planters (see table 15, columns A and B).

Expanding the analysis beyond the economic giants to include the entire merchant community reveals two quite distinct approaches to the land market. It has been possible to identify 167 county residents who between 1720 and 1776 identified themselves as merchants in the land deeds. For the purposes of this discussion, the sixty-six merchants who launched their careers between 1720 and 1759 have been labeled *traditionalists,* and the larger group of 101 who began theirs between 1760 and 1776 have been called *urbanites.*

The two groups adopted strikingly different investment patterns in Baltimore Town. Traditionalists included a disproportionately high number of speculators in urban land. That they sold urban land 177 times but bought it 102 times provides indirect evidence of speculative activity, since the typical speculator would be expected to buy a town lot or tract of suburban land, subdivide it into smaller pieces, and then resell them (see table 16, column A). Yet traditionalists behaved quite differently with respect to property they owned in the countryside: purchases of rural land greatly outnumbered sales, 374 to 282. Although the relative frequency of sales and purchases cannot by itself unveil the cultural values underlying business behavior, the data suggest that traditionalists had a stronger personal attachment to rural land than to urban land, and thus a greater reluctance to part with it. If from traditionalists' perspective the town was a place to make a living, the countryside was a place to make a life.

Thomas Sligh exemplifies the traditionalist who engaged in speculation. In 1749 and 1750 he and fellow merchant Thomas Sheredine pooled their capital in order to purchase over four hundred acres on the northeast edge of the original sixty-lot plat of Baltimore Town. This area was not laid out in regular lots until after independence, but under the direction of Sligh and Sheredine it quickly developed into an eighteenth-century suburb, only a fifteen- or twenty-minute walk from the center of town. Sheredine died soon after completing the transaction and left his interest in the enterprise to his son. Calculating that new people crowding into town would spill over onto the tract and drive up land prices, Sligh bought out his new partner and began dividing up the property for sale. Before his death in 1770, he had sold over three hundred acres in fifty-three separate parcels, ranging in size from one acre to thirty-five acres. The buyers whose occupations appeared in the deeds seem a fair cross section of a suburban community: four merchants, three gentlemen, three bricklayers, two saddlers, a physician, and a collier.[12]

Traditionalists also included a relatively large number of rentiers. They appeared as leasors of town lots 127 times but as leasees only fifteen times (see table 16, column A). Thomas Harrison provides a good example of the traditionalist rentier. Soon after emigrating from England to Maryland in 1742, he began buying land between Jones' Falls and the eastern limits of Baltimore Town—less than a mile from Sligh's tract. Within a decade his property had been surveyed into lots

Table 16. Land Transactions of Baltimore County Merchants:
1720-76

	A Traditionalists 1720-76	B Traditionalists 1760-76	C Urbanites 1760-76
Rural Transaction			
Seller	282	82	38
Buyer	374	81	83
Leasor	9	3	3
Leasee	4	2	6
Assignor	4	3	2
Assignee	6	5	10
Mortgagor	3	0	2
Mortgagee	39	10	13
SUB-TOTAL	(721)	(186)	(157)
Urban Transaction			
Seller	177	87	45
Buyer	102	39	120
Leasor	127	122	32
Leasee	15	11	73
Assignor	4	4	35
Assignee	5	5	66
Mortgagor	3	1	3
Mortgagee	3	0	12
SUB-TOTAL	(436)	(269)	(386)
TOTAL	1,157	455	543

SOURCES: Baltimore County Land Records.

NOTES: The 66 merchants who first appeared in the land records between 1720 and 1759 are defined as traditionalists; the 101 who first appeared between 1760 and 1776 are defined as urbanites. Column A includes all of the traditionalists' land transactions between 1720 and 1776. Column B refers to only the traditionalists' transactions that were registered between 1760 and 1776. Column C includes all of the urbanites' transactions between 1760 and 1776.

bordering Gay and Frederick streets and absorbed into the town. This area, together with an additional half-dozen lots acquired along the choicest stretch of waterfront, may have made Harrison the greatest single landowner in the expanded Baltimore Town. Like Sligh, Harrison initially conveyed his property outright, but the increased demand for lots in the late 1750s and early 1760s prompted him to shift to leases. The standard lease ran ninety-nine years, called for one annual payment, and required the construction of a two-story brick house within three years. Deliberately or not, Harrison helped to fashion a respectable community of middling-class tenants, for small traders and craftsmen accounted for thirty-seven of the forty-six leases and conveyances. It was a profitable venture that in 1776 yielded Harrison an annual rental income of £306 sterling.[13]

Compared to traditionalists, urbanites channeled a greater portion of their capital into town land and demonstrated a greater involvement in the physical construction of the port. From 1760 to 1776 urban property was involved in 71 percent of their transactions, compared to only 59 percent for traditionalists (computed from table 16, columns B and C). As an analysis of lease assignments reveals, urbanites dealt more extensively in improved lots. Since the best lots in Baltimore Town were taken up relatively early, newcomers wanting to locate on the waterfront or along the busiest streets had no alternative but to lease land for the standard term of ninety-nine years. Within a decade these tenants had increased the value of their leaseholds by constructing houses, stores, warehouses, alleys, gardens, wells, stables, fences, wharves, and mills. The spiraling demand for property led many of the original tenants to assign what remained of their leases (rarely less than ninety years), together with improvements on the leasehold, to a second generation of tenants who continued the process of improvement. Between 1760 and 1776 assignments comprised 26 percent of urbanites' transactions in Baltimore Town, but only 3 percent of traditionalists' (computed from table 16, columns B and C).

Assigned leaseholds contained everything from large manufacturing structures to ordinary frame houses. One of the most impressive assignments involved urbanite William Moore, Jr., who in 1772 paid £965 for a lot on the outskirts of town that included a water mill, stables, roads, and mill houses. Another big investor was urbanite Alexander McMechen, who in the same year gave £514 for a waterfront lot containing a two-story brick house, kitchen, warehouse, and stables. A more typical assignment involved Webert Judy, a German butcher, who in 1761 leased a waterfront lot for ninety-nine years, where he built two "small" frame houses and the foundations of a wharf. Ten years later he assigned what remained of the lease to urbanite William Neill for £161. Although only a handful of assignments specified improvements to the property, the average price of £117 suggests that tenants did not go much beyond the requirement that they construct a two-story house with a bottom floor of 400 square feet.[14]

The sharp contrast between the investment strategies of tradition-alists and urbanites suggests that older merchants who had established their operations and learned their trade before the meteoric rise of Bal-timore Town maintained a strong attachment to the countryside. Their contribution to Baltimore Town was, to some degree, passive and par-asitic. Traditionalists were certainly prepared to turn a profit as rentiers and speculators, but relatively few of them tied up large sums of capital improving the urban property they owned. Unlike many tra-ditionalists who watched the development of Baltimore Town from their rural estates and were satisfied to play the part of speculators and rentiers, urbanites actively fueled the construction boom by expanding the market for improved property. Hence the task of constructing homes, counting houses, wharves, and warehouses fell largely to mer-chants who swarmed into Baltimore Town after 1760.

The prosperity of Baltimore Town and its merchant community must be understood within the larger context of a major restructuring of traditional commercial patterns and marketing arrangements that occurred throughout Virginia and Maryland, but with special force in the upper Chesapeake. For generations large planters had operated through the *consignment system,* employing British merchants to sell their tobacco in exchange for a commission fee, and then charging their yearly order of goods against the proceeds of the sale that had been credited to their accounts. After the 1740s another arrangement, the *store system,* spread across large parts of the tobacco colonies and enabled small planters to sell directly to local agents of British com-merical houses. Through their chains of stores, resident factors em-ployed by Scottish merchant houses made substantial inroads into the tobacco trade by offering liberal credit and high prices to ordinary planters who did not maintain permanent accounts overseas and who frequently found themselves at the mercy of large planter-merchants in the neighborhood.

During the third quarter of the eighteenth century a new market-ing arrangement, the *cargo system,* developed alongside the older ways of doing business. Its central figure was the economically inde-pendent merchant, based in the colonies, who ordered cargoes of goods from British firms, usually on condition that he make remit-tance within a year. By selling wheat and provisions to the West Indies and southern Europe, these native merchants were able to balance their overseas accounts and to continue importing manufactures from Britain. Baltimore County encompassed a large part of the northern Chesapeake that was accessible to the cargo system, since the two

Charles Ridgely, Jr., was a
thirty-year-old ship's captain
when this portrait was
painted, about 1760. Soon
after, he opened a store in
Baltimore Town. Courtesy
of the Hampton National
Historic Site.

older trades were never as deeply rooted there as they were in southern
Maryland and Virginia. Baltimore Town, whose economic lifeblood
was the wheat trade and whose harbor teemed with ships bound for the
West Indies, soon became the regional focal point for native merchants operating through the cargo system.[15]

Charles Ridgely, Jr. (usually called "the Captain" to distinguish
him from his father, Col. Charles Ridgely, Sr.) casts light on the
changing commercial environment of the upper Chesapeake, because
his business dealings embodied elements of both the old and new. On
the one hand, as scion of one the county's preeminent gentry families,
Captain Ridgely inherited strong allegiances to the older consignment
system, established close commercial ties with London tobacco merchants, and remained generally uninterested in the burgeoning West
Indian trade whose profits fueled the cargo system. On the other hand,
as a native merchant whose operations were largely self-financed,
Captain Ridgely enjoyed the commercial independence that was the
hallmark of the cargo system.

Born in 1730, the captain was the second son of Col. Charles
Ridgely, Sr., and his wife Rachel. He grew up on the family estate at
Ridgely's Delight on the Patapsco River, where he watched his father

make a fortune in the tobacco trade before moving north to Northampton. Not surprisingly, when the captain reached his late twenties, he set out to make his own fortune along the same lines, embarking on a commercial career as a ship master in the service of James Russell, the foremost tobacco consignment merchant trading in the Baltimore vicinity. According to one report, Russell's ships carried 1,800 hogsheads of Maryland tobacco each year. Since for his Baltimore correspondents Russell usually chartered a vessel that could carry 300-650 hogsheads of tobacco, it seems that the county accounted for a substantial part of his provincial consignments, between one-sixth and one-third. The tobacco consignment trade centered on James Russell was built upon an extensive kinship network that included some of the county's leading men and oldest families. In addition to placing the captain in command of his ships, Russell enlisted the services of his brother John Ridgely, William Lux, and John Dorsey, who represented three of the most powerful gentry families in the Patapsco area. The Ridgelys, Luxes, and Dorseys had been intermarried for years.[16]

In 1762 Captain Ridgely left the ship deck and opened a store in Baltimore Town, where for the next five years he continued to act as Russell's local agent. The most important of his responsibilities, requiring both care and speed, came each spring when he supervised the loading and unloading of Russell's chartered vessels. The first ships back from the Chesapeake fetched the highest prices in the European tobacco markets, and the captain received frequent and anxious reminders from his London principal to prod the notoriously slow-placed planters. Keeping the planters in good spirits sometimes proved costly, as Captain Ridgely once complained to Russell: "I am 70 or 80 Gallons out of Pocket having so Large a Ship and The Planters always on Board and collecting her Load in Three Flats They having a Bottle every Trip." In addition to taking charge of the ships when they were in port, Captain Ridgely attempted to collect debts that local planters owed Russell, although he often had to settle for personal bonds in lieu of the hard cash. As a merchant whose family had been trading along the Patapsco for two generations, Captain Ridgely was also in a good position to supply credit ratings on local planters and to identify "safe men" whom Russell was willing to carry on his books. Further, Russell depended on his Baltimore agent to estimate the size of the local tobacco crop, so that he could charter an appropriate-sized vessel.

For these and other valuable services, Russell reciprocated by filling expeditiously the captain's orders for store goods and keeping a close eye on the quality of the merchandise consigned to him. For sev-

eral years during the 1760s Captain Ridgely conducted a difficult ne-
gotiation with a prominent London merchant over the purchase of a
large tract of land in Baltimore County, and Russell spent many thank-
less hours acting as go-between for the two men. That the captain
could always count on a comfortable bed in Russell's home when he
visited the metropolis was no small fringe benefit. But without doubt,
the most valuable service Russell performed for his Baltimore agent
was waiving the standard commission fee that he charged on store
goods sent to his colonial correspondents.[17]

The War for Independence shattered this mutually agreeable relationship. In 1786, in an effort to recover £312 sterling he claimed Captain Ridgely still owed him, Russell drew up a comprehensive account
of their transactions covering the decade after 1763. This document illuminates the commercial operations of one independent merchant in
Baltimore Town. During that decade Captain Ridgely was constantly
in debt. In May 1763, only a year after opening his shop, he had already fallen £1,857 sterling behind. Although Ridgely reduced the
debt to £797 in 1764, a year later the figure had almost doubled again.
Store goods accounted for three-fourths of the total debts that Captain
Ridgely accumulated. He apparently kept enough stock on the shelves
to last two years, for the vast majority of his purchases came in the
springs of 1763 and 1765.[18]

Captain Ridgely made four types of remittances: bills of exchange,
iron and lumber, personal services, and tobacco. The largest in value
were bills of exchange drawn on London merchants, which constituted
53 percent of his total remittances and which were probably obtained
in the retail trade at his store. The second type of credit, amounting to
39 percent of remittances, Captain Ridgely earned by consigning iron
and lumber to Russell for sale in London. In 1762 Colonel Ridgely set
aside 2,500 acres in northern Baltimore for the construction of
Northampton Iron Works, stipulating that he and his two sons, the
captain and John, would operate the business as tenants in common,
with each possessing an undivided third share of the company. Russell
marketed the company's pig and bar iron in London and then credited
one-third of the profits to the captain's account. In the process of
building the furnace and clearing nearby timber lands, Captain
Ridgely came into possession of large quantities of lumber, which his
slaves and servants cut down into staves for export abroad.

While bills of exchange, iron, and lumber comprised the overwhelming majority of the Captain's remittances, a third source of
earnings, making up 6 percent of the total, came from various services

that Ridgely performed while in Russell's employ. The final category consisted of tobacco shipped to Russell, but it represented a mere 2 percent of remittances. Rather than risk competing directly with Russell, Captain Ridgely left the tobacco trade to London consignment merchants who possessed the large-scale capital and connections to finance and market the crop. Only once was he tempted to enter the market, but the circumstances were special. In 1764, when a frost destroyed two-thirds of the local tobacco harvest, Captain Ridgely snapped up twelve hogsheads of the scarce commodity and eventually sold them in London for a £76 profit.[19]

Captain Ridgely was a man in the middle. He belonged to the traditional world of tobacco traders and consignment merchants, a world whose two poles were London and Baltimore. While the relative importance of tobacco in the larger economy of northern Maryland was clearly diminishing, enough of the broad leaf was being produced in the Patapsco area to sustain a commercial network of old gentry families like the Ridgelys, Luxes, and Dorseys. Yet Captain Ridgely also exemplified the maturation of commercial enterprise in the upper Chesapeake, for ultimately it was the profits earned through the sale of iron and lumber produced on his family's property that enabled him to establish a store in Baltimore Town.[20]

The rise of Baltimore Town, the growth of the merchant community, and the development of the cargo system combined to present a formidable challenge to the customary ways of conducting politics. During the second third of the eighteenth century Baltimore County had developed an *open plutocracy,* a method of allocating scarce political resources that proved remarkably successful at accomodating ambitious newcomers. Having a family pedigree certainly did not hurt one's chances of political advancement, but the only essential prerequisite for office was wealth. The continual stream of new arrivals circulating into and out of office prevented a handful of families from entrenching themselves in power and establishing a rigid pattern of oligarchic rule as did the provincial gentry elsewhere in the Chesapeake colonies. For two generations this open plutocracy functioned smoothly and efficiently, helping to prevent the kind of controversy that rocked the county in the late seventeenth and early eighteenth centuries.

By the 1760s, as the protest movement against imperial policy deepened and disrupted local political alignments, this flexible arrangment faced a severe test. The explosive growth of Baltimore Town threatened to unleash a struggle between established gentry families with strong ties to the countryside and newly arrived traders whose political ambitions matched, if they did not exceed, their business drive. In the end, no such confrontation occurred. The relatively smooth incorporation of new merchants into the political order testified to the resilience of the open plutocracy.

The protest against imperial policy began on an auspicious note, with both Baltimore and Annapolis joining forces to orchestrate the colonywide resistance movement against the Stamp Act in late 1765 and early 1766. Whatever tension existed in the coalition remained well out of sight, lost in the euphoria of a relatively quick victory and in the public celebrations occasioned by news that the act had been repealed. While the crisis had called into existence a new organization in Baltimore, the Sons of Liberty, it remained firmly in the hands of gentlemen accustomed to exercising power. Merchant William Lux, the driving force behind the resistance movement in Baltimore and the key figure in the Sons, belonged to that privileged group of second-generation gentlemen who built their fortunes on what their fathers had left behind. His father, Darby Lux, a British ship captain and merchant who took up residence in Baltimore Town around 1743 and died seven years later, left one of the greatest estates in the county. William parlayed his inheritance into a sprawling estate that at his death in 1778 included 2,500 acres scattered across Baltimore, Anne Arundel, and Frederick counties, one Baltimore Town lot, part-ownership in a ropewalk, forty-one slaves, and a thick portfolio of commercial interests centered on the import-export trade. In 1765 he was the logical choice as the political spokesman for Baltimore County and its merchant community, having already served as town clerk, vestryman, and justice of the peace. That Lux should seize command of the movement against imperial policy underscored the continuity in political leadership during the initial phase of the resistance struggle.[21]

But new men were in the wings. By the time the Townshend duties had become public knowledge in early 1768, Lux found himself sharing power with newcomers whose sudden rise to prominence created the potential for polarizing the local leadership at precisely the moment when unity was imperative. In March 1769, under heavy pressure from Philadelphia's merchant community, Baltimore Town adopted a nonimportation measure in retaliation against the new taxes and appointed a committee of inspection to oversee enforcement of the boycott. The merchants of Baltimore were never enthusiastic about the plan, which came at a time when business seemed to be rebounding after years of postwar depression. So when Philadelphia called off the boycott in the fall of 1770, they promptly announced their intention to follow suit. On October 5 the merchants met in Baltimore Town and appointed several spokesmen to convene in Annapolis a few weeks later with representatives from throughout the colony to consider a proposal for abandoning the nonimportation measure.[22]

An examination of the six men whose signatures appeared on the letter of appointment and who seem to have been regarded as an informal executive board of the merchant community reveals the dramatic reshuffling in local leadership that had taken place since the Stamp Act crisis. Although William Lux provided an important link to the earlier protest against imperial policy, the remaining five merchants were new figures on the political scene. John Smith and William Buchanan did not settle in Baltimore until 1759, and Samuel Purviance, Jr., arrived no earlier than 1765. William Smith registered his first transaction at the county court in 1761, and Ebenezer Mackie in 1769. Unlike Lux who was a seasoned politician with years of experience on the county bench, none of the five had held a local office before 1770. Nor had any of them served in the assembly.[23]

The sudden rise of these virtual unknowns to leadership positions in the provincialwide protest against the Townshend duties signaled the arrival of the Scotch-Irish community and created a network of new ties between Baltimore and Philadelphia. All five of the signers were Scotch-Irish Presbyterians and at least four came from Pennsylvania. John Smith can stand for the rest. Born in 1722 in County Tyrone, Ireland, Smith was six years old when he and his parents, Samuel and Sidney, joined the wave of Scotch-Irish immigrants then flooding the colony of Pennsylvania. Samuel, who kept a close eye on the rapidly developing region west of Philadelphia, finally settled his family in Lancaster County. For the young merchant success came quickly in the form of land and a flour mill, election to the assembly, and appointment as county sheriff.[24]

By 1750 Samuel had entrusted the family business to his son John. In a repetition of the earlier westward trek, the Smiths packed up their belongings and headed for the frontier community of Carlisle in the Cumberland Valley, some fifty miles from Lancaster. At the same time John Smith married Mary Buchanan, the sister of his future business partner William Buchanan, who had also made the journey from Lancaster to Carlisle. Like his father, John dealt in the wheat trade, much of which was being shipped from western Pennsylvania to

John Smith sat for this portrait sometime between 1792 and his death two years later. The painting by Charles Peale Polk captures the unpretentious self-confidence of the seventy-year-old merchant. Courtesy of the Maryland Historical Society.

Baltimore for reexport abroad. John also followed in his father's footsteps by climbing the local political ladder in Carlisle from justice to assemblyman.[25]

Everything seemed to be pointing in the direction of affluence and respectability until 1755, when the fighting of the French and Indian War suddenly appeared at the Smiths' doorstep. Four years later the thirty-seven-year-old Smith liquidated his assets in Carlisle and moved his sizable family—father, mother, wife, three sons, and daughter—to Baltimore Town. With the small fortune accumulated in Carlisle, Smith formed a partnership with his brother-in-law, purchased a lot at the corner of Gay and Water streets, undertook the construction of several wharves to load and unload his ships, and rose virtually overnight to become one of the greatest merchants in Baltimore.[26]

John Smith was not a loner. When the Smiths departed Lancaster for Carlisle, they were accompanied by three groups of neighbors—the Buchanans, Sterretts, and Spears—and these same families continued the journey to Baltimore Town. Together this clan of Scotch-Irish immigrants, whose children had been intermarrying since their days in Pennsylvania, supplied revolutionary Baltimore with some of its most successful merchants and powerful politicians. The Scotch-Irish also provided a direct link to the merchant community of Philadelphia, most notably in the person of Samuel Purviance, Jr. Both Samuel and his brother Robert were young men when they left Ireland for Philadelphia in the middle of the 1750s. Unlike the Smiths, Samuel and Robert stayed in Philadelphia, learned the merchant trade in the commercial capital of North America, and established invaluable business and political contacts that served them well after their arrival in Baltimore around 1765. The controversy over the Townshend duties ushered Samuel into the political arena, where he remained throughout the Revolution as the perennial chairman of the numerous extralegal committees formed after 1768.[27]

The deepening disaffection between Baltimore and Annapolis, which had been hidden from view in the political drama of the Stamp Act, finally burst into the open on October 25, 1770, when provincial leaders, including most members of the assembly, gathered together at the capital to consider the proposal made by Baltimore's merchants to terminate the nonimportation pact. The meeting not only lashed out at the merchants whose selfish actions jeopardized "the most Sacred Rights and Liberties of *America*," it declared a boycott on merchants who dared to resume trade with Great Britain before all the Townshend duties had been rescinded. Six weeks later an indignant Ebenezer Mackie, undoubtedly speaking for the signers of the letter of appointment, published a rebuttal in the newspapers, in which he defended his fellow merchants who had "without a Murmur, *Generously* sacrificed a considerable Part of their Fortunes in the Glorious Struggle." He accused the Annapolis meeting of base hypocrisy for not sacrificing "one Farthing of their Property in the common Cause." Without the cooperation of Baltimore's merchants, the nonimportation agreement was a dead letter. From the adoption of the boycott to its dissolution, every step Baltimore had taken was in consultation with and deference to the merchant community of Philadelphia. In the end, the provincial leadership in Annapolis could do nothing but issue empty threats.[28]

If during the next three years the political life of Maryland withdrew into its normal routine—a seemingly never-ending sparring match between governor and assembly—the bad blood between Baltimore merchants and Annapolis politicians continued to boil. The two groups crossed swords once again in May 1773 during a new round of campaigning for assembly elections. For five months the public had been treated to a spirited debate in the provincial press between

Charles Carroll of Carrollton and Daniel Dulany over whether Gov. Robert Eden had exceeded his legal powers in 1770 when he established a schedule of fees for proprietary officials. Questioning the legality of the fee proclamation and decrying the dangerous influence of the Dulanys, Carroll succeeded in rallying around him a group of ambitious politicians whose hopes for advancement had been repeatedly frustrated by proprietary favoritism.[29]

The debate may have raised important constitutional questions, but from the perspective of Baltimore's merchants it probably looked like just another squabble over patronage among the constitutionally disgruntled lawyers and planters of Annapolis. One of those lawyers, Samuel Chase, saw in the fee controversy a fine opportunity to revive the Baltimore-Annapolis coalition that had collapsed amid bitter recrimination three years before. With new assembly elections scheduled for May, Chase sent a letter to Captain Ridgely, who had declared himself a candidate in the Baltimore race, in which he proposed a carefully choreographed plan for a public demonstration against the proclamation. On election day everything went off as planned, with Ridgely joining the three other victorious delegates in a procession to the public gallows, where an effigy of the proclamation was destroyed. A few days later subscribers to the *Maryland Gazette* picked up their papers to find a letter addressed to the public from the four-man delegation, reiterating its opposition to the fee proclamation and extolling the virtues of its foremost opponent, Charles Carroll of Carrollton. But the plan backfired. A few weeks later the local papers carried another letter condemning the election-day proceedings and criticizing Baltimore's delegates for behaving "in such a manner as can only inflame instead of healing, the animosities of the publick." Over one hundred citizens signed the statement, nearly all of them merchants, including Samuel Purviance, Jr., and John Smith.[30]

The election finally exposed the political polarization that had been concealed amid the outpouring of anti-British rhetoric: new merchant families like the Smiths on one side, old gentry families like the Ridgelys on the other. It was not from any abiding respect for constituted authority or any general aversion to "tumultuous proceedings" that merchants refused to back Captain Ridgely, for only a month earlier a "great number of Merchants and Masters of Vessels" had tarred and feathered two men in the employ of an unpopular customs officer who had attempted to seize a ship in the harbor. The confrontation with Captain Ridgely ran much deeper. In his analysis of the incident, Charles Carroll of Carrollton, who had insider information, concluded that the election and its aftermath revealed a sectional split pitting Baltimore Town against Baltimore County. Right or wrong, one thing is clear: in their effort to shepherd Baltimore into the Chase and Carroll camp, the newly elected assembly delegation was striving to turn back the clock eight years to a time when Baltimore and Annapolis had allied against the Stamp Act. This initiative ran head-on into the Baltimore-Philadelphia axis that John Smith, Samuel Purviance, and so many of the new merchants were endeavoring to create.[31]

It was wholly understandable that Captain Ridgely and his three fellow delegates should resent the intrusion of the new merchants and the creation of the Philadelphia connection. With their deep roots in the county, these men epitomized a rural, native, and Anglican society that was rapidly losing ground with the expansion of Baltimore Town. None of them resided permanently in Baltimore Town, although Ridgely had many business interests there. Delegate Aquilla Hall lived as far away as the Bush River, in what would soon become Harford County. Although Ridgely and Hall were merchants, their diversified investments in agriculture and manufacturing set them apart from the specialized traders of Baltimore Town. The other two delegates, Thomas Cockey Deye and Walter Tolley, Jr., were planters plain and simple. All of the assemblymen had strong ties to the county: Ridgely and Tolley were fourth-generation Marylanders, Hall third-generation, and Deye second-generation. Further, all of them belonged to the Anglican church.[32]

By the time Captain Ridgely staged the fee proclamation protest the political locus of the county had already shifted definitively to Baltimore Town, where new merchants and their accommodationist allies controlled the machinery of government. The emergence of a cohesive mercantile leadership with its base in the port became apparent in the first committee of observation. In October 1774, six months after the assembly elections, the First Continental Congress adopted a comprehensive economic boycott against the mother country in response to the Coercive Acts. A few weeks later the citizens of Baltimore Town, following the directive of the Congress, selected twenty-nine men to serve on a committee of observation to enforce the Continental Association.[33]

The membership of the committee left little doubt that men of trade had secured a virtual stranglehold on power. It included twenty-five merchants, three lawyers, and one physician. Unlike the previous assembly election, where voters selected four delegates who lived in the county, the committeemen either came from Baltimore Town or nearby. Of the twenty-five who can be identified in a 1773 tax list, fifteen lived in town, another two at nearby Fell's Point, and the remaining eight in the vicinity of Patapsco Falls, a few miles away. With an average age of thirty-seven, the committee generally attracted young merchants in their prime, ranging from the twenty-year-old David McMechen to fifty-two-year-old John Smith. Although it was dominated by newly arrived immigrants such as John Smith, William Buchanan, and Samuel Purviance, Jr., it also included a handful of established merchants—the brothers John and Richard Moale, the brothers Andrew and Archibald Buchanan, and the ubiquitous William Lux—whose families had been instrumental in the development of Baltimore Town since its establishment. Unlike Captain Ridgely, these accommodationists had made their peace with the new political and economic order. Of the nineteen committeemen whose origins can be identified, twelve were in-migrants or immigrants: six from Pennsylvania, two from Cecil County, two from "Europe," and one each from England and Ireland.[34]

Baltimoreans who lived in the generation before the Revolution saw their world change in both subtle and profound ways. From an unremarkable village, Baltimore Town rose to become the largest urban center between Charleston and Philadelphia and one of the fastest growing ports anywhere in North America. The new merchants who poured in not only altered the commercial life of the upper Chesapeake but fundamentally transformed the distribution of power in the county. Yet these vast changes did not trigger intense social and political conflict between a traditional gentry class on the way out and a new guard of merchant arrivistes on the way up. The reason was simple—there was no traditional gentry class, there never had been. From the beginning of the eighteenth century the high rates of turnover, overall accessibility to newcomers, and shallow sense of class identity that had characterized the economic elite of Baltimore found expression in a remarkably flexible political order, in which wealthy outsiders could always find a place. In the largest sense, the relatively rapid and uncontested ascendency of new merchants in the political drama that unfolded after 1763 testified to those qualities that had always defined the county gentry: openness, fluidity, and impermanence.

Epilogue

In 1783, with the formal signing of peace between the United States and Great Britain, Captain Charles Ridgely boldly began construction of a new mansion on the grounds of "Northampton," the tract his father had purchased almost four decades before. Building the house was an act of supreme self-confidence. But it should also be seen as a gesture of angry defiance by a man who was committed to a different kind of society from the one that seemed to be gaining ascendancy in the aftermath of the revolutionary war. It had been more than a century since the first Ridgely arrived in Maryland, and during that time three generations of his descendants stood comfortably atop the social order. Yet, as his own life drew to a close, Captain Ridgely must have looked with chagrin as unfamiliar faces and noisy upstarts seemed to eclipse established gentry families who had provided their neighbors with a steady source of leadership, wisdom, and moral authority. Needless to say, such romanticizing greatly distorted the history of Baltimore since, as this study has attempted to demonstrate, the defining characteristics of the class to which Ridgely belonged were openness, fluidity, and turnover. Yet the bitter nostalgia that forms an unmistakable thread through the captain's public career and personal life only gave special poignancy to his efforts to recover a past that never was.

That Captain Ridgely was well past his prime when he launched the project did not dampen his resolve to see it through. Given the ambitious nature of the architectural plans and the uncertain conditions of the new republic, the sixty-year-old man could not have hoped to spend too many years in his new home. Further, the immensity of the logistical problems involved in supplying building materials and recruiting skilled workers only seemed to harden Ridgely's resolve. While the foundations and walls of the house were constructed of stone quarried on the estate, the captain had to look elsewhere for skilled workers. In the workshops and building sites of Baltimore Town, a twelve-mile journey from Northampton, he endeavored to se-

Hampton House was one of the last great Georgian homes built in Maryland. Featuring an imposing central structure and symmetrical wings, the mansion reflected the conservative values of its builder, Capt. Charles Ridgely. Etching by Don Swann.

cure an adequate supply of masons, carpenters, joiners, sawyers, plasterers, and glaziers. Family tradition has it that these men, who frequently returned home, quit work in the early afternoon so as to avoid walking through the wolf-infested forests after sunset.[1]

It took Captain Ridgely seven years to build "Hampton." The finished product was a monument to an architectural style already regarded as antiquated and to an ideal of genteel living Ridgely hoped to preserve amid the forests of northern Baltimore County. The Georgian colossus was 175 feet long and seventy-five feet wide. Ignoring the newer floor plans designed to maximize family privacy, Captain Ridgely envisioned his house as a grand stage for the performance of public events. The central feature of Hampton was a great central hall—seventy feet by twenty-one feet—devoted to large-scale entertaining, where Ridgely's heir was said to have once seated fifty-one guests for dinner and to have kept "the best table in America." In laying out the formal terraced gardens that stepped down from the southern portico, the masters of Hampton rejected the naturalistic designs that were then gaining popularity in favor of the older baroque pattern of symmetrical boxwood hedges. In sum, it would be difficult to imagine a house more defiantly old-fashioned or one better suited to atavistic tastes of Captain Ridgely.[2]

The man who built Hampton did not intend to retire there in embittered isolation. In the years following the revolutionary war, Captain Ridgely mobilized a political "interest" in Baltimore County dedicated to the defense of the same vision of traditional social order he had projected in stone and mortar at Hampton. As a perennial delegate to the legislature and with powerful allies in southern Maryland, Ridgely found himself embroiled in every major political controversy from the ratification of the new state constitution (on which he vacillated) to the ratification of the new federal constitution (which he opposed). The various twistings and turnings of his public life cannot be followed here. Suffice it to say that on one point he never wavered: the gravest threat to the rural, slaveholding, Anglican gentry he personified came from Baltimore Town and its merchants. It was against this threat that Captain Ridgely built his base of support in the county and entered into political alliances with the gentry-dominated delegations of southern Maryland.

The strategy emerged clearly in 1786 when he circulated a handbill among county residents urging them not to elect a merchant or lawyer to the assembly. Even proximity to Baltimore Town made one suspect, or so complained George Lux in an angry letter to Ridgely: "at that time an objection was made against me by your Men because I lived near the *Town*, & would not be a suitable Member for *Farmers*." While Lux was determined to maintain his independence, he acknowledged that many others had no choice but to make their peace with "the all powerful Family of the Ridgelys, who always do as their *Chieftain* orders them and move like a regulary Army."[3]

Farmers. In that one word was encapsulated the dilemma facing conservative gentlemen such as Captain Ridgely who struggled to assert the legitimacy of their authority even as the traditional underpinnings of gentry rule were collapsing. As the basis of the plantation economy and the badge of social status, slavery entangled gentry and yeomen in a complicated mutuality of interests. But Captain Ridgely could no longer count on that mutuality when he addressed his political constituents in 1786. Four years later slaves made up only 23 percent of Baltimore County's population and only 9 percent of Baltimore Town's. As a society of planters became a society of farmers, Captain Ridgely, a fourth-generation gentleman who owned over one-hundred slaves and over twenty thousand acres of land, found himself in the paradoxical position of arguing in defense of his own candidacy, "none but Farmers should be in Assembly."[4]

Yet in the end Captain Ridgely was fighting a losing battle, for the centrifugal forces unleashed by independence doomed his vision of a deferential social order dominated by gentlemen and even disrupted the harmony within the home he had labored so hard to construct. According to family tradition, Ridgely intended a grand opening for Hampton in the traditional gentry style, with music, dancing, and a banquet. His strong-willed wife said no. A recent convert to Methodism and a close friend of Francis Asbury, Rebecca Ridgely would have nothing to do with the kind of convivial gathering of high-spirited men and women that had always been the centerpiece of gentry culture and the crucible in which class consciousness was formed. Charles and Rebecca reached a compromise, but hardly a happy one. On the appointed day, Ridgely and his male companions celebrated in the great hall while Rebecca and her friends conducted a prayer meeting upstairs. A few months later Capt. Charles Ridgely, the master of Hampton, was dead.[5]

Appendix 1
Identifying the Elite

The economic elite of Baltimore has been defined as those individuals who ranked in the top 10 percent of inventoried decedents during the colonial era. All appraised values were adjusted with a deflator provided by Lois Green Carr and Lorena S. Walsh of the St. Mary's City Commission. I selected the richest decile for the period before 1690, and for each subsequent decade until 1776. A total of 1,810 inventories were recorded in either the county or provincial courts (usually both) before 1776.

Table 17 provides a breakdown of wealth distribution on a decade-by-decade basis for the entire decedent population and shows the cut-off point for elite ranking in each period. Table 18 is an alphabetical listing of the 181 individuals who ranked in the top 10 percent of decedents.

Table 17. Wealth Distribution of Baltimore County Decedents: 1660-1776 (in £)

Decile	1660-89	1690-99	1700-1709	1710-19	1720-29
Top	860-133	1,598-245	1,377-290	1,748-247	3,299-313
2nd	130- 98	231-174	290-144	218-125	306-209
3rd	95- 60	169-101	140-103	122- 83	203-156
4th	60- 48	97- 71	96- 71	81- 61	154-111
5th	46- 36	69- 51	71- 49	60- 49	109- 76
6th	36- 31	50- 40	48- 31	48- 31	75- 62
7th	29- 26	40- 30	31- 29	30- 23	61- 45
8th	23- 15	29- 19	23- 16	22- 15	44- 33
9th	15- 10	19- 13	16- 8	14- 8	32- 14
Bottom	9- 4	11- 3	7- 2	8- 1	13- 4

Table 17, *continued*

Decile	1730-39	1740-49	1750-59	1760-69	1770-76
Top	2,392-492	4,392- 531	8,024-603	3,799-488	2,919- 612
2nd	464-294	524-328	580-382	488-306	599-355
3rd	277-200	324- 190	366- 194	306- 196	344-238
4th	198-146	188- 141	183- 119	194- 136	234- 150
5th	140- 98	141- 107	109- 85	136- 99	146- 102
6th	95- 65	104- 74	84- 63	99- 70	101- 76
7th	65- 45	73- 57	58- 43	69- 49	76- 52
8th	45- 32	56- 36	43- 29	49- 29	52- 31
9th	31- 16	35- 17	29- 14	29- 14	30- 15
Bottom	13- 3	16- 2	13- 2	14- 1	14- 1

Table 18. Members of Baltimore Elite with Decade of Death: 1660–1776

Adair, Robert	1760s	Carnan, Christopher	1770s
Adams, Malcolm	1760s	Chamberlain, John	1770s
Ashman, Elizabeth	1710s	Chauncy, George	1710s
Ashman, George	1700s	Coale, Skipwith	1750s
Bailey, George, Jr.	1740s	Cockey, John	1740s
Bailey, Rachel	1750s	Cockey, William	1770s
Bale, Sarah	1700s	Colegate, Richard	1720s
Bale, Thomas	1700s	Cord, Thomas	1720s
Bisset, David	1750s	Cromwell, Richard	1710s
Bisset, James	1760s	Cromwell, William	1750s
Bond, Joshua	1760s	Crockett, John	1730s
Bond, Peter	1710s	Dallam, William	1760s
Boothby, Edward	1690s	Day, Edward	1740s
Boreing, John	1760s	Dorsey, Edward	1700s
Borsley, James	1760s	Dorsey, John	1710s
Boston, Samuel	-1690	Dorsey, John Hammond	1770s
Bowley, Daniel	1740s	Dorsey, Nicholas	1710s
Boyce, Roger	1770s	Draper, Lawrence	1710s
Brown, John	1710s	Drew, Anthony	1720s
Browne, Thomas	1700s	Drew, George	1730s
Buchanan, Eleanor	1750s	Eager, John	1700s
Buchanan, George	1750s	Ensor, John	1770s
Burgess, Hugh	1770s	Fell, William	1740s
Butterworth, Isaac	1720s	Ferry, John	1690s

Table 18, *continued*

Fottrell, Edward	1740s	Kemball, John	1700s
Gardner, John	1740s	Knowles, Henry	1710s
Garrett, Bennett	1740s	Lendrum, Andrew	1770s
Gibson, Miles	1690s	Legoe, Benjamin	1760s
Giles, John	1720s	Lewis, Joseph	1770s
Giles, John	1760s	Little, Guy	1760s
Gist, Richard	1740s	Longland, Richard	1700s
Glover, Ephraim	1770s	Luke, Jonathan	1700s
Goldsmith, George	1690s	Lusby, Jacob	1760s
Goodwin, Moses	1760s	Lusby, Joseph	1760s
Govane, William	1770s	Lux, Darby, Sr.	1750s
Grafton, William	1760s	Lynch, Eleanor	1760s
Greeniff, John	1700s	Lynch, Patrick	1760s
Grindall, Christopher	1740s	Lynch, William	1750s
Hall, Aquilla	1730s	McCulloch, David	1760s
Hall, Edward	1740s	MacNamara, Thomas	1710s
Hall, Edward	1760s	Marshall, Mary	1740s
Hall, Johannah	1730s	Marshall, William	1720s
Hall, John	1730s	Maxwell, James	1720s
Hall, John	1760s	Maxwell, James	1730s
Hall, Parker	1750s	Middlemore, Francis	1760s
Hammond, Thomas	1720s	Moale, John, Sr.	1740s
Hammond, William	1750s	Newman, Roger	1700s
Hanson, Jonathan	1720s	North, Robert	1740s
Hasselbach, Nicholas	1770s	Norwood, Edward	1770s
Heath, James	1760s	Norwood, Samuel	1770s
Hedge, Thomas	1690s	Onion, Stephen	1750s
Henry, John	1770s	Owings, Samuel	1770s
Hill, Moses	1760s	Paca, Aquilla	1720s
Holland, Francis	1730s	Paca, Aquilla	1740s
Holland, Francis	1740s	Paca, John	1760s
Holland, Susannah	1740s	Partridge, Buckler	1740s
Hollis, William	-1690	Payne, William	1760s
Holtzinger, Barnet	1770s	Phillips, James	-1690
Hopkins, Samuel	1760s	Phillips, James	1720s
Hughes, Barnabas	1760s	Phillips, James	1760s
Ingram, Peasly	1740s	Philpot, Brian, Jr.	1760s
Ives, James	-1690	Pickett, William	1710s
Johnson, Henry	1690s	Preston, James	1760s
Jones, David	-1690	Pumphrey, Walter	1720s
Jones, Philip	1760s	Raven, Luke, Sr.	1730s

Table 18, *continued*

Rhoades, Anthony	1760s	Stokes, George	1740s
Richardson, Mark	1700s	Stokes, John	1730s
Ridgely, Charles, Sr.	1770s	Talbot, Thomas	1770s
Ridgely, John	1770s	Tharp, Edward	1760s
Rigbie, Nathan	1750s	Tibbs, William	1730s
Risteau, Talbot	1750s	Todd, Thomas	-1690
Roberts, John	1720s	Todd, Thomas	1730s
Rogers, Nicholas	1720s	Todd, William Thomas	1720s
Rogers, Nicholas	1750s	Todd, William Thomas	1730s
Ruff, Richard	1730s	Tolley, Thomas, Sr.	1730s
Savory, William	1750s	Uty, George	1690s
Scott, Aquilla	1760s	Uty, Mary	1690s
Scott, Daniel	1720s	Uty, Nathaniel	-1690
Scott, James	1760s	Walker, George	1740s
Scott, John	1700s	Wallice, Samuel	1750s
Shute, John	1760s	Webster, Isaac	1760s
Smith, John Addison	1770s	Wells, Benjamin	1700s
Smith, Thomas	1760s	Wells, Blanche	1700s
Smith, William	1730s	Wells, George	1690s
Smith, Winstone	1740s	Wells, George	1710s
Sollers, Sabrett	1760s	Wheeler, Benjamin, Sr.	1770s
Staley, Thomas	1700s	Wheeler, Thomas, Sr.	1770s
Stansbury, Luke	1740s	Wilmottson, John	1710s
Stansbury, Thomas	1760s	Wyatt, Thomas	1770s
Stansby, John	-1690	Young, William	1770s
Stevenson, Edward	1710s		

Appendix 2
Identifying the Merchants

The merchant community was defined as including any person who at some point during his life referred to himself as a merchant in the Baltimore County land records before 1776. This search yielded a total of 201 self-designated merchants.

Figure 5 shows the number of merchants active in the county throughout the colonial era. It was constructed as follows: First, I dated the beginning of a merchant's career at the year when he first appeared in the land records. Second, for the 135 merchants who left either a will, inventory, or both, I assumed that their careers lasted until the first year they appeared in probate. Third, for the remaining sixty-six merchants, I assumed that their careers ended at the conclusion of the decade when they last transacted business at the court (for the decade of the 1770s, 1776 was selected as the end point).

Table 19 presents an alphabetical listing of merchants, together with the dates when they were active in the county. I have placed (e) after the names of the thirty-three merchants who also ranked in the elite.

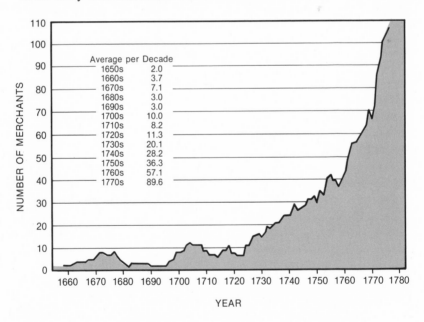

Average per Decade	
1650s	2.0
1660s	3.7
1670s	7.1
1680s	3.0
1690s	3.0
1700s	10.0
1710s	8.2
1720s	11.3
1730s	20.1
1740s	28.2
1750s	36.3
1760s	57.1
1770s	89.6

Figure 5. Number of Merchants Active in Baltimore County: 1660-1776

SOURCES: Baltimore County Land Records; Inventories; Inventories & Accounts; Baltimore County Inventories; Wills; Baltimore County Wills, Maryland State Archives.

Table 19. Merchants of Baltimore County with Approximate Career
Dates: 1660-1776

Adair, Robert (e)	1745-69	Croxall, Charles	1749-82
Alexander, Mark	1761-76	Croxall, Richard	1747-85
Allen, Solomon	1776	Dagon, George	1773-76
Appleman, Conrad	1774-76	Dallam, Richard	1761-76
Ashburner, John	1771-76	Dallam, William (e)	1734-62
Bailey, John	1742-49	Davidson, John	1773-76
Baker, Matthew	1745-49	Devilbiss, George	1733-76
Bale, Thomas (e)	1702-8	Dick, Thomas	1759-64
Beasman, Joseph	1772-76	Dillon, Henry	1769-71
Bowly, Daniel	1769-1808	Dorsey, John Hammond (e)	1756-75
Boyd, John	1762-76	Dugan, Cumberland	1771-1836
Brereton, Thomas	1770-88	Eichelberger, Bernard	1771-83
Brown, Samuel	1769-76	Eichelberger, Jacob	1774-1833
Buchanan, Andrew	1754-86	Ennals, Andrew	1775-1803
Buchanan, Archibald	1763-85	Ensor, John, Jr.	1751-71
Buchanan, William	1761-76	Ewing, Thomas	1769-80
Bull, Jacob	1726-56	Fell, Edward	1725-43
Burrough, Richard	1716-19	Fell, William (e)	1730-46
Button, Richard	1771-76	French, James	1774-76
Calvert, Joseph	1728-29	Garts, Charles	1771-1811
Carnan, Christopher (e)	1754-70	Gay, Nicholas Ruxton	1749-70
Carson, Samuel	1776	Gilbert, John	1668-77
Cary, James	1754-69	Giles, Jacob	1729-84
Chamberlain, Thomas	1703-19	Gist, Christopher	1741-59
Chamier, Daniel	1754-79	Gist, Mordecai	1772-93
Cheston, James	1772-76	Gist, Richard (e)	1693-42
Christie, Charles	1753-57	Goodwin, Lyde	1750-56
Christie, James	1760-76	Goodwin, William	1770-1808
Christie, Robert	1763-80	Govane, William (e)	1738-68
Clarke, James	1771-1814	Greene, Job	1774-76
Clendinning, Thomas	1754-62	Griffith, Benjamin	1763-99
Cole, Richard Miller	1747-67	Griffith, John	1772-94
Colegate, Richard (e)	1698-1721	Griffith, Nathan	1768-1806
Cornthwait, John	1772-82	Grist, Isaac	1767-1802
Courtenay, Hercules	1767-1816	Gunnell, Edward	1672-80
Cox, William	1754-67	Hall, Aquilla	1752-76
Cravash, Lemuel	1771-76	Hammond, William (e)	1727-52
Crockett, John (e)	1715-36	Harmer, Godfrey	1658-73
Crooke, James	1699-1727	Harris, William	1771-76
Cross, Samuel	1765-69	Harrison, Thomas	1742-82

Table 19, *continued*

Hart, John	1760-99	Morgan, Henry	1737-59
Hedge, Thomas	1698-1708	Neill, William	1771-85
Holmes, James	1771-76	Newman, Roger (e)	1697-1704
Holtzinger, Barnet (e)	1770-72	Nicholson, James	1772-76
Howard, John Beale	1776	North, Robert (e)	1724-49
Hudson, Jonathan	1772-86	O'Neil, Felix	1769-1800
Hughes, Barnabas (e)	1762-65	Owens, Richard	1704-19
Israel, John	1703-23	Paca, John	1730-85
Ives, James (e)	1670-79	Patten, George	1768-78
James, Charles	1661-98	Patterson, Robert	1762-69
Jarrett, Abraham	1759-69	Perkins, Richard	1772-76
Jones, Nicholas	1762-91	Phile, Thomas	1775-76
Jones, Thomas	1762-1811	Philpot, Brian, Jr. (e)	1753-69
Kelleher, John	1775-76	Philpot, John	1773-78
Kennedy, John	1772-1822	Place, Thomas	1771-76
King, Richard	1716-20	Plowman, Jonathan	1759-76
Landsdale, Thomas	1771-76	Purviance, Samuel	1769-76
Larsh, Valentine	1750-81	Randall, John	1751-55
Lawson, Alexander	1737-60	Reid, George	1713-19
Lemmon, Richard	1772-96	Rhoads, Anthony (e)	1753-62
Lux, Darby, Jr.	1764-1812	Richard, James	1742-59
Lux, Darby, Sr. (e)	1734-50	Ridgely, Charles, Sr. (e)	1727-72
Lux, William	1752-77	Ridgely, Charles, Jr.	1761-90
McCandless, George	1761-93	Ridgely, John (e)	1750-71
McCulloch, David (e)	1757-66	Ridley, Matthew	1773-90
McFaden, John	1772-80	Rigbie, Nathan(e)	1719-53
Mackie, Ebenezer	1769-96	Risteau, John	1732-52
McKim, John	1772-1819	Roberts, John	1738-49
McLure, Alexander	1771-86	Robinson, John	1763-69
McMechen, Alexander	1765-76	Rogers, Benjamin	1760-76
Magill, William	1769-1813	Rogers, Nicholas (e)	1752-58
Marshall, William (e)	1718-20	Rogers, Philip	1770-1836
Matthews, Bennett	1767-69	Roody, Samuel	1775-76
Merryman, John	1763-80	Russell, William	1769-76
Middlemore, Josias	1718-55	Salmon, George	1773-1807
Miles, James	1677-85	Savory, William (e)	1746-59
Miller, Thomas	1762-76	Sheaff, Henry	1774-76
Moale, John, Jr.	1755-98	Sheredine, Thomas	1724-53
Moale, John, Sr. (e)	1728-40	Sicklemore, Samuel	1695-1719
Moale, Richard	1760-86	Simm, Robert	1763-69
Moore, William, Jr.	1766-76	Sligh, Thomas	1731-74

Table 19, *continued*

Smith, John	1760-94	Thompson, John	1747-69
Smith, Nathaniel	1770-93	Thompson, Henry	1772-76
Smith, William(e)	1724-32	Thurston, Thomas	1658-92
Smith, William	1760-1814	Todd, Lancelot	1719-29
Spear, John	1773-96	Todd, Thomas (e)	1664-77
Spear, William	1771-90	Vanbibber, Abraham	1769-1805
Spencer, William	1770-87	Vanbibber, Isaac	1770-1825
Stansbury, Luke (e)	1724-42	Usher, Simon	1769-76
Stansbury, Tobias	1742-58	Usher, Thomas	1775-86
Sterrett, James	1761-96	Walsh, Robert	1773-76
Sterrett, John	1773-87	Webster, Isaac(e)	1732-55
Stevenson, Edward (e)	1700-18	Webster, John Lee	1765-76
Stevenson, John	1753-76	Wells, Charles	1769-1801
Stewart, Alexander	1757-69	Wilde, Abraham	1670-69
Swift, Mark	1697-1708	Wilson, Henry, Jr.	1771-1816
Talbot, William	1699-1713	Wilson, John	1768-76
Taylor, Brian	1733-36	Worthington, Thomas	1766-1821
Taylor, Joseph	1747-59	Young, Charles	1773-76
Taylor, Thomas	1724-49	Young, William(e)	1741-72
Thatcher, Elisha	1774-76		

Notes

Introduction

1. For two good reviews of the literature, see Thad W. Tate, "The Seventeenth-Century Chesapeake and Its Modern Historians," in Thad W. Tate and David L. Ammerman, eds., *The Chesapeake in the Seventeenth Century: Essays on Anglo-American Society and Politics* (Chapel Hill, N.C., 1979), 3-50; Lois Green Carr, Philip D. Morgan, and Jean B. Russo, "Introduction," in Lois Green Carr, Philip D. Morgan, and Jean B. Russo, eds., *Colonial Chesapeake Society* (Chapel Hill, N.C., 1988), 1-46.

2. For Jacob M. Price, see *France and the Chesapeake: A History of the French Tobacco Monopoly, 1674-1791, and of Its Relationship to the British and American Tobacco Trades,* 2 vols. (Ann Arbor, 1973); idem, *Capital and Credit in British Overseas Trade: The View from the Chesapeake, 1700-1776* (Cambridge, Mass., 1980); idem, "The Economic Growth of the Chesapeake and the European Market, 1697-1775," *Journal of Economic History* 24 (1964): 496-511; idem, "The Rise of Glasgow in the Chesapeake Tobacco Trade, 1707-1775," *William and Mary Quarterly,* 3d ser., 11 (1954): 179-99; idem, "Buchanan & Simpson, 1759-1763: A Different Kind of Glasgow Firm Trading to the Chesapeake," ibid., 40 (1983): 3-41; idem. "The Last Phase of the Virginia-London Consignment Trade: James Buchanan & Co., 1758-1768," ibid., 43 (1986): 64-98. For Edmund S. Morgan, see *American Slavery—American Freedom: The Ordeal of Colonial Virginia* (New York, 1975). For Rhys Isaac, see *The Transformation of Virginia, 1740-1790* (Chapel Hill, N.C., 1982). For Allan Kulikoff, see *Tobacco and Slaves: The Development of Southern Cultures in the Chesapeake, 1680-1800* (Chapel Hill, N.C., 1986).

3. For references to the journal articles that comprise the main body of this work, see essays in note 1. The book-length studies that have appeared include Lois Green Carr and David William Jordan, *Maryland's Revolution of Government, 1689-1692* (Ithaca, N.Y., 1974); Paul G.E. Clemens, *The Atlantic Economy and Colonial Maryland's Eastern Shore: From Tobacco to Grain* (Ithaca, N.Y., 1980); David W. Jordan, *Foundations of Representative Government in Maryland, 1632-1715* (Cambridge, 1987). For Darrett B. Rutman and Anita H. Rutman, see *A Place in Time: Middlesex County, Virginia, 1650-1750* (New York, 1984).

4. Jack P. Greene, "Society, Ideology, and Politics: An Analysis of the Political Culture of Mid-Eighteenth-Century Virginia," in Richard M. Jellison, ed., *Society, Freedom, and Conscience: The American Revolution in Virginia, Massachusetts, and New York* (New York, 1976), 14-76; idem, " 'Virtus et Libertas': Political Culture, Social Change, and the Origins of the American Revolution in Virginia," in Jeffrey J. Crow and Larry E. Tise, eds., *The Southern Experience in the American Revolution* (Chapel Hill, 1978), 55-108; idem, "Character, Persona, and Authority: A Study of Alternative Styles of Political Leadership in Revolutionary Virginia," in W. Robert Higgins, ed., *The Revolutionary War in the South: Power, Conflict, and Leadership: Essays in Honor of John Richard Alden* (Durham, 1979), 3-42; Richard R. Beeman, *The Evolution of the Southern Backcountry: A Case Study of Lunenburg County, Virginia, 1746-1832* (Philadelphia, 1984); Albert H. Tillson, Jr., *Gentry and Common Folk: Political Culture on a Virginia Frontier, 1740-1789* (Lexington, Ky., 1991); Aubrey C. Land, "Economic Base and Social Structure: The Northern Chesapeake in the Eighteenth Century," *Journal of Economic History* 25 (1965): 639-54; idem, "Economic Behavior in a Planting Society: The Eighteenth-Century Chesapeake," *Journal of Southern History* 33 (1967): 469-85; T. H. Breen, *Tobacco Culture: The Mentality of the Great Tidewater Planters on the Eve of Revolution* (Princeton, 1985); Kenneth A. Lockridge, *The Diary, and Life, of William Byrd II of Virginia, 1674-1744* (Chapel Hill, N.C., 1987); David Hackett Fischer, *Albion's Seed: Four British Folkways in America* (New York, 1989); Daniel Blake Smith, *Inside the Great House: Planter Family Life in Eighteenth-Century Chesapeake Society* (Ithaca, N.Y., 1980); Jan Lewis, *The Pursuit of Happiness: Family and Values in Jefferson's Virginia* (Cambridge, 1983); Charles S. Sydnor, *Gentlemen Freeholders: Political Practices in Washington's Virginia* (Chapel Hill, N.C., 1952); Louis B. Wright, *The First Gentlemen of Virginia* (San Marino, Calif., 1940); Thomas J. Wertenbaker, *The Planters of Colonial Virginia* (Princeton, 1922); Bernard Bailyn, "Politics and Social Structure in Virginia," in James Morton Smith, ed., *Seventeenth-Century America: Essays in Colonial History* (Chapel Hill, N.C., 1959), 63-115.

5. For Byrd, see Louis B. Wright and Marion Tinling, eds., *The Secret Diary of William Byrd of Westover, 1709-1712* (Richmond, Va., 1941); Louis B. Wright and Marion Tinling, eds., *William Byrd of Virginia: The London Diary (1717-1721) and Other Writings* (New York, 1958); Maude H. Woodfin, ed., *Another Secret Diary of William Byrd of Westover, 1739-1741: With Letters and Literary Exercises, 1696-1726*, Marion Tinling, trans. (Richmond, Va., 1942). For Carter, see Jack P. Greene, ed., *The Diary of Colonel Landon Carter of Sabine Hall, 1752-1778*, 2 vols. (Charlottesville, Va., 1965).

6. Greene, "Society, Ideology, and Politics," 16.

7. In the most careful discussion of the relationship between wealth and status among the gentry, Rutman and Rutman conclude that people with great wealth were likely to enjoy high status (defined as having an honorific or

holding office), but that people with high status were even more likely to enjoy great wealth. This probably reflected the fact that there were more wealthy people than offices to accommodate them. See Darrett B. Rutman and Anita H. Rutman, *A Place in Time: Explicatus* (New York, 1984), 133-44.

8. Historians have not reached a consensus on the numbers of gentlemen in the colonial Chesapeake. Greene suggests that the gentry "probably did not comprise much over 2 to 5 percent of the total white inhabitants, with the inner gentry group comprising no more than a fraction, perhaps a fifth, of the whole category." See "Society, Ideology, and Politics," 17. By using an estate worth £1,000 sterling as the cutoff for the elite status in Maryland, Land estimates that "great planters" increased from 1.6 percent of inventoried decedents in the late seventeenth century to 3.9 percent by the mid-eighteenth century. See "Economic Base and Social Structure," 653. Kulikoff states that the gentry comprised "perhaps a twentieth of the region's white men." See *Tobacco and Slaves*, 262. Breen calculates that the "great Tidewater planters" amounted to "anywhere from 3 to 10 percent of the white heads of households." See *Tobacco Culture*, 32. D. Alan Williams says that the "true planter gentry", those who owned real and personal property worth £1,000, made up 10 percent of the population. See D. Allan Williams, "The Small Farmer in Eighteenth-Century Virginia Politics," *Agricultural History* 43 (1969): 92.

1. Baltimore County

1. Russell R. Menard, "British Migration to the Chesapeake Colonies in the Seventeenth Century," in Carr, Morgan, and Russo, eds., *Colonial Chesapeake Society*, 102.

2. Philip L. Barbour, ed., *The Complete Works of Captain John Smith (1580-1631)*, 3 vols. (Chapel Hill, N.C., 1986), I, 148; Philip L. Barbour, *The Three Worlds of Captain John Smith* (Boston, 1964), 204-5.

3. Barbour, ed., *Complete Works of Captain John Smith*, II, 163.

4. Ibid., I, 148, II, 166; Raphael Semmes, "Aboriginal Maryland, 1608-1689. In Two Parts. Part Two: The Western Shore," *Maryland Historical Magazine* 24 (1929): 196.

5. Barbour, *Complete Works of Captain John Smith*, I, 148; Robert D. Mitchell and Edward K. Muller, "Interpreting Maryland's Past: Praxis and Desiderata," in Robert D. Mitchell and Edward K. Muller, eds., *Geographical Perspectives on Maryland's Past* (College Park, Md., 1979), 1-3; *Maryland Geological Survey* 6 (Baltimore, 1906), 55-70.

6. For secondary accounts, see Newton D. Mereness, *Maryland as a Proprietary Province* (New York, 1901); Bernard C. Steiner, *Maryland During the English Civil Wars*, Parts 1 and 2, Johns Hopkins University Studies, No. 25 (Baltimore, 1907); Bernard C. Steiner, *Maryland Under the Commonwealth: A Chronicle of the Years 1649-1659*, Johns Hopkins University Stud-

ies, No. 29 (Baltimore, 1911); Aubrey C. Land, *Colonial Maryland: A History* (Millwood, N.Y., 1981), 3-56; Jordan, *Foundations of Representative Government in Maryland*, 1-59; J. Frederick Fausz, "Present at the 'Creation': The Chesapeake World That Greeted the Maryland Colonists," *Maryland Historical Magazine* 79 (1984): 7-20.

7. Arthur E. Karinen, "Maryland Population: 1631-1730," *Maryland Historical Magazine* 54 (1959): 390; Edward B. Mathews, *The Counties of Maryland: Their Origin, Boundaries, and Election Districts*, Maryland Geological Survey, Special Publications, Vol. 6, Part 5 (Baltimore, 1907), 442-46; Francis Jennings, "Indians and Frontiers in Seventeenth-Century Maryland," in David B. Quinn, ed., *Early Maryland in a Wider World* (Detroit, 1982), 221-22.

8. Mathews, *Counties of Maryland*, 442-46.

9. Karinen, "Maryland Population," 390-91; Russell R. Menard, "Five Maryland Censuses, 1700 to 1712: A Note on the Quality of the Quantities," *William and Mary Quarterly*, 3d ser., 37 (1980): 618.

10. Baltimore County Court Proceedings, G # 1, 597, Maryland State Archives.

11. Gloria L. Main, *Tobacco Colony: Life in Early Maryland, 1650-1720* (Princeton, N.J., 1982), 81. Quote on p. 89.

12. Calculated from lists of assemblymen in Edward C. Papenfuse, Alan F. Day, David W. Jordan, and Gregory A. Stiverson, eds., *A Biographical Dictionary of the Maryland Legislature, 1635-1789*, 2 vols. (Baltimore, 1979-85), I, 23-35. For a profile of legislators stressing turnover in office, see Jordan, *Foundations of Representative Government in Maryland*, 70-80.

13. Theodore C. Gambrall, *Studies in the Civil, Social and Ecclesiastical History of Maryland* (New York, 1893), 134; Percy G. Skirven, *The First Parishes of Maryland* (Baltimore, 1923), 47-62, 71-104.

14. Nelson W. Rightmyer, *Maryland's Established Church* (Baltimore, 1956).

15. William N. Wilkins, comp., "Maryland Genealogical Notes: Early Parishes and Hundreds, Baltimore County, Md., including Tax Lists Years 1692, 1694, 1695," [typescript], Maryland State Archives; Menard, "Five Maryland Censuses," 620, 624. For accounts of transition to slavery, see Russell R. Menard, "From Servants to Slaves: The Transformation of the Chesapeake Labor System," *Southern Studies* 16 (1977): 355-90; idem, "The Maryland Slave Population, 1658 to 1730: A Demographic Profile of Blacks in Four Counties," *William and Mary Quarterly*, 3rd ser., 32 (1975): 29-54.

16. Main, *Tobacco Colony*, 105. For a fuller discussion of the transition from servitude to slavery, see chap. 3.

17. Wilkins, comp., "Maryland Genealogical Notes."

18. Ibid. For an analysis of mobility in Talbot County in the 1720s, see Clemens, *Atlantic Economy and Colonial Maryland's Eastern Shore*, 162-63. Morgan stresses the mobility of landless freemen in Virginia in *American*

Slavery—American Freedom, 215-34. For mortality rates in early Chesapeake, see Carville V. Earle, "Environment, Disease, and Mortality in Early Virginia," in Tate and Ammerman, eds., *Chesapeake in the Seventeenth Century*, 96-125; Lorena S. Walsh " 'Till Death Us Do Part': Marriage and Family in Seventeenth Century Maryland," ibid., 126-52; Darrett B. Rutman and Anita H. Rutman, "Of Agues and Fevers: Malaria in the Early Chesapeake," *William and Mary Quarterly*, 3rd ser., 33 (1976): 31-60; Lorena S. Walsh and Russell R. Menard, "Death in the Chesapeake: Two Life Tables for Men in Early Colonial Maryland," *Maryland Historical Magazine* 49 (1974): 211-27.

19. For an analysis of economic conditions, see Russell R. Menard, "The Chesapeake Tobacco Industry, 1617-1730: An Interpretation," in Paul Uselding, ed., *Research in Economic History: A Research Annual* 5 (1980): 109-77; Clemens, *Atlantic Economy and Colonial Maryland's Eastern Shore*, 36-39; John J. McCusker and Russell R. Menard, *The Economy of British America, 1607-1789* (Chapel Hill, N.C., 1985), 117-43. For decline in mobility for freedmen, see Russell R. Menard, "From Servant to Freeholder: Status Mobility and Property Accumulation in Seventeenth Century Maryland," *William and Mary Quarterly*, 3rd ser., 30 (1973): 37-64; Lorena S. Walsh, "Servitude and Opportunity in Charles County, Maryland, 1658-1705," in Aubrey C. Land, Lois Green Carr, and Edward C. Papenfuse, eds., *Law, Society, and Politics in Early Maryland* (Baltimore, 1977), 111-33; Lois Green Carr and Russell R. Menard, "Immigration and Opportunity: The Freedman in Early Colonial Maryland," in Tate and Ammerman, eds., *Chesapeake in the Seventeenth Century*, 206-42.

20. Russell R. Menard, "Economy and Society in Early Colonial Maryland" (PhD diss., University of Iowa, 1975), 284, 306-8.

21. Robert Brenner, "The Social Basis of English Commercial Expansion, 1550-1650," *Journal of Economic History* 32 (1972): 361-84; idem, "The Civil War Politics of London's Merchant Community," *Past and Present* 58 (1973): 53-107. For the successful integration of merchants into the Virginia elite, see Warren G. Billings, "The Growth of Political Institutions in Virginia, 1634 to 1676," *William and Mary Quarterly*, 3rd ser., 31 (1974): 236-38.

22. Merchants were identified in Baltimore County Land Records, Maryland State Archives. A fuller explanation is in appendix 2. For estates, see Inventories & Accounts, V, 3-6; XXIII, 98-99; XIIIA, 314-17; VIIA, 6-8, 211-12; I, 48-50, Maryland State Archives.

23. For references to sons, see Patents, XII, 202; Baltimore County Land Records, IR # PP, 65, RM # HS, 479, IS # IK, 230-35; Wills, VI, 22-23; Cecil County Land Records, I, 182. For references to occupations of the sons, see Baltimore County Land Records, HW # 2, 281-82, 307-9, TR # RA, 339; Cecil County Land Records, 1, 305, Maryland State Archives. For references to estates of sons, see Inventories & Accounts, XXXI, 2-3, 65-66; I, 603-4; WB # 3, 90-91; XXVIII, 138-39, 153.

24. "Report of Governor Johan Printz, 1664," in Albert Cook Myers, ed., *Narratives of Early Pennsylvania, West New Jersey, and Delaware, 1630-1707* (New York, 1912), 106; Patents, Q, 62, 241-44, 296-98; XV, 170-71, 250, Maryland State Archives; William B. Mayre, "Early Settlers of the Site of Havre de Grace," *Maryland Historical Magazine* 13 (1918): 201; William Hand Browne et al., eds., *Archives of Maryland* (72 vols., Baltimore, 1883-), LVII, 50, III, 411, 430.

25. Baltimore County Land Records, IR # PP, 84, 87; Inventories & Accounts, I, 48-50; Wills, I, 613-14.

26. Browne et al., eds., *Archives of Maryland*, LXVII, 197, 437-39; Patents, XV, 486-87; Baltimore County Land Records, IR # PP, 4-5; Inventories & Accounts, VIIA, 211-12.

27. Browne et al., eds., *Archives of Maryland*, LXVIII, 233-34; Baltimore County Land Records, RM # HS, 175; Testamentary Proceedings, IX, 300; XIIA, 176-77, Maryland State Archives; Baltimore County Court Proceedings, D, 254.

28. Browne et al., eds., *Archives of Maryland*, LXV, 97-101, LI, 351, LXVIII, 33-34; Patents, XV, 121-22; XVII, 402; Testamentary Proceedings, VII, 322-35; Inventories & Accounts, IV, 484-86; V, 305.

29. Nell Marion Nugent, *Cavaliers and Pioneers: Abstracts of Virginia Land Patents and Grants, 1623-1666* (Richmond, 1934), 253; Bernard C. Steiner, "Presbyterian Beginnings," *Maryland Historical Magazine* 15 (1920): 305-11, esp. 306; Louis Dow Scisco, "Notes on Augustine Herman's Map," ibid., 33 (1938): 343-51, esp. 351; Baltimore County Land Records, IR # PP, 66, 71, 74, 107. For headrights, see Patents, VII, 224-26; XII, 309-11; XIII, 40-41; XV, 287; XIX, 173-74. Calculations on investment patterns are based on the assets each man owned at the time of his death. For inventories, see Inventories & Accounts, I, 48-50; VIIA, 211-12, 279; V, 3-6.

30. Nugent, *Cavaliers and Pioneers*, 527; Testamentary Proceedings, IX, 162-66; Inventories & Accounts, V, 3-6.

31. The crop would have required thirty to forty workers; the elder Thomas Todd owned only three slaves at his death. See Wills, V, 227-28.

32. Land, "Economic Base and Social Structure"; idem, "Economic Behavior in a Planting Society," 469-85.

33. This account draws heavily on Carr and Jordan, *Maryland's Revolution of Government*, though they stress continuity over change in the period 1689-92. Lois Green Carr presents a case for the county court as an anchor of stability in "The Foundations of Social Order: Local Government in Colonial Maryland," in Bruce C. Daniels, ed., *Town and County: Essays in the Structure of Local Government in the American Colonies* (Middletown, Conn., 1978), 72-110; Lois Green Carr, "Sources of Political Stability and Upheaval in Seventeenth-Century Maryland," *Maryland Historical Magazine* 79 (1984): 44-70. For other secondary works on the revolution, see Jordan, *Foundations of Representative Government in Maryland*, 97-137; Francis

Sparks, *Causes of the Maryland Revolution of 1689*, Johns Hopkins University Studies in Historical and Political Science, ser. XIV, nos. 11-12 (Baltimore, 1896); Bernard C. Steiner, "The Protestant Association in Maryland," American Historical Association, *Annual Report of the American Historical Association for the Year 1897* (Washington, D.C., 1898), 279-353; Michael Kammen, "The Causes of the Maryland Revolution of 1689," *Maryland Historical Magazine* 55 (1960): 293-333.

34. Kammen, "Causes of the Maryland Revolution"; for Virginia, see Bailyn, "Politics and Social Structure in Virginia," 90-115.

35. Carr and Jordan, *Maryland's Revolution of Government*, 189-90.

36. These figures were computed from data presented in Carr and Jordan, *Maryland's Revolution of Government*, table 2. For petitions, see pp. 92-93.

37. Thurston's clashes with authorities can be followed Browne et al., eds., *Archives of Maryland*, III, 348-50, 352, 353, 362, 364, XLI, 268-69, 286, 287, 319, 322, 331, 334, 339, 364, 508. See also Kenneth L. Carroll, "Thomas Thurston, Renegade Maryland Quaker," *Maryland Historical Magazine* 62 (1967): 170-92; David W. Jordan, " 'Gods Candle' within Government: Quakers and Politics in Early Maryland," *William and Mary Quarterly*, 3rd ser., 39 (1982): 629.

38. Patents, XIX, 258; IX, 30, 113, 337-39; XI, 195, 209-10; Browne et al., eds., *Archives of Maryland*, LIV, 264-65.

39. Inventories & Accounts, XIIIA, 314-17; XIIIB, 86; XIV, 145.

40. Clayton Colman Hall, ed., *Narratives of Early Maryland, 1633-1684* (New York, 1910), 405; Carroll, "Thomas Thurston," 184-88.

41. Browne et al., eds., *Archives of Maryland*, VIII, 338, 378.

2. The Open Elite

1. Menard, "Five Maryland Censuses," 618, 625; Karinen, "Maryland Population," 405. The estimate for 1737 was derived by multiplying the county's taxables by 3.0, as is suggested by Karinen, p. 367. For taxables, see William N. Wilkins, comp., "Baltimore County Court Records, Joppa, Maryland: Levy Allowances and List of Taxables by Hundreds, 1737," [typescript], Maryland State Archives.

2. Distribution of slaves was calculated from Wilkins, comp., "Baltimore County Court Records, Joppa, Maryland."

3. For Chesapeake craftsmen, see Jean B. Russo, "Self-sufficiency and Local Exchange: Free Craftsmen in the Rural Chesapeake Economy," in Carr, Morgan, and Russo, eds., *Colonial Chesapeake Society*, 389-432. For the larger economic context of occupational diversification in the eighteenth-century Chesapeake, see Lois Green Carr, "Diversification in the Colonial Chesapeake: Somerset County, Maryland, in Comparative Perspective," ibid., 342-88; Lois Green Carr and Lorena S. Walsh, "Economic

Diversification and Labor Organization in the Chesapeake, 1650-1820,"
in Stephen Innes, ed., *Work and Labor in Early America* (Chapel Hill, N.C.,
1988), 144-88.

4. Mathews, *Counties of Maryland*, 445; Thomas Bacon, ed., *Laws of
Maryland* (Annapolis, 1765), Chap. XIV, Apr. 1706; Chap. XVI, Apr. 1707;
Chap. XIX, Nov. 1712.

5.For descriptions and analyses of the Virginia court, see Isaac, *Transformation of Virginia*, 88-94; Charles S. Sydnor, *Gentlemen Freeholders*,
86-91; A. G. Roeber, "Authority, Law, and Custom: The Rituals of Court
Day in Tidewater Virginia, 1720-1750," *William and Mary Quarterly*, 3rd
ser., 37 (1980): 29-52. For Ward, see Baltimore County Court Proceedings,
IS TW # 3, 200, Maryland State Archives.

6. Baltimore County Court Proceedings, IS # C, 512-13.

7. For an analysis of the social composition and political function of
the court that stresses the role of small planters, see Gwenda Morgan, "Law
and Social Change in Colonial Virginia: The Role of the Grand Jury in Richmond County, 1692-1776," *Virginia Magazine of History and Biography* 95
(1987): 461. For the 1697 petition, see Baltimore County Court Proceedings,
G # 1, 597. For other petitions from grand jury, see G # 1, 528; IS # A, 182,
288; IS A # 3, 662; IS # C, 226-28.

8. For a list of Baltimore ministers together with the approximate dates
of their incumbencies, see Rightmyer, *Maryland's Established Church*,
143-46.

9. For personal property of ministers, see Inventories, XXVII, 148-51;
CXI, 288-91; XXXI, 445-49; XVII, 296-301; XXIV, 382-88; IX, 251-53,
Maryland State Archives. The data on landholdings were calculated by tracing the ministers through the Baltimore County Land Records, Wills, Maryland State Archives. The largest landowner was Evan Evans with 1,000 acres,
but his property was located in the Philadelphia area where he lived before
settling in Baltimore. See Wills, XVII, 207-10. For town lots, see Wills,
XXII, 100-101; Baltimore County Land Records, IS # I, 74, 210.

10. William S. Perry, ed., *Historical Collections of the American Colonial Church*, 4 vols. (Hartford, Conn., 1870-78), IV, 190-92.

11. For estates of Phillips and Rogers, see Inventories and Accounts, I,
73-83, Maryland State Archives; Inventories, VIII, 195-217.

12. For patterns of consumption, see Lois Green Carr and Lorena S.
Walsh, "Changing Lifestyles in Colonial St. Mary's County," *Working
Papers from the Regional Economic History Research Center* I, no. 3
(1978): 72-118; Lois Green Carr and Lorena S. Walsh, "Inventories and the
Analysis of Wealth and Consumption Patterns in St. Mary's County, Mary-
land, 1658-1777," *Historical Methods* 13 (1980): 81-104; Lorena S. Walsh,
"Urban Amenities and Rural Sufficiency: Living Standards and Consumer
Behavior in the Colonial Chesapeake, 1643-1777," *Journal of Economic His-
tory* 43 (1983): 109-17.

13. Baltimore County Land Records, IR # PP, 22-24, 33-34, 40-41, 46, 49, 50-51, 64; IR # AM, 118, 133-34, 162-65: IS # IK, 53-54; TR # RA, 169-71, 245-48, 262-63; Inventories, I, 26-31; Papenfuse et al., eds., *Biographical Dictionary of the Maryland Legislature.*

14. Inventories, I, 26-31.

15. Baltimore County Court Proceedings, BA, 78, 615, 740; Inventories, XI, 165-68.

16. Inventories, XI, 165-68.

17. Ibid.

18. For major accounts of the rise of the tidewater gentry, see Isaac, *Transformation of Virginia;* Sydnor, *Gentlemen Freeholders;* Kulikoff, *Tobacco and Slaves,* 261-313; Morgan, *American Slavery—American Freedom;* Bailyn, "Politics and Social Structure in Virginia," 90-115; Fischer, *Albion's Seed,* 207-418.

19. Baltimore County Debt Books, 1754 through 1771, Maryland State Archives. The debt book for the year 1767 is missing. For a description of the debt books, see Elisabeth Hartsook and Gus Skordos, *Land Office and Prerogative Court Records of Colonial Maryland* (Annapolis, 1946), 33-41.

20. The biographical data were culled from three sources: Wills, Inventories, and Papenfuse et al., eds., *Biographical Dictionary of Maryland Legislators.*

21. For wills of Gover and Heath, see Wills, XXX, 518-19; XXV, 63-68.

22. In a 1754 land deed, Charles Carnan was mentioned as being "late of London Merct." See Baltimore County Land Records, BB # I, 291-92. For Heath's and Smith's fathers, see Inventories, XVII, 235-41; XX, 282-87; XLI, 126-35, 313-14; XLIX, 41; Effie Gwynn Bowie, *Across the Years in Prince George's County* (Richmond, Va., 1947), 295. For the fathers' estates, see Inventories, X, 174-91, 575-76; XXV, 289-90, 431; XVII, 235-41; XX, 282-87; XXIV, 277-79; LXXIV, 93, 292-96; XLVI, 383-84; XVIII, 161-62; VIII, 297-300.

23. Anne Arundel County Deeds, RD # 1, 219-23; IB # 2, 108-10; IHTI # 1, 373-75; Chancery Record 8 IR # 5, 820, Maryland State Archives.

24. For court proceedings, see Chancery Record 8 IR # 5, 820-68, 944-45. See also Anne Arundel County Deeds, RB # 3, 540-41; Baltimore County Land Records, B # G, 51-53; Patents, BC & GS # 7, 237; Wills, XXXVI, 675-76.

25. For wills of natives' fathers, see Wills, XXX, 24-26; XXIX, 87-88; XXIV, 81-84, 473-74; XXIII, 374-77, 566-71; XVI, 18-20; XIX, 778-79; XXII, 436-37.

26. Wills, I, 161-62, 494-98; II, 6-10; Baltimore County Debt Books, 1754 through 1771.

27. Wills, XXX, 24-26; Baltimore County Land Records, TR # D, 465; BB # I, 505, 632, 664; Patents, BT & BY # 3, 146; BC & GS # 28, 507.

28. In the most careful study of intergenerational mobility among the elite, Kulikoff stresses continuity, arguing that the richest families of Prince George's County constituted "a nearly self-perpetuating oligarchy." See *Tobacco and Slaves*, 263. Rutman and Rutman find that four of fifteen sons of fathers who had "high status" in Middlesex County also achieved high status. See *A Place in Time: Explicatus*, 149.

29. William N. Wilkins, comp., "Baltimore County Tax List, 1773", [typescript], Maryland State Archives.

30. Ibid.

31. Baltimore County Debt Books, 1754 through 1771.

32. Inventories & Accounts; Inventories, *passim*.

33. Ibid. It should be remembered that these percentages are based on a small sample: five elite sons could be identified in inventories before 1729, twenty-six between 1730 and 1759, and nine between 1760 and 1776.

34. My understanding of political recruitment patterns in tidewater areas is based primarily on Sydnor, *Gentlemen Freeholders*, 74-85, and Kulikoff, *Tobacco and Slaves*, 261-313. For high rates of turnover among justices of the peace in North Carolina, see A. Roger Ekirch, *"Poor Carolina": Politics and Society in Colonial North Carolina, 1729-1776* (Chapel Hill, N.C., 1981), 172-73. Quote is from Kulikoff, *Tobacco and Slaves*, p. 275.

35. Lists of court justices appear in Baltimore County Court Proceedings, IS # TW2; IS # TW3; IS # TW4; HWS # 6; HS # 7; HWS # 9; HWS # 1A; HWS & TR; TB # TR; TB # D; BA Pt. 1; BA Pt. 2; TB & TR; 1750; TR # 6; BB # A; BB # B; BB # C; BB # D. Data on personal wealth are from Inventories, Baltimore County Inventories, Maryland State Archives.

36. Ibid. For 1746 list of justices, see ibid., BA Pt. 2, 800; TB & TR, 1, 115, 219.

37. Ibid. For a different pattern among office holders of Prince George's County, see Kulikoff, *Tobacco and Slaves*, 271-72.

38. For assemblymen, see Papenfuse et al., eds., *Biographical Dictionary of the Maryland Legislature*.

39. Ibid.

40. Ibid.

41. Ibid.; Inventories; Baltimore County Inventories.

3. The Work Force

1. Two works in particular have shaped my understanding of slavery in the colonial Chesapeake: Morgan, *American Slavery—American Freedom* and Kulikoff, *Tobacco and Slaves*. For herrenvolk democracy, see Pierre L. van den Berghe, *Race and Racism: A Comparative Perspective* (New York, 1967); George M. Fredrickson, *The Black Image in the White Mind: The Debate on Afro-American Character and Destiny, 1817-1914* (New York, 1971), 61-68, 93-96.

2. M. I. Finley, *Ancient Slavery and Modern Ideology* (New York, 1980), 80-81. The tax lists are contained in Wilkins, comp., "Maryland Genealogical Notes"; Wilkins, comp., "Baltimore County Court Records, Joppa, Maryland." For figures on Chesapeake counties, see Richard S. Dunn, "Black Society in the Chesapeake, 1776-1810," in Ira Berlin and Ronald Hoffman, eds., *Slavery and Freedom in the Age of the American Revolution* (Charlottesville, Va., 1983), 54-59, esp. 55, 57.

3. Jean Butenhoff Lee, "The Problem of Slave Community in the Eighteenth-Century Chesapeake," *William and Mary Quarterly,* 3d ser., 43 (1986): 343 (table).

4. The figures for 1692 have been calculated from Wilkins, comp., "Maryland Genealogical Notes." For settlement patterns, see Mathews, *Counties of Maryland,* 442-46; Karinen, "Maryland Population," 390-93.

5. The phrase is borrowed from Willie Lee Rose, "The Domestication of Domestic Slavery," in William W. Freehling, ed., *Slavery and Freedom* (New York, 1982), 18-36. The literature on slavery is enormous, but among the most important general works stressing the adaptive capacities of the slave community are the following: John W. Blassingame, *The Slave Community: Plantation Life in the Antebellum South* (New York, 1979); Eugene D. Genovese, *Roll, Jordan, Roll: The World the Slaves Made* (New York, 1974); Herbert G. Gutman, *The Black Family in Slavery and Freedom, 1750-1925* (New York, 1976); Sterling Stuckey, *Slave Culture: Nationalist Theory and the Foundations of Black America* (New York, 1987). A good survey of the state of the literature is Peter J. Parish, *Slavery: History and Historians* (New York, 1989).

6. Philip D. Morgan and Michael L. Nicholls, "Slaves in Piedmont Virginia, 1720-1790," *William and Mary Quarterly,* 3d ser., 46 (1989): 242-43.

7. For the relatively small size of slaveholdings and the tenuous nature of slave community in eighteenth-century Charles County, Maryland, see Lee, "Problem of Slave Community," 333-61.

8. Kulikoff stresses the dense web of kinship ties that developed within and among slave quarters, but the slaveholdings he describes were much larger than any in Baltimore. Slaveholding among the gentry of Baltimore may have more closely resembled the pattern Kulikoff finds for smaller planters of Prince George's County: in 1776 only 18 percent of slaves on small plantations lived in units with an adult male and adult female. See *Tobacco and Slaves,* 364-71. For a critique of Kulikoff's interpretation and use of evidence, see Lee, "Problem of Slave Community," 333-61. For an analysis of the early development of the quarter system, see Main, *Tobacco Colony,* 128.

9. Maryland State Archives, Inventories, IX, 102-10; LXLVIII, 267-74.

10. For listing of workers at the ironworks, Wilkins, comp., "Baltimore County Tax List, 1773." For the iron industry of the upper Chesapeake, see Ronald L. Lewis, *Coal, Iron, and Slaves: Industrial Slavery in Maryland and*

Virginia, 1715-1865 (Westport, Conn., 1979); Keach Johnson, "The Genesis of the Baltimore Ironworks," *Journal of Southern History* 19 (1953): 157-79; Michael Warren Robbins, "The Principio Company: Iron-Making in Colonial Maryland, 1720-1781" (PhD diss., George Washington University, 1972); Charles G. Steffen, "The Pre-Industrial Iron Worker: Northampton Iron Works, 1780-1820," *Labor History* 20 (1979): 89-110.

11. Wilkins, comp., "Baltimore County Tax List, 1773." Lewis argues that slave ironworkers succeeded in overcoming many of the obstacles to family life, in part by taking advantage of the incentive system of overwork to earn something extra for their wives and children. Our conclusions are not necessarily incompatible because the ironworks he examines employed larger work forces and maintained more evenly balanced sex ratios than any of the furnaces or forges in Baltimore. See *Coal, Iron, and Slaves,* 161-69.

12. Kulikoff argues that this demographic transition underlaid the development of slave communities in the Chesapeake. See *Tobacco and Slaves,* 352-80.

13. For the larger estates, see idem, *Tobacco and Slaves,* 320-24. For evidence on the small number of slave artisans in Talbot County, see Russo, "Self-sufficiency and Local Exchange," 409-10.

14. Idem, "Self-sufficiency and Local Exchange," 373; Gerald W. Mullin, *Flight and Rebellion: Slave Resistance in Eighteenth-Century Virginia* (New York, 1972), 83-123.

15. David Walter Galenson, *White Servitude in Colonial America: An Economic Analysis* (Cambridge, 1981).

16. For a good analysis of household composition in Talbot County, see Clemens, *Atlantic Economy and Colonial Maryland's Eastern Shore,* 146. Note also the high rates of geographic mobility among the inmates of households in Lunenburg County in Beeman, *Evolution of the Southern Backcountry,* 70.

17. For leases that specified acerage and rent, see Maryland State Archives, Baltimore County Land Records, BB # I, 117-18; AL # E, 379-83; B # I, 44-46; TB # A, 161-63; IS # I, 68; TB # C, 33-34, 198-99, 248-49; TR # P, 24-25; B # Q, 188-96; B # L, 454-58; HWS # IA, 51-52, 107-9, 338-40; AL # A, 267-68; B # M, 54-56; B # N, 327-29. For studies on tenancy in the Chesapeake, see Kulikoff, *Tobacco and Slaves,* 132-35; Gregory A. Stiverson, *Poverty in a Land of Plenty: Tenancy in Eighteenth-Century Maryland* (Baltimore, 1977); Williard F. Bliss, "The Rise of Tenancy in Virginia," *Virginia Magazine of History and Biography* 58 (1950): 427-41.

18. Baltimore County Land Records, TR # C, 137-39; B # Q, 189-92; B # L, 454-58. For the shift to short-term leases, see Lorena S. Walsh, "Land, Landlord, and Leaseholder: Estate Management and Tenant Fortunes in Southern Maryland, 1642-1820," *Agricultural History* 59 (1985): 386-87.

19. The principal collections used here are Maryland Historical Society, Ridgely Account Books, MS 691; Ridgely Papers, MS 692.

20. For bequests of Robert and Charles, see Inventories and Accounts, VIII, 295-302; VII, 271-74; Will Book # 3, 703-705. For Robert's life, see Anne C. Edmonds, "The Land Holdings of the Ridgelys of Hampton, 1726-1843" (MA thesis, Johns Hopkins University, 1959), 116; Henry Ridgely Evans, *Founders of the Colonial Families of Ridgely, Dorsey, and Greenberry, of Maryland* (Washington, D.C., 1935), 14-16. For Robert's offices, see Donald M. Owings, *His Lordship's Patronage: Offices of Profit in Colonial Maryland* (Baltimore, 1953), 126, 128, 140. For Robert's legal career, see Alan F. Day, "A Social Study of Lawyers in Maryland" (PhD diss., Johns Hopkins University, 1976), 1041-43.

21. For the estate of the colonel's father, see Inventories and Accounts, Will Book # 3, 703-705. For Patapsco purchases, see Baltimore County Land Records, IS # H, 294-96; IS # L, 72-74, 80-82. For gift to John, see Baltimore County Land Records, TR # C, 18-20. For effects of high mortality rates, see Rutman and Rutman, "Of Agues and Fevers," 31-60.

22. For Gunpowder purchases, see Baltimore County Land Records, TB # D, 94-97; TB # E, 161-71, 286-89, 292-303, 474-78, 481-83, 487-89, 642-44, 658-62; B # H, 98-100. For total landholdings, see "Land in Quit Rent Book of 1757, Charged to Chas. Ridgely," box 15, Ridgely Papers.

23. Wilkins, comp., "Baltimore County Court Records, Joppa, Maryland."

24. Ibid.

25. For the Arnall households, see idem, "Baltimore County Court Records, Joppa, Maryland," 28, 37, 46. For debt to Okeson, see Ledger 1735, box 1, 42, Ridgely Account Books. For Arnall accounts, see Ledger 1734, box 1, 20, 24, 31.

26. Baltimore County Court Proceedings, HWS # TR, 11-12.

27. Daybook 1745, box 1, ca. Oct. 1745; Daybook 1748, box 2, on back leaf. All daybooks are located in Ridgely Account Books.

28. Daybook 1746-47, box 1, Dec. 8, 1747.

29. Daybook 1746-47, Dec. 8, 1747. The contracts were written on the back of pages that were later bound up in Daybook 1741, box 1. For the importance of the convict trade in Maryland, see Richard S. Dunn, "Servants and Slaves: The Recruitment and Employment of Labor," in Jack P. Greene and J.R. Pole, eds., *Colonial British America: Essays in the New History of the Early Modern Era* (Baltimore, 1984), 170-71; A. Roger Ekirch, *Bound for America: The Transportation of British Convicts to the Colonies, 1718-1775* (Oxford, 1987), 142.

30. Daybook 1746-47, Nov. 7, July 20, Nov. 2, 1747, Jan. 13, 23, 1748; Forest Daybook 1748, box 1, Mar. 1, 23, 1748. The Forest Daybook is bound with the Daybook 1746-47.

31. Forest Daybook 1748, Feb. 1748.

32. Daybook 1748, Jan. 13, 1748; Daybook 1746-47, Oct. 26, 1747.

33. Daybook 1746-47, Feb. 8, 29, 1748; Clarence P. Gould, *The Land System in Maryland, 1720-1765,* Johns Hopkins University Studies, XXXI, no. 1 (Baltimore, 1913), 74.

34. Daybook 1747-47, Oct. 26, 1747, Feb. 22, 1748. For the importance of free craftsmen on large plantations in Talbot County, see Russo, "Self-sufficiency and Local Exchange," 426-29.

35. Daybook 1742-43, 1745, box 2, Mar. 28, 1743; Daybook 1745, Aug. 22, 1745; Daybook 1746-47, Dec. 12, Nov. 9, Sep. 24, June 15, 1747.

36. Daybook 1746-47, June 2, 27, 1747, Nov. 30, 1748; Daybook 1742-43, 1745, Apr. 29, May 4, 1745; Daybook 1753-55, box 2, Aug. (?), Dec. 8, 12, 1755; Baltimore County Court Proceedings, BB # C, 66-69. For Pennsylvania labor practices, see Paul G.E. Clemens and Lucy Simler, "Rural Labor and the Farm Household in Chester County, Pennsylvania, 1750-1820," in Innes, ed., *Work and Labor in Early America,* 106-43. For a description of Robert Carter's relationship with his tenants, see Louis Morton, *Robert Carter of Nomini Hall: A Virginia Tobacco Planter in the Eighteenth Century* (Charlottesville, Va., 1941), 74-75.

37. Daybook 1753-55, box 2, Feb. 7, Sep. 6, 1755.

4. The Landed Estate

1. Maryland State Archives, Baltimore County Debt Books, 1754 through 1771 .

2. Ibid.

3. These data have been drawn from an analysis of Baltimore County Land Records, Maryland State Archives. For the speculative activities of two prominent provincial gentlemen, see Aubrey C. Land, *The Dulanys of Maryland: A Biographical Study of Daniel Dulany, the Elder (1685-1753) and Daniel Dulany, the Younger (1722-1797)* (Baltimore, 1955); Morton, *Robert Carter of Nomini Hall.*

4. Baltimore County Land Records.

5. Ibid.; Wilkins, comp., "Baltimore County Court Records, Joppa, Maryland."

6. Baltimore County Land Records.

7. Ibid.; Wilkins, comp., "Baltimore County Court Records, Joppa, Maryland."

8. For Webster-Giles transactions, see Baltimore County Land Records, HWS # M, 12-14, 394-97; TB # C, 349-51; TB # A, 121-23; HWS # 1A, 1-2, 7-12, 18-19, 126-28, 133-34, 173-84, 222-24, 226-30, 432-34; TB # E, 392-94, 412-14; IS # IK, 373-76, 385-90, 520-26, 528-32. For the decline in land speculation on the Eastern Shore, see Clemens, *Atlantic Economy and Maryland's Eastern Shore,* 70-76. Nor has Beeman found evidence of speculation among the Lunenburg County elite. See *Evolution of the Southern Backcountry,* 71.

9. For the gentry as profit-maximizing capitalists, see Land, "Economic Base and Social Structure," 639-54; idem, "Economic Behavior in a Planting Society," 469-85. For an argument that both small and large planters in western Virginia were speculators, see Robert D. Mitchell, *Commercialism and the Frontier: Perspectives on the Early Shenandoah Valley* (Charlottesville, Va., 1977), 79-80.

10. For evidence on the prevailing pattern of partible inheritance in the colonial Chesapeake, see Jean Butenhoff Lee, "Land and Labor: Parental Bequest Practices in Charles County, Maryland, 1732-1783," in Carr, Morgan, and Russo, eds., *Colonial Chesapeake Society*, 306-41; C. Ray Keim, "Primogeniture and Entail in Colonial Virginia," *William and Mary Quarterly*, 3d ser., 25 (1966): 545-86; Joan R. Gundeersen and Gwen Victor Gampel, "Married Women's Legal Status in Eighteenth-Century New York and Virginia," ibid., 39 (1982): 122; Daniel Blake Smith, *Inside the Great House*, 231-48; Linda E. Speth, "More Than Her 'Thirds': Wives and Widows in Colonial Virginia," in Linda E. Speth and Alison Duncan Hirsch, *Women, Family, and Community in Colonial America: Two Perspectives* (New York, 1982), 5-42; James W. Deen, Jr., "Patterns of Testation: Four Tidewater Counties in Colonial Virginia," *American Journal of Legal History* 16 (1972): 158-59. Martin H. Quitt links the practice of partible inheritance among the gentlemen of early Virginia to their unhappy experiences in England. See "Immigrant Origins of the Virginia Gentry: A Study of Cultural Transmission and Innovation," *William and Mary Quarterly*, 3d ser., 45 (1988): 648. For the logic of partibility in a patriarchal setting, see Kulikoff, *Tobacco and Slaves*, 199-200. The pattern of partibility seems to have continued among antebellum planters. See James Oakes, *Slavery and Freedom: An Interpretation of the Old South* (New York, 1990), 90-91.

11. For a discussion of intestacy law, see Lee, "Land and Labor," 314-15, 330. Quote from Gundersen and Gampel, "Married Women's Legal Status," 120.

12. Unless otherwise noted, the data in this chapter have been derived from an examination of the elite's wills found in Wills; Baltimore County Wills, Maryland State Archives.

13. For the factors behind the practice of leaving land to the youngest son, see James A. Henretta, "Families and Farms: *Mentalité* in Pre-Industrial America," *William and Mary Quarterly*, 3d ser., 35 (1978): 27.

14. For a similar pattern in Virginia, see Deen, "Patterns of Testation," 158.

15. Wills, XXVII, 280-82.

16. For daughters, see Wills, XVII, 230-32; XXV, 561-63; Baltimore County Wills, II, 6-10, 191-92; III, 46-47, 89-90, 267. Lee finds that 23 percent of daughters received land in eighteenth-century Charles County. See "Land and Labor," 323. The lower figure undoubtedly reflects the fact that she has aggregated all wills, irrespective of the testator's economic standing,

whereas I have focused on the richest 10 percent of decedents who had more land to devise to their sons and daughters.

17. For the status of colonial widows, see Marylynn Salmon, *Women and the Law of Property in Early America* (Chapel Hill, N.C., 1986); Alexander Keyssar, "Widowhood in Eighteenth-Century Massachusetts: A Problem in the History of the Family," *Perspectives in American History* 8 (1974): 82-119; Christine H. Tompsett, "A Note on the Economic Status of Widows in Colonial New York," *New York History* 55 (1974): 318-22; Kim Lacy Rogers, "Relicts of the New World: Conditions of Widowhood in Seventeenth-Century New England," in Mary Kelley, ed., *Woman's Being, Woman's Place: Female Identity and Vocation in American History* (Boston, 1979), 26-52; Lois Green Carr and Lorena S. Walsh, "The Planter's Wife: The Experience of White Women in Seventeeth-Century Maryland," *William and Mary Quarterly,* 3d ser., 34 (1977): 542-71.

18. Baltimore County Wills, I, 142-43, 494-98; II, 297-99; III, 205-8.

19. Ibid., III, 214-16, 299-303, 317; Wills, XXXIV, 526-28.

20. Baltimore County Wills, III, 206. For a similar pattern in Charles County, where testators increasingly granted their daughters land in fee simple or as tenants until their marriage or death, see Lee, "Land and Labor," 324-25, 341.

21. Baltimore County Wills, III, 46-47, 174, 200-201, 314-15.

22. Ibid., I, 215; II, 60-61, 203-205; III, 56-57.

23. Unless otherwise noted, data on deeds of gift have been derived from an examination of Baltimore County Land Records, Maryland State Archives. For a sweeping interpretation of the rise of the companionate family in England, see Lawrence Stone, *Family, Sex and Marriage in England, 1500-1800* (New York, 1977).

24. For Buchanan, see Baltimore County Land Records, TR # C, 369-70; TR # D, 307-308; Wills, XXVII, 280-82.

25. For gifts of slaves, see Baltimore County Land Records, TR # C, 369-70; B # H, 420-24; HWS # 1A, 50, 333-34; IS # L, 334, 335; HWS # M, 249-56, 301; IS # G, 196; TR # A, 368-69; IS # H, 202, 237; TR # RA, 421; TB # C, 636, 640.

26. Ibid. For Ravens see, HWS # M, 249-53; IS # H, 268-72. For Wheeler, see B # P, 388-91. For Tolley, see, IS # L, 181-83.

27. Ibid. For gifts to daughters see, BB # I, 31-32, 210-12; TR # RA, 421; HWS # M, 253-56; AL # E, 357-61; TB # C, 636, 640; IS # G, 196; HWS # 1A, 334. For gifts to sons-in-law see, AL # B, 29-31; RM # HS, 569-71; TR # A, 207; HW # 2, 50-51; IS # H, 202. For gifts to sons-in-law and daughters jointly see, BB # I, 32-33, 424-25; IS # H, 200-202.

28. Ibid. For Stokes see, IS # H, 202. See also Speth, "More Than Her 'Thirds', " 9; Marylynn Salmon, "Equality or Submersion? Femme Convert Status in Early Pennsylvania," in Carolyn R. Berkin and Mary Beth Norton, eds., *Women of America: A History* (Boston, 1979), 98-101, 108-11.

29. For gifts to extended kinsmen, see Baltimore County Land Records, AL # B, 27-28; HWS # 1A, 50; IS # G, 218-19. For gifts to friends see, TR # RA, 343, 350-51, 377-78, 444-46; TR # A, 79.

30. Ibid., Al # B, 27-28; B # H, 420-24; BB # I, 31-33, 210-12; TR # C, 18-20; AL # A, 682-85; B # L, 83-88. For an interesting parallel with a Georgia planter, see Alan Gallay, "Jonathan Bryan's Plantation Empire: Land, Politics, and the Formation of a Ruling Class in Colonial Georgia," *William and Mary Quarterly,* 3d ser., 45 (1988): 266.

5. The Merchant Community

1. My understanding of the larger institutional and economic context within which Baltimore's merchants operated is based chiefly on the scholarship of Jacob M. Price. See especially his *France and the Chesapeake; Capital and Credit;* "Economic Growth of the Chesapeake"; "Rise of Glasgow"; "Buchanan & Simpson"; and "Last Phase of the Virginia-London Consignment Trade."

2. On planter-merchants, see the essays by Aubrey C. Land: "Economic Base and Social Structure"; and "Economic Behavior in a Planting Society." It is impossible to speak precisely about the numerical distribution of merchants in the Chesapeake colonies, but one study suggests that between 250 and 300 merchants were active in Virginia in 1773. At the same time Baltimore County alone could boast of around one hundred merchants. See Peter V. Bergstrom, *Markets and Merchants: Economic Diversification in Colonial Virginia, 1700-1775* (New York, 1985), 219.

3. For overviews of these economic developments, see Price, *France and the Chesapeake,* I, 509-30; Paul G.E. Clemens, *The Atlantic Economy and Colonial Maryland's Eastern Shore,* 29-40; McCusker and Menard, *The Economy of British America, 1607-1789,* 117-43.

4. The ten merchants who left inventories were Richard Colegate, Thomas Bale, Edward Stevenson, Roger Newman, William Marshall, John Israel, James Crooke, Mark Swift, Richard King, and Thomas Hedge. Of these, the first eight also left accounts, from which it was possible to determine net worth. See Inventories and Accounts, Maryland State Archives.

5. Maryland State Archives, Baltimore County Land Records, TR # RA, 316, 329-31; HW # 2, 106-107, 152, 196-98; TR # A, 231-33; IR # PP, 156-58; IR # AM, 15-17; RM # HS, 220-22, 300-302, 368; IS # G, 254-55; Patents, XVII, 463, Inventories and Accounts, XIX, 142-44.

6. Baltimore County Land Records, TR # A, 231-32; Maryland State Archives, Inventories, IX, 102-10. For first-generation cargos, see Inventories and Accounts, XVI, 121-123; Browne et al., eds., *Archives of Maryland,* LXVIII, 33-34.

7. Baltimore County Land Records, HWS # M, 386-88; TR # A, 231-33. It was possible to locate most of the merchants' residences, which clus-

tered around the Patapsco, from their land patents and deeds. In some instances there is an explicit reference: Richard Colegate "Mercht. in Patapsco River" or Roger Newman's "dwelling plantation" on the Patapsco. See Baltimore County Land Records, HW # 2, 321; Maryland State Archives, Wills, III, 258-59.

8. Wills, XVII, 230-33; Inventories, IX, 102-10.

9. For guardians, see Maryland State Archives, Baltimore County Court Proceedings, IS # TW4, 32; IS # H, 322, 326; HWS # 1A, 100, 139. For Benjamin's estate, see Inventories, LXLVII, 77-79; Accounts, LVIII, 400-403. For problems of orphans, see Darrett B. Rutman and Anita H. Rutman, " 'Now-Wives and Sons-in-Law': Parental Death in a Seventeenth-Century Virginia County," in Tate and Ammerman, eds., *Chesapeake in the Seventeenth Century,* 153-82; Lois Green Carr, "The Development of the Maryland Orphans' Court, 1654-1715," in Land, Carr, and Papenfuse, eds., *Law, Society, and Politics in Early Maryland,* 41-62.

10. For the emergence of this native elite, see Bailyn, "Politics and Social Structure in Virginia," 90-115; Jordan, *Foundations of Representative Government in Maryland,* 141-82; David W. Jordan, "Political Stability and the Emergence of a Native Elite in Maryland," in Tate and Ammerman, eds., *Chesapeake in the Seventeenth Century,* 243-73; Carole Shammas, "English-Born and Creole Elites in Turn-of-the-Century Virginia," ibid., 274-96.

11. These data have been calculated from lists of assemblymen in Papenfuse et al., *Biographical Dictionary of the Maryland Legislature,* I, 35-43.

12. These data have been calculated from lists of justices in Baltimore County Court Proceedings, IS # B, IS # A, IS # C, IS # TW1.

13. Gregory A. Stiverson and Phebe R. Jacobsen, *William Paca: A Biography* (Baltimore, 1976), 25-31.

14. See notes 11 and 12.

15. For analyses of similar confrontations elsewhere in the Chesapeake, see John C. Rainbolt, "The Alteration in the Relationship between Leadership and Constituents in Virginia, 1660 to 1720," *William and Mary Quarterly,* 3d ser., 27 (1970): 411-34; Kulikoff, *Tobacco and Slaves,* 280-300.

16. Bacon, ed., *Laws of Maryland,* Chap. XIV, Apr. 1706; Chap. XVI, Apr. 1707; Mathews, *The Counties of Maryland,* 445.

17. Baltimore County Court Proceedings, IS # A, 71.

18. Ibid., 96-97.

19. Ibid., 182, 185.

20. Ibid., 288; Browne et al. eds., *Archives of Maryland,* XXIX, 51.

21. Baltimore County Court Proceedings, IS # A, 313.

22. Browne et al., eds., *Archives of Maryland,* XXIX, 88, 136, 144 (quote).

23. Ibid., LXLVII, 149-50, 193 (quote), 272, 274-75. For law, see Bacon, ed., *Laws of Maryland,* Chap. XIX, Nov. 1712.

24. Baltimore County Court Proceedings, IS # A, 334.

25. These data have been calculated from analysis of Inventories; Account; Baltimore County Land Records.

26. Kulikoff, *Tobacco and Slaves*, 109-16; Mary McKinney Schweitzer, "Economic Regulation and the Colonial Economy: The Maryland Tobacco Inspection Act of 1747," *Journal of Economic History* 40 (1980): 551-69. For the importance of debts receivable in merchant estates, see Carville V. Earle, *The Evolution of a Tidewater Settlement System: All Hallow's Parish, Maryland, 1650-1783*, University of Chicago Department of Geography Research Papers No. 170 (Chicago, 1975), 75.

27. In addition to Wills, the biographical information has been culled from Dielman File, Maryland Historical Society.

28. For property holdings of fathers, see Wills, II, 162-66; III, 238-39; XVIII, 350-51; Baltimore County Land Records, TR # DS, 254; IS # G, 395; RM # HS, 453, 601; IR # AM, 3, 5, 181-83, 193-95; TR # RA, 534; TR # A, 241, 249; Patents, CC # 4, 141; DD # 5, 136, 211; DS # F, 411; PL # 6, 292; WC # 2, 66. For personal estates, see Inventories & Accounts, WB # 3, 287-89; Inventories, XI, 196-98, 458-63; Will Book # 3, 703-705. For younger sons, see Wills, XVIII, 350-51, 429-30; XXIX, 274-75; Edmonds, "The Land Holdings of the Ridgelys of Hampton," 116.

29. Baltimore County Land Records, IS # L, 218, 367-69; HWS # M, 339-43; IR # PP, 192-95; TR # RA, 482-84; Dielman File; *Maryland Gazette*, Apr. 12, 1753.

30. Wills, XXIII, 150-55; Baltimore County Land Records, IS # H, 253-64; HWS # 1A, 84-85; IS # IK, 509-13; TB # E, 41-42; HWS # M, 75, 114-15; IS # I, 178-81, 224-27; Baltimore County Court Proceedings, HWS # 9, 206; Inventories, XXIII, 1-3; Accounts, IX, 469; *Maryland Gazette*, Mar. 15, 1755; Ethan Allen, *The Garrison Church: Sketches of the History of St. Thomas' Parish, Garrison Forest, Baltimore County, Maryland, 1742-1852* (New York, 1898), 144.

31. Wills, XXV, 561-63; John Ridgely to Charles Ridgely, Jr., May 26, 1758, box 1, Ridgely Papers, Ms 692.1. Most of the marital connections and church affiliations can be traced through Fred Barnes, comp., *Maryland Marriages, 1634-1777* (Baltimore, 1975).

32. Wilkins, comp., "Baltimore County Court Records, Joppa, Maryland." In the inventory of merchant Isaac Webster, fourteen desperate debtors were listed as dead, eleven as "ranaway," and one as a "Begar." See Inventories, LXX, 20-21. For similar credit networks in early Maryland, see James Horn, "Adapting to a New World: A Comparative Study of Local Society in England and Maryland, 1650-1700," in Carr, Morgan, and Russo, eds., *Colonial Chesapeake Society*, 167-68.

33. These data have been calculated through an examination of Baltimore County Court Proceedings.

34. Maryland Historical Society, Ridgely Account Books, Ms 691, box 1, Ledger 1734, Ledger 1735.

35. For Parrish, see Ledger 1734, pp. 29, 30; Ledger 1735, pp. 10, 24, 27. For a discussion of eighteenth-century bookkeeping, see Baxter, *The House of Hancock*, 11-38.

36. Ledger 1735, pp. 5, 9, 17; Ledger 1734, pp. 2, 27.

37. Wilkins, comp., "Baltimore County Court Records"; Baltimore County Land Records; Rent Rolls, Maryland State Archives.

38. Ledger 1734, pp. 19, 25, 29; Ledger 1735, p. 49. For artisans, see Earle, *Evolution of a Tidewater Settlement System*, 64-68; Russo, "Self-sufficiency and Local Exchange."

39. Wilkins, comp., "Baltimore County Court Records."

40. Clemens, *Atlantic Economy and Colonial Maryland's Eastern Shore*, 136-61. For a sensitive analysis of the "etiquette of debt," see Breen, *Tobacco Culture*, 95-96.

41. The data on Ridgely's court cases have been compiled from Baltimore County Court Proceedings; Maryland State Archives, Anne Arundel County Court Judgments. For Hopkins, see Baltimore County Court Proceedings, HWS # 1A, 32-34.

42. Baltimore County Court Proceedings; Anne Arundel County Court Judgments; Ledger 1734; Ledger 1735.

43. Baltimore County Court Proceedings, HS # 7, 52; HS # 9, 132; TB # TR, 151.

44. Baltimore County Court Proceedings; Anne Arundel County Court Judgments.

6. The Established Church

1. David C. Skaggs and Gerald E. Hartdagen, "Sinners and Saints: Anglican Clerical Conduct in Colonial Maryland," *Historical Magazine of the Protestant Episcopal Church* 47 (1978): 177-95.

2. University of Maryland Library, College Park, Fulham Papers, Lambeth Palace Library, [microfilm], General Correspondence, Vols. 2-3, item 215. For an account of Reverend Tibbs, see Francis F. Beirne, *St. Paul's Parish, Baltimore: A Chronicle of the Mother Church* (Baltimore, 1967), 261-72.

3. Fulham Papers, General Correspondence, Vols. 2-3, item 216. When Todd died in 1716, his estate was appraised at £657, making him the fourth richest among 131 probate decedents in the period 1700-19. See Maryland State Archives, Baltimore County Inventories, V, 7-9, 312-13,

4. Maryland State Archives, Baltimore County Court Proceedings, IS A # 3, 605; GM, 25; *Maryland Historical Magazine* 15 (1920): 306-10.

5. Perry, ed., *Historical Collections of the American Colonial Church*, IV, 309-10; Maryland State Archives, Wills, XX, 449-50.

6. Baltimore County Court Proceedings, HWS # 6, 69-70; Maryland State Archives, St. George's Parish, Vestry Minutes, 1718-1771, 24, 37.

7. Maryland State Archives, Baltimore County Land Records, HWS # 1A, 494-95; TB # C, 12; IS # K, 283-89; St. George's Parish, Vestry Minutes, 1718-1771, 53-55; Rightmyer, *Maryland's Established Church,* 219.

8. For Reverend Chase's career, see Rosamond Randall Beirne, "The Reverend Thomas Chase: Pugnacious Parson," *Maryland Historical Magazine* 59 (1964): 1-14. For moderate Enlightenment, see Henry F. May, *The Enlightenment in America* (New York, 1976), 3-101.

9. My understanding of Reverend Cradock owes a great debt to David Curtis Skaggs, whose studies include: "The Great Chain of Being in Eighteenth-Century Maryland: The Paradox of Thomas Cradock," *Historical Magazine of the Protestant Episcopal Church* 45 (1976): 155-64; "Thomas Cradock and the Chesapeake Golden Age," *William and Mary Quarterly,* 3d ser., 30 (1973): 93-116; *The Poetic Writings of Thomas Cradock, 1718-1770* (East Brunswick, N.J., 1983).

10. Skaggs, ed., *The Poetic Writings of Thomas Cradock,* 25-43; Allen, *Garrison Church,* 8-26; J. A. Leo Lemay, *Men of Letters in Colonial Maryland* (Knoxville, Tenn., 1972), 229-30.

11. Sermon on II Peter 3:3, 4, f. 3; Sermon on Malachi 3:6, ff. 8, 9, 25. Many of these sermons have not been cataloged. When uncataloged sermons do not carry a title or date, they have been identified by the Scriptural passage that is the subject of the text. All sermons are in Maryland Diocesan Archives, on deposit in Maryland Historical Society.

12. Reverend Eversfield's comments are contained in a work apparently intended as a textbook in philosophy, whose title page reads: "A Small Treatise of Morality interspersed with usefull observations relating to the Expediency & Benefit of a Revelation Design'd for the Instruction of Religious & Honest Planters in their Duty to God their Neighbors & themselves according to the Law of Nature [1735]", f. 143, Maryland Diocesan Archives. For Reverend Addison, see Sermon, ca. 1760, ff. 15-16.

13. Sermon on Rejoicing, f. 4; Sermon on Acts 24:25, ff. 9, 10, 11.

14. Reverend Cradock's sermon was published in *Two Sermons, with a Preface Shewing the AUTHOR's Reason for Publishing Them* (Annapolis, 1747), 2. For Reverend Chase, see Sermon on 1 Tim. 6:1, ff. 10-12, 14-15; Sermon on Matthew 14:23, f. 17.

15. A Small Treatise, ff. 105, 129. Reverend Eversfield wrote that on this topic the works of John Locke and Samuel Clarke were "the best of any writing I ever met with" (f. 138).

16. Sermon on Matthew 11:5, f. 11; Sermon on Luke 16:29, f. 21; William B. Sprague, *Annals of the American Pulpit; or Commemorative Notices of Distinguished American Clergymen of Various Denominations, from the Earliest Settlement of the Country to the Close of the Year Eighteen Hundred and Fifty-five,* 8 vols. (New York, 1859-65), V, 115.

17. Sermon on 1 Thess. 5:21, ff. 3-4; Sermon on Acts 24:25, 26, f. 2.

18. Perry, ed., *Historical Collections of the American Colonial Church,* IV, 190-92.

19. Skaggs, ed., *Poetic Writings of Thomas Cradock.*

20. Maryland State Archives, Wills, XX, 345-47.

21. Ibid., XXII, 249-50; Baltimore County Inventories, VI, 217-25; Maryland State Archives, Inventories, XXVIII, 422-27.

22. For Young and Smith, see Inventories, XVII, 558-69; CXIX, 193-201; CXX, 1-13, 29-30.

23. For Crockett, see Inventories, XXII, 92-103.

24. For Heath, see Baltimore County Inventories, II, 183-94; V, 149-56.

25. Ibid.

26. For the conventional reading tastes of Virginia gentlemen, see Greene, "Society, Ideology, and Politics," 43-44.

27. For example, Rhys Isaac explains the appeal of Anglicanism to "humbler persons" in this way: "Such persons might take pleasure in admiring the magnificence of the great and in deferentially receiving attentions bestowed on them from above." See *Transformation of Virginia, 1740-1790* (Chapel Hill, N.C., 1982), 65.

28. For a list of lay officers of St. Paul's Parish, see Beirne, *St. Paul's Parish, Baltimore,* 261-72. The data on office and wealth holding have been derived from an examination of Inventories and Accounts, Inventories, and Baltimore County Court Proceedings. In the older parts of the colonies, about half of the white families attended Anglican service. See Kulikoff, *Tobacco and Slaves,* 234.

29. Sermon on 1 Thess. 5:21, ff. 3-4; Sermon on Ecc. 4:9, f. 5.

30. Sermon on 1 John 4:8 (1768), f. 1.

31. Sermon on Job 29:11, 12, 13, ff. 1, 2.

32. Sermon on Reputation, ff. 1, 2; Sermon on Lev. 19:12 (1763), f. 3.

33. Sermon on Wealth, ff. 3, 4.

34. Sermon on Prov. 13:11, ff. 3, 4, 5, 7-8, 12, 13.

35. Sermon on Christian Conduct, ff. 5, 6, 7. For the convergence of gentry and yeomen religious beliefs in South Carolina, see Rachel N. Klein, *Unification of a Slave State: The Rise of the Planter Class in the South Carolina Backcountry, 1760-1808* (Chapel Hill, N.C., 1990), 271.

7. Baltimore Town

1. For accounts of the early development of Baltimore Town, see J. Thomas Scharf, *The Chronicles of Baltimore; Being a Complete History of "Baltimore Town" and Baltimore City from the Earliest Period to the Present Time* (Baltimore, 1874); Clarence P. Gould, "The Economic Causes of the Rise of Baltimore," in *Essays in Colonial History Presented to Charles*

McLean Andrews by His Students (New Haven, Conn., 1931), 225-51; Paul Kent Walker, "The Baltimore Community and the American Revolution: A Study in Urban Development, 1763-1783" (PhD. diss., University of North Carolina at Chapel Hill, 1973).

2. The activities of the town commissioners and the sale of lots can be followed in *First Records of Baltimore Town and Jones' Town, 1729-1797* (Baltimore, 1905).

3. In addition to works cited in note 1, see McCusker and Menard, *Economy of British America*, 144-68, 189-208.

4. These data have been derived from an examination of all transactions involving Baltimore Town land recorded in the Baltimore County Land Records, Maryland State Archives.

5. Ibid., TR # D, 265-67; B # Q, 342-48; B # H, 219-21; B # M, 43-50. For Croxall, see B # H, 25-26.

6. Ibid., TR # D, 518-20.

7. For Lot No. 47, see ibid., B # N, 298-301; B # P, 657-60; AL # A, 100-103, 379-80; B # H, 9-10; IS # L, 192-93; B # L, 379-82, 473-80, 483-90; B # M, 1-5, 18-23, 43-50, 328-33.

8. For a synthesis of major developments in eighteenth-century urban society, see Gary B. Nash, *The Urban Crucible: Social Change, Political Consciousness, and the Origins of the American Revolution* (Cambridge, 1979).

9. Maryland State Archives, Baltimore County Debt Books, 1754-71.

10. These figures have been computed from Wilkins, comp., "Baltimore County Court Records, Joppa, Maryland"; idem, "Baltimore County Tax List, 1773." See table 4; For 1782 figures, see Dunn, "Black Society in the Chesapeake." For Prince George's, see Kulikoff, *Tobacco and Slaves*, 137 (table).

11. Based on analysis of Baltimore County Land Records.

12. Ibid., TR # C, 419-22; TR # D, 61-63; BB # I, 539-40, 568-70, 679-81; B # G, 25-26, 292-93, 312-15, 359-61, 368-71, 442-49, 461-64, 488-90; B # H, 4-5, 14-16, 32-48, 56-57, 83-84, 100-101, 169-71, 210-12, 309-11; B # I, 3-12, 65-66; B # K, 122-26, 153-55, 185-87, 275-78, 299-301; AL # A, 218-20, 323-24; B # L, 303-306; B # O, 133-36, 321-25; B # P, 131-35, 383-85; B # Q, 11-14, 607-609; AL # B, 674-76.

13. Papenfuse et al., eds., *Biographical Dictionary of the Maryland Legislature*, I:414. For land transactions, see Baltimore County Land Records, BB # I, 90-91, 205, 245-46, 263-64, 285-87, 369-70, 372-73, 545, 622, 629, 672-73; B # G, 8, 137, 342-45, 520-21; TR # D, 306-307, 378-80; B # M, 453-58; B # P, 87-91; B # H, 11-14, 24-25, 76-78, 93-95, 107-109, 132-34, 156-58, 179-81, 284-87, 288-89, 261-67, 395-98, 442-45, 460-63; B # K, 79-84, 98-102, 263-64, 290-91; AL # G, 19-22; B # O, 278-82, 343-47, 352-55, 375-79; B # I, 56-59, 84-87, 91-94, 117-23, 130-32, 137-40, 144-50, 212-22, 346-50, 376-80; B # L, 180-83, 253-57, 336-40, 458-64; B # N,

73-77; AL # I, 345-59, 427-34; AL # F, 467-73, 481-88; AL # B, 292-99, 400-402; AL # N, 451-58; AL # D, 224-32, 238-43, 285-89, 295-99, 312-21; AL # O, 449-55; AL # H, 185-93, 328-35; AL # K, 139-49, 402-14; AL # A, 240-43, 368-71; AL # H, 380-85; AL # C, 37-40; AL # M, 1-8, 124-31.

14. Baltimore County Land Records, AL # D, 52-57, 301-306; AL # E, 13-18.

15. Price has developed these points in the following: *Capital and Credit;* "Buchanan & Simpson," "The Last Phase of the Virginia-London Consignment Trade"; "The Rise of Glasgow"; "The Economic Growth of the Chesapeake." For other studies of the store system, see J. H. Soltow, "Scottish Factors in Virginia, 1750-1775," *Economic History Review* 12 (1959): 83-98; John W. Tyler, "Foster Cunliffe and Sons: Liverpool Merchants in the Maryland Tobacco Trade, 1738-1765," *Maryland Historical Magazine* 73 (1978): 246-79; Bergstrom, *Markets and Merchants,* 163-87. For a good study of an independent merchant community, see Rutman and Rutman, *Place in Time: Middlesex County,* 204-33. The first "Scotch store" was not established in Baltimore until 1768. See Pamela Satek, "William Lux of Baltimore: 18th Century Merchant" (Master's thesis, University of Maryland, College Park, 1974), 78.

16. William Molleson to Charles Ridgely, Jr., Oct. 25, 1765; James Russell and Molleson to Charles Ridgely, Jr., Nov. 20, 1763; Joseph Grundill to Charles Ridgely, Jr., Sept. 9, 1765; James Russell to Charles Ridgely, Jr., Dec. 10, 1765; all in box 1, MS 692.1, Ridgely Papers, Maryland Historical Society; Satek, "William Lux of Baltimore," 80. On Russell, see Jacob M. Price, "One Family's Empire: The Russell-Lee-Clark Connection in Maryland, Britain, and India, 1707-1857," *Maryland Historical Magazine* 72 (1977): 165-225.

17. Charles Ridgely, Jr., to Russell and Molleson, [Sept.?], 1763; Russell and Molleson to Charles Ridgely, Jr., Nov. 12, 1763; Charles Ridgely, Jr., to Mildred and Roberts, July 25, 1764; Charles Ridgely, Jr., to Russell and Molleson, Oct. 8, 1764; all in box 1, Ridgely Papers.

18. "Mr. Charles Ridgely in Accot. Curt. with James Russell," [1786], box 2, Ridgely Papers.

19. Charles Ridgely, Jr., to Mildred and Roberts, Sept. 28, 1764; Russell to Charles Ridgely, Jr., March 3, 1766; both in box 1, Ridgely Papers. Baltimore County Land Records, B # L, 83-88; Maryland State Archives, Chancery Record, BT # 1, 84-90.

20. For similar commercial careers in Virginia, see Bergstrom, *Markets and Merchants,* 187-88.

21. Walker, "Baltimore Community and the American Revolution," 131-42; Ronald A. Hoffman, *A Spirit of Dissension: Economics, Politics, and the Revolution in Maryland* (Baltimore, 1973), 36-43. For the Luxes, see Maryland State Archives, Wills, XXVII, 403-4; Box 6, folder 2; Satek, "William Lux of Baltimore."

22. *Maryland Gazette,* Oct. 11, Nov. 1, 1770; Walker, "Baltimore Community and the American Revolution," 142-59; Hoffman, *Spirit of Dissension,* 80-91.

23. For John Smith, Buchanan, and Purviance, see Papenfuse et al., eds., *Biographical Dictionary of the Maryland Legislature.* For William Smith and Mackie, see Baltimore County Land Records, B # I, 225-29; AL # B, 31-33.

24. "A sketch of the life of General Samuel Smith during the war of the Revolution," Box 6, Samuel Smith Papers, Library of Congress; Frank A. Cassell, *Merchant Congressman in the Young Republic: Samuel Smith of Maryland, 1752-1839* (Madison, 1971), 3-5.

25. Ibid.

26. Ibid.

27. For Purviance, see Papenfuse et al., eds., *A Biographical Dictionary of the Maryland Legislature.* For the Scotch-Irish, see Leroy James Vott, "Social Dynamism in a Boom-Town: The Scots-Irish in Baltimore, 1760 to 1790" (Master's thesis, University of Virginia, 1969).

28. *Maryland Gazette,* Nov. 1, Dec. 6, 1770; Walker, "The Baltimore Community and the American Revolution," 152-54; Hoffman, *Spirit of Dissension,* 90-91.

29. Hoffman, *Spirit of Dissension,* 92-125.

30. Samuel Chase to Charles Ridgely, May 26, 1773, Box 10, Ridgely Papers; *Maryland Gazette,* June 10, 24, 1773. Quote from *Maryland Gazette,* June 17, 1773. See Walker, "Baltimore Community and the American Revolution," 157-59; Hoffman, *Spirit of Dissension,* 116-17.

31. Browne et al., eds., *Archives of Maryland,* LXIII, 428; "Extracts from Carroll Papers," *Maryland Historical Magazine* 15 (1920): 274-75.

32. For biographical information on the assemblymen, see Papenfuse et al., eds., *Biographical Dictionary of the Maryland Legislature.*

33. *Maryland Journal,* Nov. 30, 1774.

34. Biographical information was assembled from Papenfuse et al., eds., *Biographical Dictionary of the Maryland Legislature;* Baltimore County Land Records; Dielman File, Maryland Hall of Records. For tax list, see Wilkins, comp., "Baltimore County Tax List, 1773."

Epilogue

1. Katherine Scarborough, *Homes of the Cavaliers* (New York, 1930), 146.

2. Ibid., 137; John H. Scarff, " 'Hampton,' Baltimore County, Maryland," *Maryland Historical Magazine* 53 (1948): 99, 105.

3. George Lux to Charles Ridgely, Dec. 27, 1786, box 3, MS 692, Ridgely Papers, Maryland Historical Society.

4. Ibid.; Edmonds, "Land Holdings of the Ridgelys of Hampton," 45-46.

5. Scarborough, *Homes of the Cavaliers,* 141.

Index